Interfacing to the IBM
Personal Computer
Second Edition

Interfacing to the IBM Personal Computer

Second Edition

Lewis C. Eggebrecht

International Standard Book Number: 0-672-22722-3
Library of Congress Catalog Card Number: 90-61027

Acquisitions Editor: *Richard Swadley*
Development Editor: *C. Herbert Feltner*
Manuscript Editor: *Susan Pink, Techright*
Cover Concept: *Mitchell Waite*
Cover Illustration: *Bob Johnson*
Indexer: *Brown Editorial Services*
Production Assistance: *Sally Copenhaver, Tami Hughes, Bill Hurley, Charles
    Hutchinson, Jodi Jensen, Jennifer Matthews, Dennis Sheehan, Bruce
    Steed, Mary Beth Wakefield, Nora Westlake*
Compositor: *Shepard Poorman Communications Corp.*

Printed in the United States of America

Trademarks

Contents

Preface   *xv*

1 The PC Family   *1*

    The Original PC *3*
    PC XT *3*
    PC AT *7*
    386 AT Bus Systems *9*
    PS/2 Systems *9*
        PS/2 Model 25 *11*
        PS/2 Model 30 *12*
        PS/2 Model 30 286 *14*
        PS/2 Models 50 and 50Z *15*
        PS/S Model 55SX *17*
        PS/2 Model 60 *19*
        PS/2 Model 70 *21*
        PS/2 Model P70 *22*
        PS/2 Model 80 *23*
        486-Based Systems *26*

2 PC Options and Enhancements   *27*

    Displays and Display Adapters *27*
    Diskette Drives *30*

Fixed Disks *31*
    Fixed Disk Selection Criteria *32*
    Fixed Disk Adapters *33*
Printers *34*
Printer Interfaces *36*
Communications Adapters *37*
Memory Expansion Adapters *39*
Performance Accelerator Adapters *40*
Image Capture Devices *40*
Mouses *41*
Mass Storage Devices *42*
Backup Devices *42*
Interfacing Adapters *42*
Multifunction Adapters *43*

3 PC Microprocessors

45

8088 Microprocessor *47*
    Interface Signal Pins *50*
    Memory Addressing *53*
    Registers *55*
    Effective Memory Address Generation *58*
8086 Microprocessor *58*
286 Microprocessor *59*
386 Microprocessor *60*
386SX Microprocessor *65*
486 Microprocessor *66*
Instruction Set Summary *67*

4 PC Systems Performance and Bus Architectures

73

Microprocessor Type *74*
Wait States *75*
Memory Speed and Location *77*
Memory Subsystem Architecture *79*
ROM Shadowing *81*
Display Adapters *81*
Hard Disk Subsystem Performance *82*
Communications Performance *83*
LAN Performance *84*

Numeric Processor Performance *85*
Benchmark Evaluation of System Performance *85*
Bus Architectures *87*

5 PC and XT Systems and Bus Architecture   *89*

PC/XT Expansion Bus Description *89*
Memory-Read Bus Cycle *92*
Memory-Write Bus Cycle *92*
I/O-Port-Read Bus Cycle *93*
I/O-Port-Write Bus Cycle *94*
DMA Bus Cycle *95*
  DMA Memory-Write Cycle *97*
  DMA Memory-Read Cycle *98*
  Memory-Refresh DMA Cycle *99*
Wait-State Generation *100*
  8088 Wait-State Generation *100*
  Wait-State Generation in DMA Bus Cycles *103*
System-Bus Signal Descriptions *107*
  OSC *108*
  CLK *108*
  RESET DRV *109*
  A0–19 *109*
  D0–7 *109*
  ALE *110*
  I/O CH CK *110*
  I/O CH RDY *111*
  IRQ2–7 *111*
  IOR *111*
  IOW *112*
  MEMW *112*
  MEMR *113*
  DRQ1–3 *113*
  DACK0–3 *113*
  AEN *114*
  TC *114*
Bus Power and Ground *114*
System-Bus Timings *115*
System-Bus Loading and Driving Capabilities *117*
  System-Bus Drive Capability *117*
  System-Bus Load in Card Slots *121*

Capacitive Bus Loading *124*
General Rules *124*
System-Bus Mechanical and Power Characteristics *124*
System-Bus Card Slots *124*
PC Card Size *125*
System Unit Power and Power Decoupling *127*

6 PC and XT Interrupts, DMA, and Timer Counters   *129*

System Interrupts *129*
PC Interrupt System *130*
The Interrupt Controller *131*
Sequence of Events in an Interrupt *132*
Interrupt Housekeeping *134*
System Initialization for Interrupts *135*
Interrupt Initialization *136*
Interrupt Vector Table Initialization *137*
8259A Interrupt Controller Initialization *138*
Initialization Command Words *140*
Operation Control Words *144*
Impact of Changing ICWs and OCWs *148*
Interrupt Performance *148*
Circuit for Interfacing to an I/O Bus
Interrupt-Request Line *149*
Expanding Interrupts on the PC *150*
Initialization of the Expansion 8259A Device *151*
Software Service Routine for Expansion Interrupts *152*
Further Interrupt-Level Expansion *152*
System Direct Memory Access *153*
DMA Usage in the PC *156*
DMA Operation *156*
Initialization of the 8237-5 Controller *159*
Control and Status Register Definitions *159*
Address and Count Registers *166*
DMA Page Registers *167*
DMA Performance *168*
Reusing a DMA Channel *169*
Terminal Count Signal *170*
High-Speed Data Transfer *170*
Programmed I/O Data Transfer *170*
DMA Data Transfer *173*

Other Data-Transfer Techniques *174*
System Timer Counters *175*
    Channel 0 *176*
    Channel 1 *177*
    Channel 2 *177*
    Programming the Timer Counters *178*
    Timer-Counter Modes of Operation *181*
    Adding Extended Timing and Counting Functions *182*
    Timer-Counter Design *183*

7 PC and XT I/O, Memory, and Decoding *193*

Port Addressing *193*
I/O Port Address Map *195*
I/O Port Address Decoding Techniques *196*
    Fixed Address Decode *197*
    Switch-Selectable Decode *197*
    PROM Select Decode *199*
Expanding Port Addressing on the PC *201*
    High-Order Address Bit Usage *201*
    Indirect Port Addressing *201*
    Memory-Mapped I/O Port Addressing *202*
Memory Usage Map *205*
Memory Address Decoding *206*
Dynamic Memory Refresh Function *208*

8 PC Interfacing Techniques *211*

DI/DO Registers *212*
    Register Address Decoding *213*
    Decode and Bus Buffer Circuit *213*
    DO Register Design *215*
    DI Register Design *218*
    Level-Latching DI Register *219*
    Transition-Detection DI Register *221*
    Interrupts from the DI Register *223*
    Bidirectional DI/DO Registers *223*
    Pulsed-Output Port Design *223*
    DO Register Output Drive *224*
    Setting and Resetting Bits in a DO Register *225*

Testing Bits in a DI Register *226*
Other DI/DO Devices *226*
Cards and Ports for Interfacing *227*
Interfacing with the Cassette Port *227*
Interfacing with the Parallel Printer Port Card *229*
Interfacing with the Game Control Card *232*
Interface Signal Conditioning *233*
RS-232C Interface *234*
RS-423 Interface *234*
RS-422 Interface *235*
Current-Loop Data Transmission *236*
Switch Sensing *237*
Indicator Driving *239*
Relay Driving *240*
Stepper Motors *240*
Permanent-Magnet Stepping Motor *241*
Bifilar Stepping Motor *242*
Variable-Reluctance Stepping Motor *242*
Pulse Stepper Motor *242*
Analog-to-Digital Conversion *243*
Digital-to-Analog Conversion *244*
Manufacturers of DAC and ADC Devices *244*

9 PC and XT Bus Extension and Monitoring

247

A Simple Bus Extender Design *247*
An Enhanced Bus Extender Design *251*
Hardware and Software for Testing Designs *254*
Smart Card Extender Design *254*
DOS Debug Program *264*

10 PC AT System and Bus Architecture

267

PC AT and ISA Bus Slot Configuration *267*
Signal Additions and Changes in XT Slots *268*
AT Extension Slot Signal Definitions *270*
SBHE *270*
MEMR *271*
MEMW *271*
DRQ5–7 *271*

$\overline{\text{DACK5–7}}$ *271*
$\overline{\text{MEM CS16}}$ *272*
$\overline{\text{I/O CS16}}$ *272*
$\overline{\text{MASTER}}$ *272*
IRQ10, 11, 12, 14, 15 *272*
LA17–23 *273*
SD8–15 *273*
+5VDC *273*
GND *273*
Adapter Board Size *273*
Expansion Slot Bus Cycles *274*
Bus Timing *276*
Bus Loading and Drive *279*
Bus Wait States *280*
Wait-State Generation Hardware *281*
Programmable Bus and System Parameters *283*
EISA and ISA Bus Standard *284*
Power Supply Specifications *284*

11 PC AT Interrupts, DMA, Timer Counters, I/O, and Memory

287

Direct Memory Addressing *287*
Interrupts *289*
Timer Counter *291*
Real-Time Clock and CMOS Memory *291*
Memory Map *292*
I/O Map *293*

12 PS/2 Micro Channel Architecture

297

Capabilities and Characteristics *298*
    Family of Buses *298*
    Asynchronous Bus Operation *298*
    Programmable Option Select *301*
    Bus Arbitration Feature *303*
    MCA Interrupts *303*
    Physical Characteristics of MCA Adapters *305*
    MCA Power and Ground *305*

MCA Signal Definitions *307*
    A0–23 *307*
    D0–15 *307*
    ALD *307*
    M/I/O *308*
    S0 and S1 *308*
    CMD *308*
    SBHE *309*
    MADE24 *309*
    CD DS 16 *309*
    DS 16 RTN *309*
    CD SFDBK *309*
    CD CHRDY *310*
    CHRDYRTN *310*
    PREEMPT *310*
    ARB/GNT *310*
    ARB0–3 *310*
    BURST *310*
    TC *311*
    CD SETUP *311*
    CHCK *311*
    IRQ3–7, 9–12, 14, 15 *311*
    AUDIO *311*
    AUDIO GND *312*
    REFRESH *312*
    CHRESET *312*
32-Bit Extension Bus Signal *312*
    A24–31 *312*
    D16–31 *312*
    BE0–3 *312*
    CD DS 32 *313*
    DS 32 RTN *313*
MCA Video Extension Signal *313*
Basic MCA Bus Cycle *313*
MCA Enhancements *315*

13 PS/2 Interrupts, DMA, Timer Counters, I/O, and Memory   *317*

Interrupts *317*
DMA *318*

Timer Counters *323*
Real-Time Clock and the Audio System *323*
Parallel Port *324*
Memory and I/O Maps *326*

Bibliography *329*

Index *331*

Preface

As the design team leader and architect/designer on the original PC, I am astounded at the family of PC products that have grown from this initial system design. The PC has fostered an entire industry that provides enhanced and compatible systems and products. It is amazing that an adapter board designed in 1981 for the original 4.77-MHz 8088 PC will plug into and operate properly in a 33-MHz 386 AT bus PC. The industry has performed well in establishing and adhering to de facto standards created by the PC and its products. The open architecture of the PC family has contributed to its success by encouraging suppliers to invest in new designs and products. Even the IBM PS/2 Micro Channel Architecture, although not compatible with the older PC, XT, and AT buses, is still an open architecture with published specifications.

As the range of system price and performance design points increased to cover the wider requirements of PC users, pressure was placed on the single architecture approach. Intel Corporation also provided a wide range of new microprocessors with ever increasing capabilities and performance, from the original 4.77-MHz 8088 to the new 33-MHz 486, which offers more than fifty times the processor performance. Now PCs are produced with a family of bus architectures and microprocessors; some are software and hardware compatible, and others are not.

This book summarizes the PC product family by comparing capabilities, performance, microprocessors, system architectures, bus architectures, compatibility, peripherals, and enhancements products. Then it provides detailed information of the system architecture and bus architectures for the PC XT, PC AT, PC 386 AT, PS/2 286, and PS/2 386 Micro Channel systems. Information on how to use the system's DMA, interrupts, and timer counters is provided. Design examples illustrate how to develop adapter boards for these buses. By providing a comprehensive review of the PC family of products, readers can make informed decisions as to the type of system that best fits their application and needs.

Engineers and scientists will find the book invaluable in providing key technical information about performance and interfacing capabilities and in identifying additional information sources. Those who want to design adapters to the bus architectures of the PC product family will find detailed information and design examples to assist them in their endeavor.

Sorting through the maze of PC system architectures and capabilities can be a bewildering task. I hope this book makes that task a little easier.

Chapter 1

The PC Family

SINCE THE INTRODUCTION of the IBM PC in September 1981, many models of the PC have been marketed by IBM and numerous other suppliers. Describing each product line would be a formidable task—and beyond the scope of this book—but we can describe the major models introduced by IBM and others over the years. The following models of the PC incorporated major enhancements in microprocessor usage and expansion slot architecture:

- IBM PC
- PC XT
- PC AT
- PC 386 AT bus
- PS/2 XT/AT bus
- PS/2 Micro Channel
- EISA bus systems

The PC 386 AT bus system is not an IBM product; it is an industry extension of the AT systems to the newer 386 processor technology. IBM chose to implement the 386 processor technology using their proprietary Micro Channel Architecture. IBM chose also to drop the PC 286 AT systems from their product line in favor of Micro Channel 286 system architectures. This is often viewed as a major marketing mistake because it opened the way for third-party suppliers to fill the void created by IBM's decision to drop the PC AT. The industry adopted the AT bus as a standard and further extended its use to 386 processor-based systems. Thus, IBM fathered its own competition for 286/386 systems. In a later move, IBM reintroduced the AT bus in the PS/2 model 30 286. To further complicate the systems architecture issue, several major compatible systems manufacturers have cooperated on the development of a new system bus architecture that competes with the capabilities of the IBM Micro Channel but retains compatibility with the industry standard AT bus. This standard is called EISA, Extended Industry Standard Architecture. Figure 1-1 illustrates the evolution of the PC family with respect to major architecture enhancements.

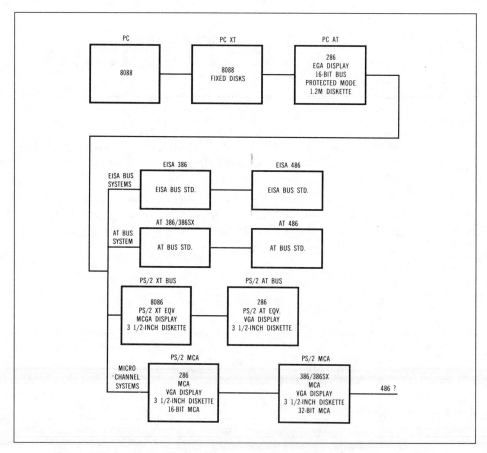

Figure 1-1. PC systems family by major architecture enhancements.

With the exception of the original PC, all models of the PC are still in production and offered by numerous suppliers. Although PC XT and AT models have been on the market for some time, new models with lower cost and higher performance combined with huge software libraries make these machines very popular for a number of applications.

The PC family can be categorized also according to packaging. All major enhancement versions of the PC are available in desktop, portable, floor-standing tower, and laptop packages. These packages usually represent different variations in mechanical and power packaging to achieve a more compact and portable system design. The portable and laptop design often limits the number of features available on one system by providing few or no expansion slots and limited diskette and disk capacity. The floor-standing tower design often offers more expansion capacity than the tabletop designs by providing more expansion slots, power supply capacity, and disk and diskette capacity options.

New PC models generally follow the introduction of new Intel microprocessors, which provide the PCs with new microprocessors, expanded bus capacity, and high system clock rates. When you evaluate the merits of a specific PC model, consider the following key attributes:

- System microprocessor and clock rate
- Type of disks and diskettes supported
- Type of bus architecture and number of expansion slots
- Type of display adapter and display supported
- Type of packaging
- Standard and maximum RAM capacity
- Degree of compatibility with IBM

The Original PC

The original PC was a floppy-based system with 32K of memory on the system board and five expansion slots. See Figure 1-2. The PC supported one or two internal 5 1/4-inch floppy diskettes, each with a capacity of 160K. Two additional floppy drives could be added externally. Shortly after its introduction, the system board was changed to support 64K RAM and the EPROM BIOS was changed to scan the upper 256K for ROM device drivers on adapter boards. The original PC used the Intel 8088 5-MHz microprocessor running at 4.77 MHz.

PC XT

The PC quickly needed several enhancements to keep up with the rapid pace of software development and the need for more RAM and disk capac-

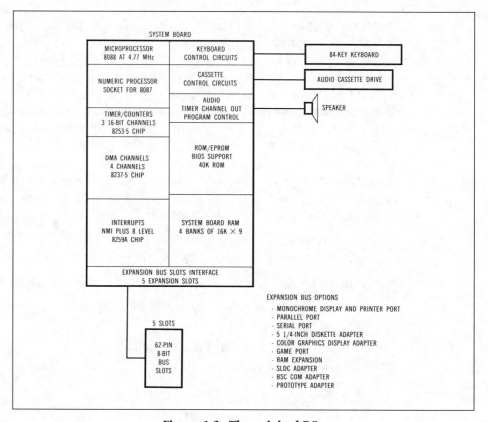

SYSTEM BOARD

MICROPROCESSOR 8088 AT 4.77 MHz	KEYBOARD CONTROL CIRCUITS
NUMERIC PROCESSOR SOCKET FOR 8087	CASSETTE CONTROL CIRCUITS
TIMER/COUNTERS 3 16-BIT CHANNELS 8253-5 CHIP	AUDIO TIMER CHANNEL OUT PROGRAM CONTROL
DMA CHANNELS 4 CHANNELS 8237-5 CHIP	ROM/EPROM BIOS SUPPORT 40K ROM
INTERRUPTS NMI PLUS 8 LEVEL 8259A CHIP	SYSTEM BOARD RAM 4 BANKS OF 16K × 9

84-KEY KEYBOARD

AUDIO CASSETTE DRIVE

SPEAKER

EXPANSION BUS SLOTS INTERFACE
5 EXPANSION SLOTS

EXPANSION BUS OPTIONS
- MONOCHROME DISPLAY AND PRINTER PORT
- PARALLEL PORT
- SERIAL PORT
- 5 1/4-INCH DISKETTE ADAPTER
- COLOR GRAPHICS DISPLAY ADAPTER
- GAME PORT
- RAM EXPANSION
- SLDC ADAPTER
- BSC COM ADAPTER
- PROTOTYPE ADAPTER

5 SLOTS

62-PIN
8-BIT
BUS
SLOTS

Figure 1-2. The original PC.

ity. This need was met by the introduction of the PC XT, shown in Figure 1-3. The original PC XT added the following enhancements:

- The number of expansion slots was increased to 8.
- A hard disk and disk adapter were added.
- A serial port and a parallel port were added as standard equipment.
- The system board RAM capacity was increased to 256K.
- The system unit power supply was increased from 65 to 135 watts.
- Diskette capacity was upgraded from single-sided, 9 sectors per track to two-sided, 9 sectors per track for a total capacity of 360K.

The physical size and mechanical style of the box remained the same as the original PC. To accommodate the additional three expansion slots, the spacing between the expansion slot connectors was reduced from 1.0 inch to 0.75 inch. The eighth slot was different because it supported only a short adapter board and was used only for the serial and parallel expan-

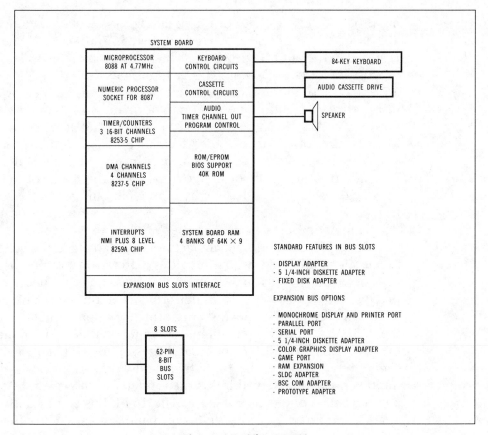

Figure 1-3. The PC XT.

sion adapter boards. Later in the production, the diskette and disk drives were converted to half-height designs to allow multiple drives in one system unit.

The IBM PC XT did not increase the processor performance level; the processor remained the 4.77-MHz 8088. The performance of the PC XT was extended, however, by a number of manufacturers. The simplest modification was to increase the clock speed of the 8088 microprocessor. PC XT compatibles are now commonly available with clock speeds of 8 MHz and 10 MHz, which more than doubles the processor's performance. In some compatibles, clock speed was increased, but wait states were added to the processor's memory cycles to allow the use of less expensive RAM chips.

The 8088 microprocessor requires four clock cycles to execute a memory cycle. With the addition of one wait state, five clock cycles are required. At 4.77 MHz, a clock cycle is 210 nanoseconds (ns) and a zero wait-state memory cycle is 4 times 210 ns, or 840 ns. A 10-MHz processor has processor clock cycles of 100 ns and zero wait-state memory cycles of 400 ns, or 2.1 times faster than the original 4.77-MHz PC. If one wait state is added in the 10-MHz processor's memory access, the cycle time is five processor clocks, or 500 ns. This is 1.68 times the original PC's speed at 4.77 MHz. The addition of the single wait state in the memory cycle appears to have a significant effect on performance. Measured performance, however, indicates that a single wait state in a 10-MHz machine will result in an average of 1.8 times the performance of a 4.77-MHz processor system. The difference between the measured and calculated effects of wait-state addition in processor memory cycles is the result of the 8088 bus interface design, which has a 4-byte prefetch buffer. This lessens the effects of wait-state insertion in bus cycles. This same effect occurs on the 286 family of processors used in the PC AT systems.

Some XT compatible manufacturers also changed the system microprocessor to the 8086, which provides a 16-bit bus to memory. A 16-bit memory access versus an 8-bit memory access does not necessarily result in a twofold increase in system performance at the same processor clock rates. On average, the effect is a performance improvement of 1.6. Again, the 8086 has a 6-byte prefetch buffer, which masks some of the effect of the 16-bit bus. In addition, most data accesses are 8 bit, not 16 bit, and thus cannot effectively use the 16-bit bus bandwidth. Significant performance improvement is observed in instruction fetches, however, because most are more than one byte in length. The 16-bit bus significantly increases system performance also in interrupt handling and subroutine calls because push and pop instructions used to save and restore system context information are 16-bit operations. A zero wait-state 8086 at 10 MHz would exhibit a 2.1 performance increase due to clock speed and a 1.6 increase due to the 16-bit bus. Thus, a total performance increase of 3.36 times the original 4.77-MHz PC could be realized. The AT&T family of XT compatible systems used the 8086.

PC XT systems are still useful and inexpensive solutions for applications such as word processing, terminal emulation, spreadsheets, accounting, and LAN terminals. A 10-MHz zero wait-state machine with 640K RAM, a serial port, parallel port, Hercules monochrome graphics adapter and display, 20M disk and adapter, 360K disk and adapter, and keyboard can be purchased for under $1000.00. With a little effort assembling the basic system pieces yourself, this system can be purchased for under $750.00.

Contrary to popular belief, the PC XT was not killed by IBM. The PS/2 model 30 is a PC XT in a PS/2 cover. The model 30 still retains the PC bus and uses an 8-MHz 8086 processor. The diskette drives have been converted to 3 1/2-inch, but otherwise the system is a PC XT!

PC AT

The introduction of the PC AT marked the use of the new generation Intel 286 microprocessor. To accommodate the 16-bit bus of the 286 micro-processor, the AT extended the PC XT bus to 16 bits for data and 24 bits for the memory address. Backward compatibility was essentially maintained on the AT bus slots with adapters designed for the PC and XT. The additional bus signals were added in a second bus slot connector. The original IBM AT supported a clock rate of 6 MHz with one bus cycle wait state. IBM later increased this to 8 MHz. Many manufacturers of AT clones have increased the clock rates to 10, 12, 16, 20, or 25 MHz operation. An AT with a higher clock rate and no wait states challenges the 386-based machines in many applications.

The 286 microprocessor provided its higher performance with a higher clock rate, fewer clocks per bus cycle, fewer clock cycles per instruction, new instructions, and a 16-bit bus width. Depending on the clock speed and number of wait states, the new AT systems offered 4 to 10 times the performance of the 4.77-MHz PC and XTs. The 286 supports two modes of operation: real mode and protected mode. Real mode emulates the 8088/8086 program environment of 1M of address space, which allows existing PC and XT software to execute unmodified. In protected mode, support is provided for multitasking environments. The full 16M address space of the 286 and a virtual address space of 1 GB per task mapped to the 16M real address space also are supported in protected mode. Memory management also supports four-level memory protection. Unfortunately, because little PC software is available in protected mode, the capability of the 286 microprocessor in protected mode has been largely unrealized.

In addition to introducing the 286 and AT bus extensions, the AT introduced 1.2M high-density diskettes and 20M hard disks as standard features on the AT. The AT added also a clock/calendar with battery backup and the new EGA (Enhanced Graphics Adapter) display adapter and monitor. The EGA display adapter dramatically increased the graphics resolution and color capabilities of the PC. (The EGA also could be retrofitted into older XTs.) Figure 1-4 is a block diagram of a typical AT system.

When first introduced by IBM, the PC AT used no custom silicon chip devices on the system board. Manufacturers of clones quickly produced custom chip sets that integrated many of the discrete devices on the system board. These chip sets dramatically reduced the size and cost of AT motherboards and allowed more I/O features and memory to be resident on the motherboard. As more memory was added to the motherboard, the

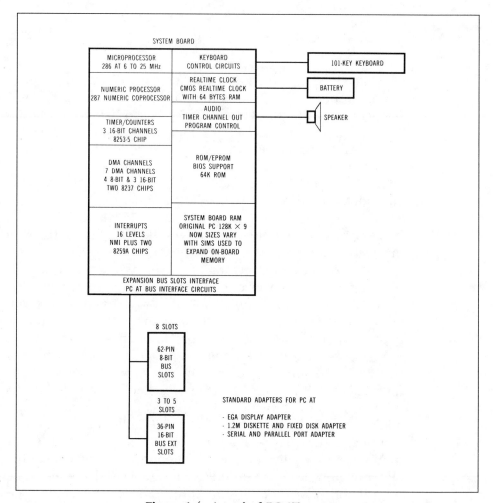

SYSTEM BOARD

MICROPROCESSOR 286 AT 6 TO 25 MHz	KEYBOARD CONTROL CIRCUITS
NUMERIC PROCESSOR 287 NUMERIC COPROCESSOR	REALTIME CLOCK CMOS REALTIME CLOCK WITH 64 BYTES RAM
TIMER/COUNTERS 3 16-BIT CHANNELS 8253-5 CHIP	AUDIO TIMER CHANNEL OUT PROGRAM CONTROL

101-KEY KEYBOARD

BATTERY

SPEAKER

DMA CHANNELS
7 DMA CHANNELS
4 8-BIT & 3 16-BIT
TWO 8237 CHIPS

ROM/EPROM
BIOS SUPPORT
64K ROM

INTERRUPTS
16 LEVELS
NMI PLUS TWO
8259A CHIPS

SYSTEM BOARD RAM
ORIGINAL PC 128K × 9
NOW SIZES VARY
WITH SIMS USED TO
EXPAND ON-BOARD
MEMORY

EXPANSION BUS SLOTS INTERFACE
PC AT BUS INTERFACE CIRCUITS

8 SLOTS

62-PIN
8-BIT
BUS
SLOTS

3 TO 5
SLOTS

36-PIN
16-BIT
BUS EXT
SLOTS

STANDARD ADAPTERS FOR PC AT

- EGA DISPLAY ADAPTER
- 1.2M DISKETTE AND FIXED DISK ADAPTER
- SERIAL AND PARALLEL PORT ADAPTER

Figure 1-4. A typical PC AT system.

clock rates could be increased because special buses could be created between the 286 and memory, which eliminated bus buffer delays.

Today, a PC AT motherboard with a 12.5-MHz clock rate with zero wait state, an integrated real-time clock, a serial port, a parallel port, and 2M RAM is a commodity. Systems with this type of motherboard and 1M RAM, 1.2M 5 1/4-inch diskette, 40M hard disk, and EGA adapter and monitor are available from many manufacturers for under $1500. These 286-based systems have the added advantage of supporting protected mode software such as UNIX and OS/2. Thus, they can run new application software designed for the larger address and memory of the protected mode environment.

386 AT Bus Systems

The next major development was the introduction of the Intel 386 32-bit microprocessor. IBM introduced the 386 in the PS/2, a family of PCs that utilized a new and proprietary bus architecture called Micro Channel Architecture. The rest of the industry stuck with the AT bus and produced 386 systems with AT buses.

Until this time, PC-compatible manufacturers had followed IBM's moves in lockstep. Systems produced by these manufacturers varied little from IBM's basic system architecture but provided more integrated features and higher performance at a lower cost. The 386 AT bus system marked the industry's first departure from compliance with IBM architecture standards. The 386 AT bus compatible systems are simply PC ATs with the 286 replaced with the 386. Many early 386 systems were built using PC AT chip sets with high-speed RAM or interleaved RAM. Now, 386 PC AT systems are built with chip sets customized to the 386, utilizing cache controllers coupled to 32-bit dynamic RAM. By placing the system memory on the system board and on a separate local bus, the 386 PC AT system enjoys 32-bit memory access performance, AT bus compatibility, and access to the huge family of PC, XT, and AT peripheral adapter boards. This split bus architecture allows an optimized bus for memory and a lower cost PC AT bus for low-speed I/O and PC bus compatibility.

The 386 microprocessor offers 12 to 50 times the performance of the original 4.77-MHz 8088 PC and 2 to 10 times the performance of an 8-MHz 286 system. These performance improvements are realized by higher clock rates, fewer clocks per bus cycle, fewer clocks per instruction, new instructions for 32-bit operations, and 32-bit data buses. The 386 also supports the real modes of the 8088, 8086, and 286. In protected mode, it supports 286 protected mode and extended 386 protected mode. A key new capability of protected mode is virtual 8086 real mode, which allows multiple tasks, each running 8086 real mode operating systems and applications. Figure 1-5 is a block diagram of a typical 386 AT bus system.

PS/2 Systems

In 1987, IBM introduced a new family of PCs designated the PS/2 family. The following features were common to all the family members:

- Integration of the display adapter on the system board
- Integration of the diskette controller on the system board

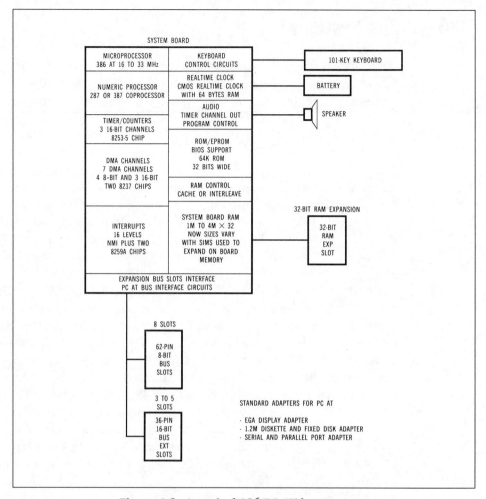

Figure 1-5. A typical 386 PC AT bus system.

- Integration of the serial and parallel ports on the system board
- Integrated mouse port
- Use of 3 1/2-inch diskette drives
- Introduction of the new VGA graphics adapter standard

The initial offering supported three basic architecture machines: the PS/2 models 25 and 30 using the 8086 microprocessor with the PC XT bus, the 286 machines using the new Micro Channel Architecture, and the 386 machines using the new Micro Channel Architecture. Notably absent was any machine based on the AT bus architecture. IBM partially remedied this problem later with the introduction of the PS/2 model 30 286, which incorporated the PC AT bus with three expansion slots. IBM has never produced a 386 AT bus machine. At present there are ten models of the PS/2 product family. Table 1-1 summarizes the PS/2 family according to microprocessors, clock rate, memory and memory expansion capability, bus architecture, and coprocessor capability. Table 1-2 summarizes the PS/2 family according to packaging, expansion slots, diskette drives, fixed disk capacities, display capability, and keyboard type and size. All models of the PS/2 family come with an integrated display adapter, serial port, parallel port, mouse port, and real-time clock/calendar.

Table 1-1. PS/2 Systems Comparison Chart A

PS/2 Model	Micro Type	Clock Speed	Base Memory Size	Expansion Memory Size	Bus Type	NPU Type
Model 25	8086	8 MHz	512K	640K	XT	8087
Model 30	8086	8 MHz	640K	640K	XT	8087
Model 30 286	286	10 MHz	512K	16M	AT	287
Model 50	286	10 MHz	1M	16M	MCA	287
Model 50Z	286	10 MHz (0 WS)	2M	16M	MCA	287
Model 55SX	386SX	16 MHz	4M	16M	MCA	387SX
Model 60	286	10 MHz	1M	16M	MCA	287
Model 70	386	16, 20, 25 MHz	2M	16M	MCA	287/387
Model 70P	386	20 MHz	4M	16M	MCA	387
Model 80	386	16, 20 MHz	2M	16M	MCA	287/387

PS/2 Model 25

The PS/2 model 25 is the entry-level model in the PS/2 family. It is packaged as a desktop unit with an integrated display. The model 25 uses the 8086 microprocessor running at 8 MHz and supports two PC compatible expansion slots. See Figure 1-6. The model 25 comes standard with

- 512K RAM (expandable to 640K)
- 720K 3 1/2-inch diskette and adapter (a second drive is optional)
- Serial, parallel, and mouse ports
- Two expansion slots (one full, one 8 inches long)
- MCGA video adapter and integrated monochrome monitor display (color monitor is optional)
- 8087 math coprocessor socket

- 84-key keyboard (101-key keyboard optional)
- Real-time clock/calendar

Optional features available on the model 25 are a 20M fixed disk, math coprocessor, and token ring adapter (model 25LS). Naturally, any PC bus adapter board can be used in the expansion slots of the model 25.

PS/2 Model 30

The PS/2 model 30 is a desktop system with a separate display; it is similar to the old PC and XT package, except the three expansion slots are horizontal in the model 30. The model 30, like the model 25, uses the Intel 8086 running at 8 MHz and supports the PC/XT bus. There are two sub-models of the model 30; one provides two 720K 3 1/2-inch diskette drives, and the other supports one 720K 3 1/2-inch diskette drive and one

Table 1-2. PS/2 Systems Comparison Chart B

PS/2 Model	Packaging Style	Bus Slots	Diskette Drives	Fixed Disks	Display Type	Keyboard Size
Model 25	Desktop	2 XT	2 720K, 3 1/2 inch	20M Opt	MCGA	84/101
Model 30	Desktop	3 XT	720K	20M	MCGA	101
Model 30 286	Desktop	3 AT	1.44M, 3 1/2 inch	20M	VGA	101
Model 50/50Z	Desktop	3 MAC, 16-bit	1.44M, 3 1/2 inch	20M, 60M	VGA	101
Model 55SX	Desktop	3 MCA, 16-bit	1.44M, 3 1/2 inch	30M, 60M	VGA	101
Model 60	Tower	7 MCA, 16-bit	1.44M, 3 1/2 inch	44M, 70M, 115M	VGA	101
Model 70	Desktop	3 MCA, 2 16-bit, 1 32-bit	1.44M	60M, 120M	VGA	101
Model 70P	Portable	2 MCA, 1 16-bit, 1 32-bit	1.44M, 3 1/2 inch	60M, 120M	VGA	101
Model 80	Tower	7 MCA, 4 16-bit, 3 32-bit	1.44M, 3 1/2 inch	44M, 70M, 115M, 314M	VGA	101

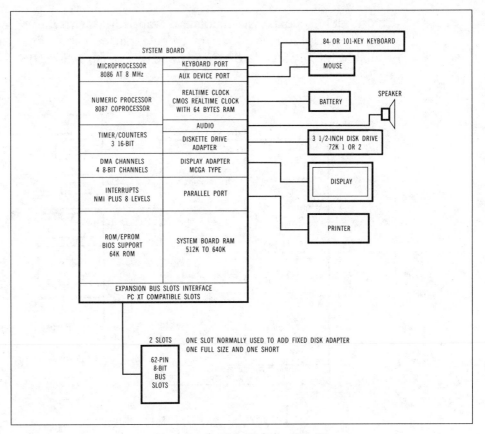

Figure 1-6. The PS/2 model 25.

20M hard drive. See Figure 1-7. The following are standard features of the model 30 system:

- 640K RAM (maximum available)
- Integrated diskette controller and 720K diskette drive
- Integrated serial, parallel, and mouse ports
- Integrated MCGA display adapter
- Three full-length PC expansion slots
- 8087 math coprocessor socket
- 101-key keyboard
- 20M hard disk and adapter (model 30-021)
- 70-watt power supply
- Real-time clock/calendar

The model 30's expansion slots are compatible with the PC and XT. The hard disk adapter uses one of the three expansion slots; thus, two slots are available for any standard PC or XT feature adapter board.

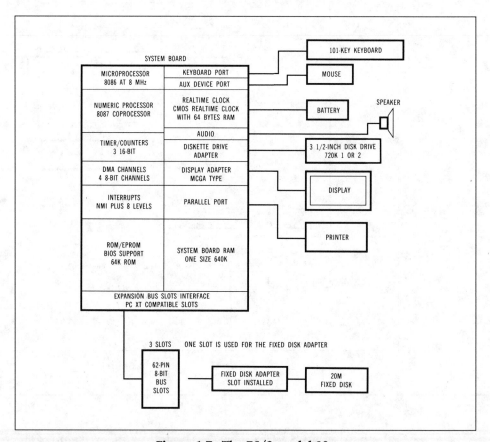

Figure 1-7. The PS/2 model 30.

The model 30 is generally viewed as the PS/2 replacement for the popular PC XT with a performance improvement of 2.5, better display capability, a 3 1/2-inch diskette drive, smaller footprint packaging, and expansion slot compatibility with the PC and XT buses.

PS/2 Model 30 286

The PS/2 model 30 286, announced in late 1988, was not in the original PS/2 product plans. It appears to be IBM's reaction to the continued popularity of the PC AT 286 systems after IBM dropped the AT from its product line. It is significant in that it is the only IBM system that presently supports the PC AT bus architecture.

The PS/2 30 286 is available in two versions. One version has a 1.44M 3 1/2-inch diskette drive; the second version added a 20M hard drive. This system is packaged as a desktop system with a separate display. The model 30 286 uses the Intel 286 microprocessor running at 10 MHz and supports three PC AT dual 8-bit/16-bit expansion slots. The base systems come with 512K RAM, expandable to 4M on the system board. A total of 16M can be supported using the expansion slots. See Figure 1-8. A key new feature of this system is the integrated VGA display adapter supporting 640-by-480 resolution, 16-color graphics. Following are the key features of the PS/2 model 30 286:

- Intel 286 microprocessor at 10-MHz clock rate
- 512K RAM expandable to 4M on the system board
- Serial, parallel, and mouse ports
- 101-key keyboard
- Socket for optional 287 math coprocessor
- Integrated diskette controller and 3 1/2-inch 1.44M diskette drive
- Integrated VGA display adapter
- Real-time clock/calendar
- Three PC AT dual 8-bit/16-bit expansion slots
- Socket for 287 math coprocessor

The model 30 286 offered more than twice the performance of the standard model 30 with its 8-MHz 8086. The model 30 286 is the lowest cost IBM system to use the VGA display adapter as a standard feature. Because its expansion slots are compatible with the popular AT bus, a wide variety of adapter boards are available to add features and enhance the system.

PS/2 Models 50 and 50Z

The PS/2 model 50 is the Micro Channel Architecture version of the PC AT. It utilizes the Intel 286 operating at 10 MHz. The model 50 is nearly identical in features and performance to the model 30 286; the main differentiating features are the use of the 16-bit version of the Micro Channel for its four expansion slots and the 1M standard memory size. The standard disk for the model 50 is a 20M drive with a slow 80 ms access time.

To provide greater performance than that found in the model 30 286 and model 50, IBM introduced the model 50Z. The *Z* stands for zero

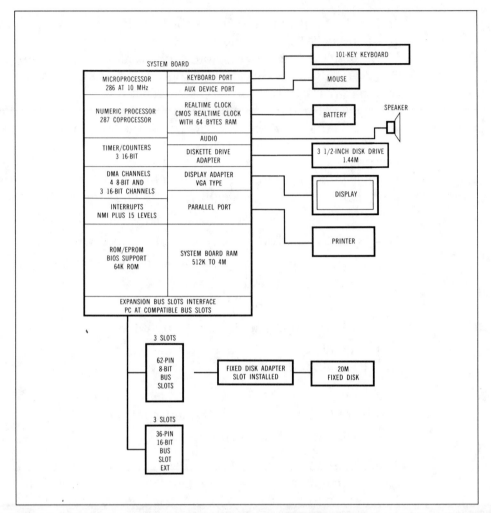

Figure 1-8. The PS/2 model 30 286 system.

wait-state memory accesses. The 30 286 and 50 models use one wait state in all memory accesses. At 10 MHz, a memory bus cycle on a 286 microprocessor is two clock cycles (or 200 ns) with no wait states. The addition of a single wait state increases the cycle time to 300 ns. Thus, the model 50Z enjoyed a significant performance improvement over the models 30 286 and 50. The model 50Z supports system board memory expansion to 2M, and significantly improves fixed disk capability by providing 30M and 60M drives with 39 ms access times. Following are the key features of the models 50 and 50Z:

- Intel 286 microprocessor running at 10-MHz clock rate (model 50 with one wait state; model 50Z with zero wait states)

- System board RAM of 1M for the model 50 and 2M for the model 50Z
- Serial, parallel, and mouse ports
- Integrated diskette controller and 1.44M 3 1/2-inch disk drive
- Integrated VGA display adapter
- Hard disk adapter (takes an expansion slot); 20M drive with 80 ms access time for model 50, and 30M and 60M drives with 39 ms access time for model 50Z
- 101-key keyboard
- Four 16-bit Micro Channel expansion slots (three unused)
- Real-time clock/calendar
- Socket for 287 math coprocessor

The Micro Channel expansion slots allow the addition of memory and other expansion features and devices to the models 50 and 50Z systems. Figure 1-9 is a block diagram of the PS/2 models 50 and 50Z.

PS/S Model 55SX

In May of 1989, IBM announced a new addition to the PS/2 systems product line. The PS/2 model 55SX, shown in Figure 1-10, is at the low end of 386 architecture PS/2 systems. It utilizes the 386SX, a special low-cost version of the 386 microprocessor that uses a 16-bit bus instead of the 32-bit bus in the 386. The model 55SX uses the 386SX at a clock rate of 16 MHz, which gives a performance improvement of 1.5 over the model 50Z.

The 386SX with its significant lower cost was intended to replace the older 286 in PC AT designs. However, the 286 has several second-source manufacturers pushing down its price. In addition, 286 microprocessors with clock rates as high as 25 MHz are now available. Further, most existing PC software does not take advantage of 32-bit instructions. This combination of factors has put severe pressure on the 386SX.

The model 55SX is packaged as a desktop system using the model 30 enclosure. It uses the 16-bit version of the Micro Channel Architecture to support three expansion slots. Following is a summary of the key features of the PS/2 model 55SX:

- Intel 386SX microprocessor running at 16-MHz clock rate
- 2M system board RAM (expandable to 4M on the system board)
- Serial, parallel, and mouse ports
- Integrated diskette adapter and 3 1/2-inch 1.44M diskette drive
- 101-key keyboard

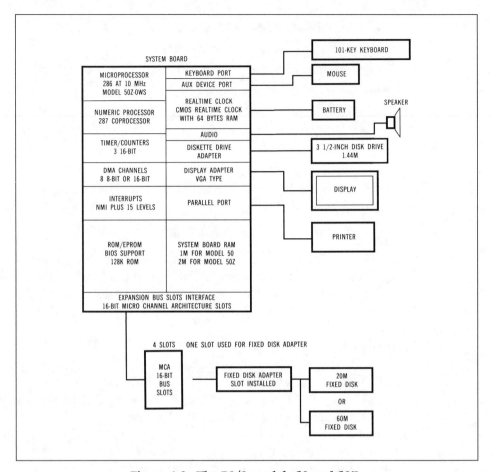

Figure 1-9. The PS/2 models 50 and 50Z.

- Integrated VGA display adapter
- Three 16-bit Micro Channel Architecture expansion slots
- Socket for 287 math coprocessor
- 30M or 60M hard disk and adapter
- Real-time clock/calendar

The three Micro Channel expansion slots allow the addition of up to 16M system RAM or other Micro Channel compatible adapter boards.

Although the 386SX has very little performance advantage over 286 systems with equivalent clock rates, it does fully support all the extended protected mode memory management features of the 386. As more 386 32-bit specific software is developed to take advantage of the large address space in protected modes, the more desirable the 386SX is to the 286.

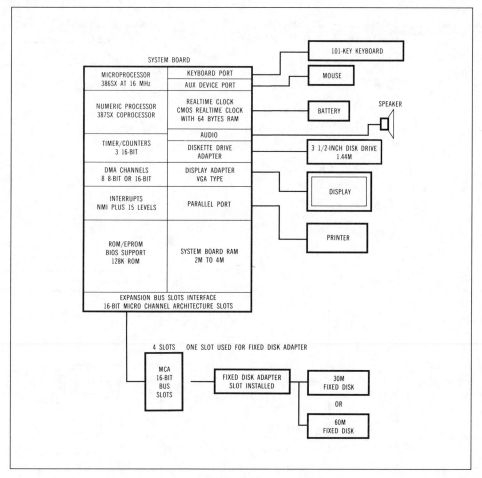

Figure 1-10. The PS/2 model 55SX.

Eventually, 386SX-based systems for both the Micro Channel and AT bus will become the standard low-end PC systems.

PS/2 Model 60

The PS/2 model 60 is similar to the model 50 because it uses the Intel 286 microprocessor running at 10 MHz and it uses a 16-bit version of the Micro Channel Architecture. But the model 60 is designed to be a more expandable system than the model 50. First, it is packaged as a floor-standing tower unit. Second, seven expansion slots are provided for memory and adapter board expansion. Third, the model 60 supports up to two 1.44M 3 1/2-inch diskette drives and one or two hard drives. The first hard drive is 44M with a 40 ms access time; the second hard drive can be a 70M or a

115M drive providing a maximum mass storage capacity of 159M. See Figure 1-11. The following is a summary of model 60 features:

- Intel 286 microprocessor running at a clock rate of 10 MHz
- Seven 16-bit Micro Channel Architecture expansion slots
- 1M RAM on the system board
- Serial, parallel, and mouse ports
- Real-time clock/calendar
- Integrated diskette controller and 3 1/2-inch 1.44M diskette drive expandable to a second drive
- Integrated VGA display adapter

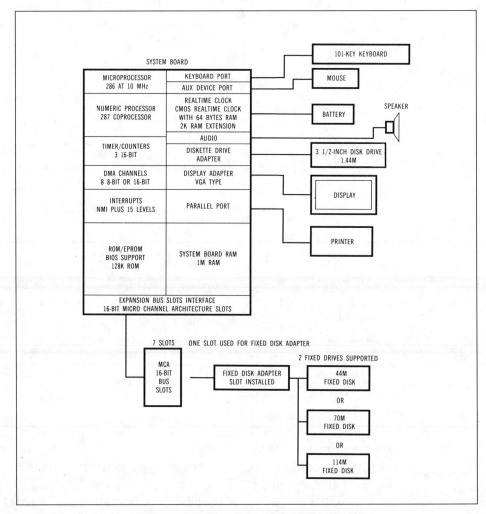

Figure 1-11. The PS/2 model 60 system.

- Floor-standing tower mechanical package design
- Hard disk adapter and support for two hard disks (44M, 70M, and 115M drives)
- 101-key keyboard

The model 60 supports a total system memory size of 16M by the addition of memory boards in the Micro Channel expansion slots.

PS/2 Model 70

The PS/2 model 70, shown in Figure 1-12, is presently IBM's most powerful desktop computer using the Intel 386 microprocessor. The model 70 is packaged in the same size desktop enclosure as the model 50 and comes with 2M system board memory and a 1.44M 3 1/2-inch diskette drive and controller. The model 70 is available in three different clock speed versions, 16 MHz, 20 MHz, and 25 MHz. Hard disks are available in 60M or 120M sizes with an access time of 29 ms. The model 70 uses the Micro Channel Architecture to support three 32-bit expansion slots.

The model 70 is the closest comparable system to the standard 386 AT desktop system offered by many manufacturers. The model 70 has the unique position of being the first IBM system upgraded to the new Intel 486 microprocessor. IBM now offers a 486 upgrade kit for the model 70-A21 (25-MHz 386 version); the 25-MHz 386 processor board is replaced with a 25-MHz 486 board. The upgrade is available only for the 25-MHz model 70. The 486 is software compatible with the 386 but includes an on-chip math coprocessor, 8K cache and controller, support for a secondary cache, single clock cycle burst bus operations, and fewer clock cycles per instruction execution. In general, a 486 running at the same clock rate as a 386 will exhibit twice the performance as the 386. The following is a summary of the features of the model 70:

- Intel 386 microprocessor at 16-MHz, 20-MHz, or 25-MHz clock speed (optional 486 processor board at 25 MHz)
- System board RAM up to 2M (up to 16M using expansion slots)
- Serial, parallel, and mouse ports
- Integrated VGA display controller
- Integrated diskette controller and 3 1/2-inch 1.44M drive
- Socket for 387 math coprocessor
- Real-time clock/calendar
- Three available Micro Channel 32-bit expansion slots

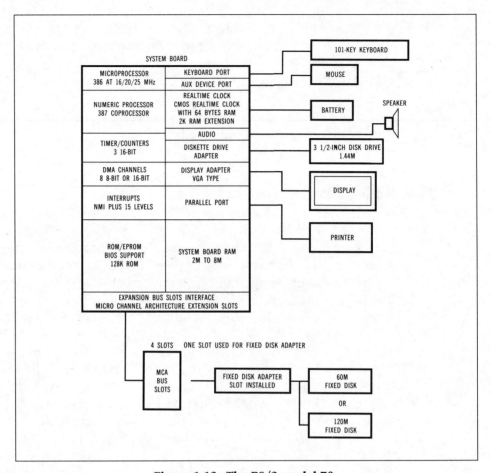

Figure 1-12. The PS/2 model 70.

- 101-key keyboard
- Hard disk controller and 60M or 120M disk drive

The model 70 will likely be the basis of the new 486 PS/2 system. With the 486 upgrade kit, the model 70 is IBM's highest performing Intel processor architecture system.

PS/2 Model P70

The PS/2 model P70 is a 386 Micro Channel Architecture portable computer. This model measures 5 by 18 by 12 inches, weighs 21 pounds, and incorporates an incredible amount of function and power. The model P70 runs the 386 at 20 MHz and provides 4M RAM on the system board, expandable to an additional 4M. It supports two Micro Channel expansion slots. One slot is full size and supports 16-bit and 32-bit operations; the second slot is half size and supports 16-bit operations. The 32-bit slot can accept an additional 8M RAM board, increasing the total memory size to 16M. A key feature of the system is a high contrast, 10-inch diagonal, gas plasma display to support the full resolution of the integrated VGA adapter (640 x 480 with 16 shades of orange). A connector is provided for the external attachment to VGA compatible displays. The model P70 supports a 60M or 120M hard disk drive. A standard 1.44M 3 1/2-inch diskette drive is provided along with a connector for interfacing to an IBM external 5 1/4-inch diskette drive. The following is a summary of the features of the PS/2 model P70:

- Intel 386 microprocessor running at 20-MHz clock rate
- 4M system board memory expandable to 8M (additional 8M with expansion slot)
- Integrated diskette controller and 1.44M 3 1/2-inch drive
- Integrated serial, parallel, and mouse ports
- Two Micro Channel expansion slots (one full-size 32-bit and one half-size 16-bit)
- Integrated VGA adapter and 10-inch diagonal, orange 640 x 480, gas plasma display with 16 levels of gray scale
- Connectors for an external VGA display and a 5 1/4-inch diskette drive
- Real-time clock/calendar
- 101-key keyboard
- Hard disk controller and 60M or 120M disk drive
- Socket for 387 math coprocessor
- Portable packaging, 21 pounds, 5 by 12 by 18 inches

Figure 1-13 is a block diagram of the PS/2 model P70.

PS/2 Model 80

The PS/2 model 80 is the top of the line for the PS/2 family. See Figure 1-14. It is packaged similar to the model 60 using a floor-standing tower approach. This packaging permits a total of seven Micro Channel expansions slots (three 32-bit slots and four 16-bit slots), two diskette drives, and two hard disk drives, with a total capacity of 628M. The model 80 utilizes the Intel 386 at a clock speed of 16 MHz or 20 MHz. The system

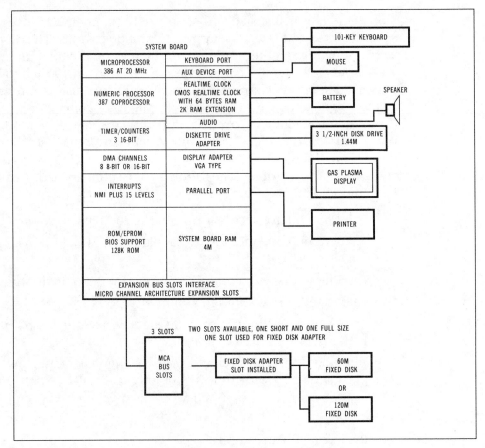

Figure 1-13. The PS/2 model P70.

board supports up to 2M RAM. Up to 16M system RAM can be configured using the 32-bit expansion slots. The following is a summary of the features of the PS/2 model 80:

- Intel 386 microprocessor at clock speeds of 16 MHz or 20 MHz
- Up to 2M system board RAM
- Seven Micro Channel expansion slots (three 32-bit and four 16-bit slots)
- Integrated diskette controller with one or two 1.44M 3 1/2-inch diskette drives
- Integrated serial, parallel, and mouse ports
- Real-time clock/calendar
- Socket for 387 math coprocessor

- Integrates VGA display adapter
- 101-key keyboard
- Hard disk drive controller and 44M, 70M, 115M, or 314M hard drives (two drives supported); maximum capacity of 628M

The model 80 represents the most expandable PS/2 system offered by IBM. At present, the 486 upgrade option is not available on the model 80; this is probably due to the maximum 20-MHz clock speed in the model 80, which is incompatible with the 486's 25-MHz operation in the model 70. IBM will most likely offer a 486 version of the model 80 in the future.

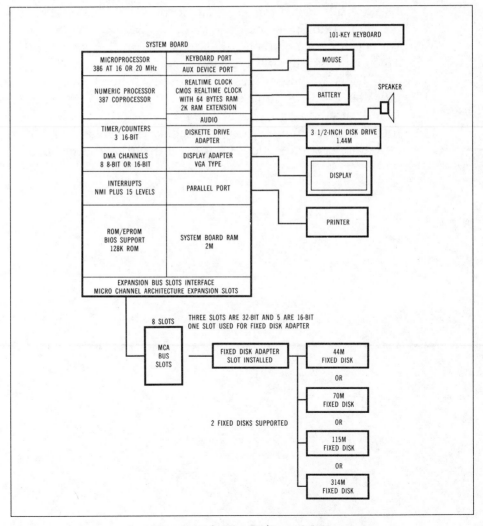

Figure 1-14. The PS/2 model 80.

486-Based Systems

With the introduction of the higher performance Intel 486 micro-processor, a number of 486 systems have been announced and a few have been shipped with early versions of the 486 microprocessor. These systems will likely be based on three different system bus architectures:

- PC AT
- IBM Micro Channel Architecture
- EISA bus architecture

In general, these systems will offer twice the computational performance of 386 machines at the same clock speeds. As has occurred with the PC, XT, and AT and now the PS/2 model 70, vendors will offer 486 coprocessor accelerator boards for these systems so that existing PC owners can enjoy much of the 486's capabilities.

The 486 microprocessor is presently offered in 25-MHz and 33-MHz clock speeds with rumored versions of up to 50 MHz. These speeds combined with the single clock cycle memory access capability of the 486 will force innovation in memory interfacing and cache design to allow slower and more cost-effective RAM to be utilized by the systems.

Chapter 2

PC Options and Enhancements

AS PC SYSTEMS and bus architectures have proliferated, the number of peripheral devices, options, and hardware enhancements has exploded. This chapter describes the key characteristics and capabilities of the most important product classifications. The following products are covered:

- Displays and display adapters
- Diskette drives
- Hard disk drives
- Printers
- Communications adapters
- Memory expansion boards
- Performance accelerator adapters
- Image capture devices
- Mouses
- Mass storage devices
- Fixed disk backup devices
- Interfacing adapters
- Multifunction adapters

Displays and Display Adapters

Perhaps the most confusing aspect of PC selection and configuration is the choice of the display and the display adapter. The original PC was offered with two types of displays and display adapters. The CGA, or Color Graphics Adapter, supported All Points Addressable (APA) color graphics with color-character text mode. This adapter had low resolution (640 x 200 pixels) and supported TV-quality monitors and displays. It supported attachment to displays using a direct-drive digital RGB (Red Green Blue) interface or a composite video interface both at standard TV scan frequencies. The second adapter, the MDA, or Monochrome Display Adapter, supported text-mode screens of 80 x 25 characters and high-resolution character presentation with a character box size of 9 x 14 pixels. It also incorporated a parallel printer port. This adapter provided high-quality text-only displays on the monochrome display furnished by IBM. It interfaced to the display through a direct-drive interface at IBM proprietary scan and refresh frequencies.

The next member of the PC display adapter family strangely enough did not come from IBM. The Hercules company, recognizing that the monochrome display used with the MDA had a graphics resolution capability of 720 x 350 pixels, soon introduced an adapter with 720 x 350 monochrome APA graphics. For high-resolution monochrome graphics applications, the HMGA (Hercules Monochrome Graphics Adapter) remains a best buy for PCs today. It costs less than $50.00 for the adapter and less than $70.00 for the display, yet provides pixel resolution greater than the more advanced EGA adapters and greater than the Apple Macintosh and Macintosh SE.

The CGA adapter was quickly viewed as inadequate in its support of color graphics applications and was followed by the IBM EGA (Enhanced Graphics Adapter). The EGA supported resolutions up to 640 x 350 pixels, with 16-color pixels from a palette of 64 colors. The EGA preserved software compatibility by continuing to support the text and graphics modes in the MDA and CGA. The EGA supported a 640 x 350 monochrome mode similar to the Hercules graphics mode. The EGA could interface to all existing direct-drive monitors used by the CGA and MDA. In addition, the EGA had new scan and refresh rates to support its higher resolution capabilities. To support these high-resolution modes, the EGA display was introduced.

With the announcement of the PS/2 family of products, IBM supported two new display adapters. Both are integrated into the PS/2 systems boards and support analog RGB color interfaces to their compatible displays. The MCGA (Multi Color Graphics Adapter) was incorporated in the PS/2 models 25 and 30 and supported all modes of the older CGA, plus 640 x 480 2-color and 320 x 200 256-color modes. All other PS/2 systems use an integrated VGA (Video Graphics Array). The VGA is available from IBM and others also packaged as a standard adapter board for use in PC and AT systems. The VGA supports all the older EGA graphics and text modes plus the new modes of the MCGA and a new 640 x 480 16-color mode. A new VGA display is required for use with the VGA adapter.

Display manufacturers responded to the different scan and refresh frequencies, different color encoding schemes, and direct drive versus analog interfaces by supplying a new type of display. Multisync displays can accept different signal frequencies and be configured for different types of display adapter interfaces. To incorporate these features, the cost of the multisync display is significantly higher than the EGA- or VGA-only compatible display. The VGA display and display adapter probably give the best performance and resolution for the price. The VGA supports all PC display modes, and the VGA display costs less than a multisync display.

Table 2-1 summarizes the display modes supported by each PC video adapter. Table 2-2 summarizes the display type interfaces required for each adapter. Many more display modes are possible by custom programming the display adapter. For example, in text modes on the EGA, MCGA, and VGA, a 132-character line can be selected with up to 43 lines per screen. In addition, all adapters after the MDA and CGA support user-definable character fonts by using a programmable character generator. EGA and VGA on PC XT or AT compatible bus interface boards carry their own BIOS support. These adapters can be used in older PCs and retain software compatibility. For detailed information on programming the

Table 2-1.   Display Modes Supported by PC Video Adapters

Display Mode	Colors/Gray Scales	Video Adapter Type
40 x 25 text	16	CGA, EGA, MCGA, VGA
80 x 25 text	16	CGA, EGA, MCGA, VGA
80 x 25 text	Monochrome	CGA, EGA, MCGA, VGA, HMDA
720 x 350 graphics	Monochrome	HMDA (not in BIOS)
320 x 200 graphics	4	CGA, EGA, MCGA, VGA
640 x 200 graphics	2	CGA, EGA, MCGA, VGA
320 x 200 graphics	16	EGA, VGA
640 x 200 graphics	16	EGA, VGA
320 x 200 graphics	256	MCGA, VGA
640 x 350 graphics	Monochrome	EGA, VGA
640 x 350 graphics	16	EGA, VGA
640 x 480 graphics	2	MCGA, VGA
640 x 480 graphics	16	VGA

Table 2-2. Video Interfaces Supported by Video Adapters

Display Adapter	Interface Type	Horizontal Sync Rate
CGA	RGB direct-drive composite	15.75 KHz
MDA/HMDA	Direct drive	18 KHz
EGA	RGB direct drive	21.8, 18, 15.75 KHz
MCGA	Analog RGB	31.5 KHz
VGA	Analog RGB	31.5 KHz

alternate modes of operation of these adapters, consult the IBM *Technical Reference* manuals.

The display adapters and displays listed in Tables 2-1 and 2-2 are now manufactured by many suppliers; in many instances, these adapters offer enhanced modes sometimes called Super EGA or Super VGA modes. Additional resolution and color are often provided in a compatible manner with the standard display modes.

Diskette Drives

Diskette drive size and capacity have also proliferated in the PC family. In most instances, the change was driven by new and better technology. The original PC was announced with single-sided, 5 1/4-inch diskette drives with 160K capacity and a double-sided version that provided 320K. In the next DOS release, the number of sectors per track was changed from 8 to 9, increasing the 160K drive to 180K and the 320K drive to 360K. Today, almost all PC XTs use the double-sided, 360K diskettes. When the PC AT was introduced, the 1.2-megabyte diskette and drive was introduced. This nearly tripled the capacity of the 5 1/4-inch diskette. The PC AT was still capable of reading and writing 160K, 180K, 320K, and 360K diskettes, but if the diskette was formatted in these modes and written to using the 1.2M drive, the data could not be read in a 1.2M drive. Naturally, 1.2M diskettes cannot be used in a 160K, 180K, 320K, or 360K drive.

With the announcement of the PS/2 systems, IBM abandoned the use of the 5 1/4-inch diskette in favor of the 3 1/2-inch diskette. This was a bold step because all industry software was distributed on 5 1/4-inch diskettes. Now, most software is available in both 5 1/4-inch and 3 1/2-inch diskettes. (Some companies provide both sizes in the same package.) The 3 1/2-inch diskettes have several benefits. First, the size of the drive allows smaller, more compact systems. Second, the small, rigid, enclosed diskettes are more sturdy and reliable than the thinly protected 5 1/4-inch floppy diskettes.

IBM introduced the 3 1/2-inch diskettes in two capacities: 720K and 1.44M. The smaller capacity drive is used exclusively on the PS/2 models 25 and 30. All other PS/2 models use the higher 1.44M drive and diskettes. Other manufacturers use the 3 1/2-inch diskette in PC XT and PC AT compatible systems, but most use the diskettes in portables and laptops. In these implementations, the capacities are mapped to the PC XT and AT 5 1/4-inch capacities. To support the migration of applications using 5 1/4-inch diskettes, IBM provides a 5 1/4-inch drive that interfaces to the PS/2 systems.

All diskette drive adapters in the PC systems family use Direct Memory Access (DMA) to transfer data between the diskette and system memory. One DMA channel is used because transfers are half duplex and the same channel can be used for reading from and writing to the diskette. The PC and PC XT add the diskette controller through a bus expansion slot. In the PC AT, the diskette controller is combined with the hard disk adapter, and takes one bus expansion slot. In all PS/2 models, the diskette controller is integrated on the system board and does not take a bus expansion slot. Table 2-3 defines the diskette drive types and sizes used in the PC systems family.

Table 2-3. PC Diskette Drive Size and Capacity

Diskette Size	Tracks/ Side	Heads (Sides)	Sectors/ Track	Total Capacity	System Use
5 1/4-inch	40	1	8	160K	PC, XT
5 1/4-inch	40	1	9	180K	PC, XT
5 1/4-inch	40	2	8	320K	PC, XT
5 1/4-inch	40	2	9	360K	PC, XT
5 1/4-inch	80	2	15	1.2M	PC AT
3 1/2-inch	80	2	9	720K	PS/2 models 25, 30
3 1/2-inch	80	2	18	1.44M	PS/2 models > than 30

Fixed Disks

Hard or fixed disks come in all shapes, sizes, and performance levels. Table 2-4 is a sampling of the types of diskettes typically used on some PC systems. The PS/2 family alone supports eight different fixed disk sizes and performance levels. Table 2-5 summarizes PS/2 fixed disks according to model.

Table 2-4.   Fixed Disk Capacities and Formats for PC Systems*

PC System	Typical Capacity	Cylinders	Sectors/ Track	Heads
PC XT	10M	306	17	4
PC AT	30M	733	17	5
PS/2 model 30	20M	612	17	4
PS/2 model 60	44M	732	17	7

* These are typical disk drives; the systems are not limited to these drives or capacities.

Table 2-5.   Fixed Disk Drives for PS/2 Systems

Drive Capacity	Access Time	System Usage
20M	80 ms	Models 30, 30-286, 50
30M	39 ms	Models 50, 55SX
44M	40 ms	Models 60, 80
60M	29 ms	Models 50Z, 55SX, 70, P70
70M	30 ms	Models 60, 80
115M	23 ms	Model 80
120M	23 ms	Models 70, P70
314M	23 ms	Model 80

Fixed Disk Selection Criteria

Along with cost and reliability, disk performance is a key consideration. Disk performance is typically summarized by the average access time. This number represents the average amount of time a seek to a specific track and sector will take on the drive. The time for a specific seek for a read or write operation depends on the initial track and sector location of the head relative to the new track and sector location. The actual access time is a summation of the following parameters:

- Number of tracks to the nearest head times the track-to-track access time
- Head settle time

- Rotational delay to the desired sector
- Sector transfer rate

From the preceding, the key disk parameters that determine disk performance are

- Number of heads (reduces number of track steps)
- Track-to-track access time (typically 2 ms)
- Head settle time (typically 10 ms)
- Rotational speed of disk (typically 3600 rpm)
- Data transfer rate (typically 5 or 10 megabits/second)

Fixed disk drives are available with three types of interfaces to the PC's system controller. The most common is the ST506 interface standardized by Segate Technologies for small Winchester technology fixed disks. This interface operates at 5 megabits per second and is the most commonly used disk interface. On newer and higher performance disks, there is ESDI (Enhanced Small Device Interface). This interface supports disk data rates in excess of 10 megabits per second and error correction. SCSI (Small Computer Systems Interface) is a high-level, I/O channel disk interface. The disk drive usually contains the SCSI subsystem controller. SCSI drives are more expensive but present significantly less control load and less processing load to the PC system. To support a SCSI drive, a SCSI adapter must be installed in the PC. For PC XTs, the ST506 interface is standard. For PC ATs, the ST506 is used by some controllers to also support ESDI. SCSI disks and controllers are often used on 386/486 systems designed as LAN servers.

Fixed Disk Adapters

The PC XT fixed disk adapter uses an 8-bit expansion slot in the PC XT and is DMA driven using channel 3. Fixed disk BIOS is integrated in ROM on the adapter. The adapter supports one or two drives with an ST506 compatible interface.

The PC AT combines the diskette controller and fixed disk controller on a single 16-bit AT bus expansion slot board. The diskette controller uses DMA for data transfers, but the fixed disk controller uses programmed I/O. Programmed I/O operates more efficiently than DMA because the fixed disk data is buffered in 4K RAM. This RAM is accessed using 16-bit, 286 Repeat I/O instructions, which operate at AT bus bandwidth and require no program instruction fetches once inside the 286 instruction queue. The PC AT fixed disk adapter supports the attachment of two ST506 compatible drives. The adapter contains no BIOS ROM; fixed disk BIOS support is in system board ROM.

The PS/2 adapter is a 16-bit Micro Channel Architecture board that uses one 16-bit micro channel slot in the system. The adapter supports the ESDI interface to one or two disk drives. The adapter and system speed often are the limiting factor in fixed disk performance. If the adapter and system cannot operate on data in consecutive sectors, the disk is operated in an interleave mode. This involves formatting the disk in such a manner that the physical sector numbers and logical sector numbers do not correspond. A disk with an interleave factor of 4, for example, would number the sectors such that four real sectors are between each logical sector. This allows the adapter four real sector times between adjacent logical sector operations.

Depending on the processing time between sectors, adjusting the interleave factor on the fixed disk can have a significant impact on performance. With an interleave factor of 4, for example, four rotations of the disk are required to access all the data on the track. If the system and adapter can support an interleave factor of 1, you will get the best performance on large file operations. Generally, the lower the interleave factor, the better the adapter design and performance. Some applications with small length records requiring significant processing time, however, can perform better with larger interleave factors.

Printers

The original IBM PC was announced with an 80 characters per second (CPS) speed, an 8 x 8 character box, and no graphics support. To support letter-quality printing, third parties provided daisywheel impact printers with speeds typically around 30 CPS. Today, a wide variety of printers are available, ranging from low-cost dot-matrix technology to high-resolution laser printers. In this section, we will review the printer technologies on PC systems today, comparing the capabilities of each.

Dot-matrix printers are still providing low-cost, near-letter quality printing with graphics support, although several other printer technologies may be more appropriate for certain applications. 80-column dot-matrix printers with 9-wire heads supporting 200 CPS in draft mode and 30 CPS in near-letter quality (NLQ) mode and providing full graphics support are now available for under $200.00. Dot-matrix printers at speeds of 350 CPS in draft mode and 80 CPS in NLQ mode are available also at reasonable prices. Letter-quality (LQ) modes are available on the more expensive printers. Key items to investigate when selecting a dot-matrix printer are summarized in the following list:

- Number of wires in the head. The more wires per head, the higher the resolution of characters printed in a single pass. Printers with 8 to 24 wires per head are available.
- Bidirectional printing capability. This reduces the print head movement to the next line and increases throughput.
- Form feed slew rate. This indicates how fast a printer can advance the paper line-to-line. Fast line printing can be defeated by a slow form feed slew rate.
- Type of form feed mechanism. Pressure feeds are best for single sheet operations, whereas tractor feeds are better for multiple sheet jobs. Some printers support both.
- Paper width sizes supported.
- Number of columns that can be printed. Some printers can control the font size and can print variable length columns.
- Maximum dot resolution capability, usually expressed in dots per inch. This is crucial to the printer's capability to display graphic images and produce near-letter quality and letter-quality output. Some printers have different resolutions in the horizontal and vertical directions.
- Types and number of character fonts supported. Some printers support multiple fonts, character sizes, and styles. Does the printer support proportionately spaced fonts?
- Does the printer support the full IBM standard character set? Some printers support alternate character sets, foreign character sets, multiple fonts, or user-programmed character sets and fonts.
- Variable line spacing support. This is often controlled by Escape character programming sequences.
- What are the printer speeds (in CPS) in draft, NLQ, and LQ modes? Note that these numbers can be greatly inflated if a small size font with narrow character box size is selected.
- Is the APA graphics mode supported?
- Can the printer support both portrait and landscape printing?
- Does the printer support any high-level graphics language such as PostScript of HPL?

Many of these questions and specification issues are valid independent of the printer technology selected.

IBM has introduced a new twist on the dot-matrix printer in their

Quietwriter series of printers. This printer uses a resistive ribbon thermal transfer technique. The print head wires selectively pass an electrical current through the ribbon, melting the ink and transferring it to the paper. This technique significantly reduces mechanical wear and noise while providing dot-matrix levels of resolution and performance.

Even with all the advances in dot-matrix technology, much of the best looking printing is produced by engrave printers. Engrave printers are similar to a typewriter in the way they form characters; an engraved character on a chain or disk strikes a ribbon, transferring the ink to the paper. Many still consider this the best high-quality printing available, exceeding laser printer quality. This technology, however, has some drawbacks. First, changing a font or character set typically involves changing a print wheel disk. Second, graphics are not easily supported. Third, the printers are usually expensive and difficult to maintain.

With the introduction of low-cost laser printers, high-quality printing and graphics were combined. This has resulted in the creation of desktop publishing. Laser printers support resolutions of 300 x 300 dots per inch with APA bit-map memories from 0.5 to 4.0 megabytes, and print at speeds in the range of 8 to 20 pages per minute. The large memories permit simultaneous use of user-defined soft fonts and the printer's built-in hard fonts. An entry-level laser printer costs less than $1000.00.

Printer Interfaces

Most printers support either an RS-232C serial asynchronous port interface or a Centronix parallel printer port interface. Some support both. If the printer is near the PC, the parallel port should be used, if possible, because parallel ports transfer data faster than serial ports. The printer controls the rate using an Acknowledge or Busy signal on the parallel port interface. It is particularly important to use the parallel port if the printer supports APA bit-map graphics, in which the volume of transferred data is high.

Serial port attachment to the printer is usually through the PC's COM1 or COM2 port, which normally operates at speeds up to 19.2K baud. The advantage of using the serial port is that the printer can be farther from the PC. Without a modem, a distance of 50 feet is possible. With a modem, the distance is nearly unlimited, but the data rate has to be adjusted down to meet the maximum speed capability of the modem.

Standard PCs have one serial port and one parallel port. If you use the serial port to attach the printer, a second serial port must be added to support communications applications and to support some mouse models. When a serial port is used to directly connect to a printer, a special cable called a modem eliminator may be required if both the PC and the printer "think" they are DTE (Data Terminal Equipment) and thus are transmitting and receiving on the same signal leads.

Communications Adapters

As the community of PC users increased, the desire to communicate with each other over greater distances using the telephone network naturally increased. In addition, PCs quickly became intelligent terminals to host computers, which required connections over phone lines. The standard communications interface for the PC is through the RS-232C COM1 or COM2 asynchronous data communications port. DOS supports data rates of up to 9600 baud on COM ports. Through custom programming of the hardware, data rates of up to 115.2K baud can be obtained. (These rates violate the communications chip and driver/receiver specifications; the maximum safe rate is generally considered to be 57.6K baud.)

To interface serial ports to analog telephone lines, modems are typically used. The actual data rate achieved over phone lines with modems depends on the modem and the quality of the telephone line. A typical 2400-baud modem costs less than $200.00. You also can purchase communications adapters that incorporate the modem and attach directly to the phone line. These adapters fit directly in the PC bus expansion slots and are called "under-the-cover" modems. An under-the-cover, 1200-baud modem adapter costs less than $100.00.

The COM ports on the PC are often used to attach user terminals in multitasking, multiuser operating system environments such as UNIX. In this case, multiple COM ports are normally required. Several vendors supply adapter boards with as many as eight ports per board. On the PS/2, IBM offers a dual COM port adapter board that fits in a Micro Channel Architecture bus expansion slot.

Attachments to IBM hosts often require synchronous protocols such as BSC (Binary Synchronous Communications), SDLC (Synchronous Data Link Control), and HDLC (High-level Data Link Control). The PC's asynchronous COM ports do not support these protocols; special adapters are required and are available from IBM and many other vendors. For the PS/2, IBM offers a multiprotocol adapter that supports all of the previously mentioned protocols on a single Micro Channel Adapter board.

The increase in performance levels of PCs has resulted in a desire for data communications support at speeds greater than those provided by the analog telephone network. The trend is to high-performance digital networks in which modems are not required and data rates up to T1 carrier speeds of 1.5 megabits per second are available. These are synchronous networks and therefore work best with synchronous protocols such as SDLC and HDLC. Table 2-6 lists some of the synchronous digital service network types now available.

Table 2-6. Synchronous Digital Networks

Network Type	Data Rates Supported
DDS (Digital Dataphone Service)	56K bits/sec
Switch 56/64	56K and 64K bits/sec
ISDN Basic Rate Interface	16K, 56K, and 64K bits/sec Three channels per line: D channel = 16K bits/sec B1 channel= 56K or 64K bits/sec B2 channel= 56K or 64K bits/sec
T1 or ISDN primary rate	1.5 megabits/second
Fractional T1	64K x N (N=1 to 24) bits/second

PCs interfacing to these networks require special network interface units called CSUs (Customer Service Units). To obtain the maximum throughput allowed by these networks, the PCs must use synchronous adapters and protocols. Unfortunately, most PC software uses ASCII asynchronous protocol. To use PC asynchronous software on these networks, the asynchronous data must be converted to synchronous mode. Several standards are used to perform the rate adaption conversion. All have drawbacks; the most severe drawback is the loss of performance. Most rate adaption conversion techniques will support only a 19.2K baud asynchronous transfer on a 56K or 64K bits per second synchronous line. Following is a list of typical standard conversion protocols:

- X.3/X.28/X.29 PAD (converts asynchronous to X.25)
- DMI mode 2 (converts asynchronous to HDLC)
- V.120 (converts asynchronous to X.25 layer 2 LAPB or LAPD)
- V.110 (converts asynchronous to 80-bit synchronous frame)

Trillium Network Systems, located in Evergreen, Colorado, markets a PC asynchronous COM port adapter board that allows direct attachment to synchronous digital networks and sends PC asynchronous data without rate adaption overhead. This permits existing PC asynchronous software to take full advantage of the performance of the new digital networks. The Trillium Network Systems COM 64 adapter supports data rates up to 256K bits per second. In addition, Trillium provides a family of communication adapters supporting direct connection to ISDN Basic Rate Interfaces.

Memory Expansion Adapters

A popular PC upgrade is memory expansion. Memory upgrades can take the form of chips installed in sockets on the system board, SIMMs (Single In-line Memory Modules) installed in slots on system boards or on memory boards, and memory boards installed in bus expansion slots on PC system boards. The most important consideration in the selection of a memory upgrade feature is its performance compatibility with the target system; the memory must be fast enough to operate at the system clock rate. To ensure proper operation in the system, some memory expansion boards insert wait states in the bus cycles to slow the cycle time.

Today, most PC XTs, ATs, and compatibles come with a minimum 640K RAM, and upgrades take the form of more memory on the system board either in sockets, SIMMs, or memory-expansion specific board slots. (The standard is 640K because this is the most DOS will directly address.) Memory on the system board does not have to be attached through the expansion slot bus; it can more efficiently attach to the local microprocessor bus, thus permitting greater microprocessor clock speeds and saving an expansion slot.

If you install memory boards in the bus expansion slots of many high clock rate PC XTs, ATs, and PS/2 systems, the system cannot operate at maximum clock rates without inserting extra clock cycles (wait states) in the bus cycles. In general, it is best to select a system that permits memory expansion on the system board because this allows an optimized connection directly to the local bus of the microprocessor.

In an attempt to overcome the 640K limit of DOS, several expanded memory schemes are now in practice. In general, these schemes involve the mapping of blocks of paged memory into the real address space of DOS. Many memory expansion boards support some version of expanded memory. Care should be taken to understand the capabilities of the system and the memory expansion features relative to your applications that are capable of using expanded memory. With 286-based systems, a full 16 megabytes of RAM can be addressed. Only operating systems capable of running in protected mode, such as UNIX and OS/2, are capable of directly using this increased memory capacity; DOS is still limited to 640K. However, extended memory was used for RAM drives, print spoolers, and disk sector caching. Some system and memory expansion features for PC AT systems permit the use of memory above 1M as either expanded memory or extended memory. If all of this is confusing, I suggest that you consult *MS-DOS Beyond 640K, Working with Extended and Expanded Memory* by James Forney.

Performance Accelerator Adapters

Performance accelerator adapters typically are high-speed processors and memory subsystems that plug into a PC's bus expansion slot and take over the execution of system software. The most popular performance accelerator is a 386 processor with RAM installed in older PC XT and AT systems. All system memory is on the accelerator board because the board normally cannot use the memory already installed in the PC. This type of accelerator board is a very cost-effective way to increase the performance of an older system. With the advent of the 486, 486 performance accelerator boards will be available with this enhanced processor. IBM has recently announced a 486 performance accelerator board for their PS/2 model 70 system. When you select an accelerator board (as when you select a system), consider how much memory is supported on the adapter and what memory expansion schemes are supported.

Image Capture Devices

The advent of low-cost laser printers, high-resolution color displays, and desktop publishing has fueled the need to capture images for PC processing. Several vendors offer Video Frame Capture adapters that use standard TV cameras as image input devices. The images are digitized and available for PC processing, such as scaling, rotating, and editing. Some adapters perform image data compression and decompression, thus supporting efficient transmission and storage of high-resolution color images.

Several vendors now offer small, low-cost, hand-held image scanners that can capture APA grey-scale images from photographs, magazines, and the like. With many popular word processing and desktop publishing software packages, you can import digitized image data, then incorporate the data in documents. Image capture systems are often used with PC fax boards to facilitate image transfer on phone lines. PC fax boards are now available for reception and transmission of PC graphic and text images at group three data rates of 9600 bits per second.

Mouses

The mouse has become the preferred pointing device for PC applications. Many user application interfaces are dramatically improved with the use of the mouse to point to menus and images and to position data and images on the display. The PS/2 family incorporates a standard pointing device port on all models. Four features of the mouse require consideration:

- Bus versus serial
- Mechanical versus optical
- Resolution
- Number of buttons

On most PC XT and AT systems, you can attach a mouse in two ways. First, you can attach a mouse to one of the RS-232C asynchronous communication ports of the PC. If the PC has a spare COM port, this is the least expensive way to attach a mouse. If a serial port is not available, you can buy a mouse with a bus interface adapter that plugs into one of the system bus expansion slots. Either attachment method works fine. The pointing device port of the PS/2 system can be attached only to an IBM compatible mouse. The serial and bus mouse interfaces between the PS/2 and the PC XT and AT are not compatible.

Two types of technology are used to detect direction and motion in the mouse: mechanical and optical. The mechanical mouse uses a large rubber ball that rotates as the mouse is moved. The rotation is detected and sent to the PC through the interface attachment cable. In an optical mouse, an LED sends the mouse pad a light beam, which is reflected to a receiver that measures the distance and direction traveled. Generally, an optical mouse is more expensive and more reliable, and may require a special pad to operate on.

The resolution of the mouse is an important specification that indicates how small a movement can be detected. As displays get larger with greater resolution, the selection of small items and regions using the mouse will require higher resolution. Standard mouse resolution today is between 100 and 200 dots per inch (DPI). A high-res mouse supporting EGA and VGA displays should be between 200 and 350 DPI.

The number of button switches on the mouse should be considered; some applications require three buttons and others only two. The number of buttons indicates the number of optional signals that can be sent to an application when a mouse has reached a position. The three-button mouse can send three different signals to the application. The IBM PS/2 provides a two-button mechanical mouse.

Mass Storage Devices

PCs often need to store and have access to large amounts of data. In the past, this was accomplished using large magnetic media fixed disk drives or magnetic tape drives. But the disk drives were expensive, and the tape drives had slow sequential access. Laser disk technology was long viewed as a potential alternative, but until recently, data had to be placed on the disk at the time it was manufactured, making updates and changes expensive and impractical. Now, laser disk technology supports a write once, read many (WORM) capability. IBM has introduced with the PS/2 family the IBM 3363 optical disk drive, which provides WORM capability on 200M disks. Several vendors now supply optical disk WORM technology that supports adapters and drives for PC XT, AT, and Micro Channel bus systems.

Backup Devices

Periodically backing up fixed disk data on another type of media is required in many user environments where loss of data is critical. Backup using floppy diskettes is tedious and not practical for larger disks. Most backup devices are 1/4- or 1/2-inch tape units. The fastest and least expensive tape unit is a streaming tape unit, which backs up an entire fixed disk drive in a non-selective manner. Streaming tape units cannot selectively retrieve portions of data.

Backup devices using VCR tapes are also available. They use standard TV VCR tape and drive technologies converted to store digital information. Backup units using fixed disk cartridges are also available. Although they are fast and support selective retrieval, they generally have a lower capacity and higher cost than tape units.

Interfacing Adapters

In many applications, the PC is interfaced to real-world environments. Examples include sensing data and controlling external events through devices such as relays and actuators. For the PC to perform this external environment interfacing, different types of interfacing adapter boards are required. Vendors have responded with adapter boards that meet nearly every imaginable interfacing need.

Multifunction Adapters

Many PCs have a limited number of bus expansion slots. Users often run out of available expansion slots. To relieve this problem, vendors have produced numerous multifunction adapters, in which a board incorporates several functions. Multiple serial and parallel ports combined with memory are very popular because they save slots and reduce adapter costs.

Chapter 3

PC Microprocessors

THE PC'S MAJOR ENHANCEMENTS in performance and function can be traced back to the major innovations in the Intel microprocessor family. The PC product line now spans four generations of Intel microprocessors, starting with the 8088/8086 to the 286 to the 386 and now to the 486 microprocessor. This chapter describes these microprocessors and compares their capabilities and features. But first a little history.

As the architect and design team leader for the IBM PC project, I am often asked why the 8088 microprocessor was selected for the original PC design. At the time of the PC's development, IBM viewed the major competition as the Apple II and a growing family of Z80 CPM-based systems, with Radio Shack the low-cost price leader. The goal was a better performing and expandable machine starting at the Apple II price. This goal immediately ruled out a number of competing microprocessors, including all IBM proprietary designs, which at this time were very expensive, and multichips, which had nonstandard power requirements, required significant TTL glue chips to form a system design, had few companion peripheral chips, and were difficult to package using low-cost circuit board technology.

Some of the competitors were the IBM Series 1 processor, the System 3 mainstore processor, and the communication microprocessor in the IBM 37xx product line. A major problem with these microprocessors was the lack of IBM or third-party software development tools that ran on the target microprocessors. You needed an IBM mainframe to do software development, which was somewhat beyond the target developer's means. The 6502 family of microprocessors was ruled out due to its use in the Apple product line; the last thing IBM wanted was to be viewed as an Apple-compatible manufacturer.

The Z80 was a strong competitor with its high performance, large user base, and third-party development tools, as well as its good language, operating system (CPM), and application support. But the Z80 had four basic problems. First, if IBM used the Z80, it would be viewed as a follower endorsing again the architecture and operating system of a number of small competitors. Second, the Z80 architecture supported a limited address space of 64K, without a paging scheme implemented external to the microprocessors. Third, there was no visible migration path to higher performance, larger address space systems using the Z80. Fourth, the Z8000 microprocessor (next generation Z80) had a totally different architecture. IBM Japan proposed a dual-processor PC using the Z80 to support existing applications and a Z8000 for new applications, which was an expensive hardware solution requiring the support of two software environments. The Intel 8048 single-chip microprocessor used in a multiprocessor architecture was also proposed by an IBM group in the Northeast. This was never given serious consideration due to the software limitations of the 8048.

We have now ruled out IBM microprocessors and the classic 8-bit microprocessors of the time. This left only one other competitor, the Motorola 68000. The 68000 supported a large linear address space and a register-based instruction set that was very attractive to software developers. An excellent architecture chip, it has proven to be a worthy competitor to the Intel-based architecture microprocessors. But at the time, the 68000 was viewed as having many of the same drawbacks as the IBM proprietary microprocessors.

There were four major concerns with the 68000. First, because it was a true 16-bit data and 24-bit address device, it would require a more expensive system board design, including more bus buffer chips and TTL glue chips, larger expansion slot connectors, and a more complex circuit board design (more layers). Second, the 16-bit bus required twice the memory chips (ROM and RAM) for a minimum system implementation; the minimum memory size and memory increments would always be twice the size and cost of an 8-bit bus. Third, benchmark analysis of the 68000 indicated a performance edge over the 8086, but it was not as memory efficient as the 8086 architecture, making a small-system implementation less competitive. Fourth, the 68000 lacked companion peripheral and support chips comparable to what was provided by Intel and third-party vendors for the Intel bus compatible microprocessors.

The most damaging concern with the 68000 was its lack of software support, including development tools, languages, operating system, and applications. This was also somewhat true of the 8088/8086 processors. Intel, however, provided a migration strategy from the 8080 architecture and software to the 8086 architecture. The 8086 preserved the 8080 register architecture and condition codes and provided a software utility that converted 8080-based code to 8086 code. This provided the opportunity to convert the existing 8080 software base to the 8086, and in actuality, most initial PC software was converted 8080 software.

A number of other circumstances affected the decision to use the 8088. The PC design is often viewed as IBM's first encounter with Intel, but IBM had an ongoing relationship with Intel. IBM was using Intel processors in a number of products prior to the PC design. The 8080 was used as a communications controller in the IBM 5100 portable computer, the 8086 was used in the IBM Display writer, the 8085 was used in the 5250 terminals for the System 3X mainframes and the IBM Data Master, and the 8048 was used in IBM keyboards. Thus, IBM had extensive experience with Intel and Intel technology. To be used in IBM products, Intel parts had to pass IBM's quality standards and tests. Another strong motivation was Intel's capability to offer a kit price for the majority of the PC chip set.

In summary, the 8088 was selected because it allowed the lowest cost implementation of an architecture that provided a migration path to a larger address space and higher performance implementations. Because it was a unique choice relative to competitive system implementations, IBM could be viewed as a leader rather than as a follower. It had a feasible software migration path that allowed access to the large base of existing 8080 software. The 8088 was a comfortable solution for IBM. Was it the best processor architecture available at the time? Probably not, but history seems to have been kind to this decision.

The following sections define the key architectural differences between the microprocessors in the PC system product family and identify which systems use which processors. For detailed information on a processor's architecture, instruction sets, and hardware interfacing details, consult Intel's *Microprocessor and Peripherals Handbook, Volume 1, Processors*. Figure 3-1 illustrates the Intel microprocessor family; note that not all members are used in the PC product line. Table 3-1 summarizes the types of Intel microprocessors used in PC systems. To define the base capabilities of these microprocessors, the architecture of the 8088/8086 is presented next.

8088 Microprocessor

The 8088 microprocessor is a derivation of the 8086 microprocessor; the major difference is the data-bus width. The 8086 has both an internal data-

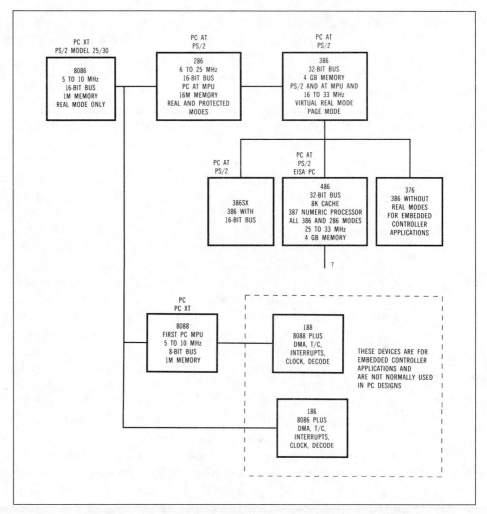

Figure 3-1. Intel 8086 architecture microprocessor family.

path and an external memory data-bus width of 16 bits, whereas the 8088 has an internal data-path width of 16 bits but a memory interface of only 8 bits. Code written for either processor will execute on the other processor with no changes. Code written on a different 8088- or 8086-based system, however, will not necessarily run without change. This is because the code may be dependent on system resources or functions other than those of the processor.

The difference in bus width between the 8086 and 8088 could lead you to conclude that the 8086 is twice as fast as the 8088 processor. In general, this is not true. The 8088 executes its instructions from an internal queue that is filled as soon as there is an empty location; thus, it is possible to overlap execution cycles and instruction-fetch bus cycles. As

Table 3-1.   Intel Microprocessor Usage in PC Systems

PC System	Microprocessors
PC	8088
PC XT	8088, 8086
PC AT	286, 386, 386SX, 486
PS/2 models 25 and 30	8086
PS/2 model 30 (286)	286
PS/2 models 50, 50Z, 60	286
PS/2 model 55SX	386SX
PS/2 models 70 and 80	386
PS/2 model 70 (486)	486
PS/2 model P70	386
EISA bus systems	286, 386, 386SX, 486

long as instructions are executed from the internal queue and do not have to wait for a bus cycle, they execute as fast as they would on an 8086 processor. If data cycles are 16 bits long, however, they will take two memory cycles; in an 8086 microprocessor, it will take only one cycle. Thus, if an application is oriented heavily toward 8-bit data, it will perform nearly as well on an 8088 microprocessor as it will on an 8086 processor. If the application is 16-bit in nature, the 8088 will perform less well, but not usually at half speed.

The following is a summary of the highlights of the 8088 microprocessor, all of which are described in greater detail later in this chapter:

- 16-bit internal architecture
- Supports 1 megabyte of attached memory
- 8- and 16-bit signed and unsigned arithmetic in both binary and decimal notation, including multiply and divide
- 14 16-bit registers
- Maskable and nonmaskable interrupt capability
- 24-operand addressing modes
- Direct-memory access capability
- Supports for local bus coprocessors
- Supports both memory-mapped I/O and I/O-mapped I/O
- String operations

The instruction set of the 8088 microprocessor is very large and could by itself be the subject of a book. It is only summarized in this book—see Table 3-7 at the end of this chapter. If you require detailed descriptions and timing information on the 8088 instruction set, obtain one of the following books:

> *iAPX 88 Book*, published by Intel Corporation
> *iAPX 86, 88 User's Manual*, published by Intel Corporation
> *Macro Assembler*, published by IBM

Interface Signal Pins

A good way to learn about the 8088 microprocessor is to learn about the functions of its interface signal pins. Figure 3-2a is a functional block diagram of the 8088 CPU. Figure 3-2b is a pin definition diagram of the 8088's signals; note that some pins have two definitions.

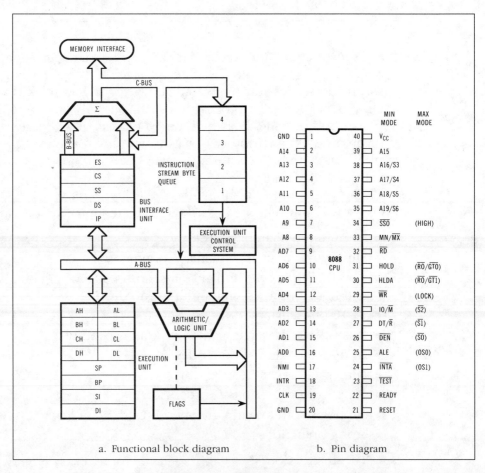

a. Functional block diagram   b. Pin diagram

Figure 3-2. The 8088 microprocessor. *(Courtesy Intel Corporation)*

The 8088 processor has two modes of operation that are selected by strapping pin 33 (MN/MX). When the pin is held high, the 8088 is in minimum mode and its interface pins are compatible with those of an 8085 microprocessor; it can be directly attached to any of the 8085 family of support devices. When in minimum mode, a bus controller chip is not needed because the bus commands are decoded and available from the 8088. The request/grant interface is not supported in minimum mode and, thus, you cannot attach coprocessors, such as the 8087 math coprocessor. In the PC design, pin 33 is strapped low so that it operates in maximum mode. Therefore, only maximum mode pin definitions will be described here.

AD0–AD7   Signal pins AD0–AD7 (pins 9–16) transmit memory and I/O address information on each bus cycle. These signals, however, are multiplexed; they carry address bits A0–A7 at the beginning of the bus cycle and, later in the cycle, are used as the processor's data bus. In the PC design, the address information on A0–A7 is latched off from this bus. These signals are then repowered and become the system-bus address bits A0–A7. These signals are also repowered and become the system's data bus D0–D7.

A8–A15   Signal lines A8–A15 (pins 2–8 and pin 39) output memory and I/O address bits A8–A15 on each bus cycle. These lines are not multiplexed, and they remain stable throughout the bus cycle. In the PC design, these lines are latched, repowered, and then become the system-bus address bits A8–A15.

A16/S3–A19/S6   At the beginning of each memory bus cycle, signals A16/S3–A19/S6 (pins 35 through 38) carry memory address bits A16–A19. During the remainder of the cycle, these bits present the 8088 internal status. When S6 is set low, S5 gives the status of the interrupt enable flag, and S4 and S3 are encoded to tell which segment register is being used for the bus cycle. The PC design does not use this status information. These lines are latched, repowered, and then become the system-bus address bits A16–A19. Table 3-2 defines the decoded values of the S4 and S3 status bits, which identify the segment register used during an 8088 bus cycle.

CLK   The CLK input line (pin 19) provides the basic timing information for the 8088 microprocessor. In the PC design, this line comes from the 8284A clock chip and is a 4.77-MHz signal with a 1/3 duty cycle.

RQ/GT0   The RQ/GT0 is a bidirectional signal used by other local bus masters to request the use of the local bus. In the PC design, this line (pin 31) is tied to the RQ/GT0 line on the auxiliary processor socket. This socket is compatible with the 8087 numeric processor manufactured by

Table 3-2.   S4 and S3 Status Bit Decodes

S4	S3	Segment
0	0	Alternate data segment
0	1	Stack segment
1	0	Code segment
1	1	Data segment

Intel. The RQ/GT0 signals allow the auxiliary processor to take over the local bus and, consequently, the stem to perform its functions.

RQ/GT1   The RQ/GT1 line (pin 30) performs the same function as the RG/GT0 line, but it has a lower priority level. In the PC design, this line is not used and tied up.

LOCK   The LOCK line (pin 29) is activated by a lock instruction prefix and remains active until the end of the next instruction. It is used to indicate to other bus masters that they should not attempt to gain control of the bus. Because the PC design is not a multimaster bus design, this line is not used.

NMI   The NMI input line (pin 17) generates a nonmaskable interrupt to the 8088 microprocessor. In the PC design, it is masked outside the processor with a programmable port bit. This interrupt request input is used to report parity errors in the system board memory, accept interrupt requests from the auxiliary processor socket, and accept interrupt requests from devices on the system bus.

INTR   The INTR input signal (pin 18) is the maskable interrupt input to the 8088 processor. In the PC design, it is attached to the 8259A interrupt controller, which expands the input to 8 system interrupt inputs.

READY   The READY input line (pin 22) is used to insert wait states in the 8088 microprocessor bus cycles and, thus, extend the length of a cycle. This signal is used to slow the 8088 processor when it is accessing an I/O port or memory that is too slow for a normal 8088 bus cycle. In the PC design, this line comes from the 8284A clock chip, which synchronizes it with the system clock. The PC uses the READY function to insert one wait state in all I/O port accesses and DMA cycles, and to provide a wait-state generation function on the system bus.

RESET   The RESET signal (pin 21) is used to halt the microprocessor. In the PC design, this signal comes from the 8284A clock chip, which receives its input from the system's power supply. The system power supply generates a signal called *power good*, which indicates that the power levels are at their proper levels and RESET can be removed from the 8088 processor.

QS0 and QS1   The QS0 and QS1 output lines (pins 24 and 25) give the status of the 8088's internal instruction queue. In the PC design, these lines are wired to the auxiliary processor socket in such a manner that it can track the status of the 8088's queue.

TEST   The TEST input pin (pin 23) is tested by the *wait for test* instruction. If TEST is low, execution continues; if TEST is high, the 8088 waits in an idle state until the pin goes low. In the PC design, the TEST input is wired to the BUSY output pin of the 8087 coprocessor socket.

S0, S1, and S2   The S0, S1, and S2 output pins (pins 26 through 28) present status information that pertains to the type of bus cycle that will be performed. This status is valid at the beginning of each bus cycle. In the PC design, these bits are wired to the 8288 bus controller chip, where they are decoded. The 8088 decoded output signals become the control lines on the system bus. The following signals are generated from the status lines by the 8288 bus controller and are present on the system bus: IOR, IOW, MEMR, MEMW, and ALE. Table 3-3 defines the decoding of the S0, S1, and S2 status output lines.

Table 3-3.   Bus Cycle Type from Status Decodes

S0	S1	S2	Bus Cycle Type
0	0	0	Interrupt acknowledge
0	0	1	I/O port read
0	1	0	I/O port write
0	1	1	Halt
1	0	0	Code access
1	0	1	Memory read
1	1	0	Memory write
1	1	1	Passive

Memory Addressing

One of the unique characteristics of the 8088 microprocessor is its capability to address the more than 65,536 bytes of data specified by a 16-bit address field. The 8088 has a 20-bit address capability that allows a physical memory size of 1,048,576 bytes. Because most 8088 memory reference instructions permit the specification and manipulation of only a 16-bit address field, it would appear as though only 65,536 bytes of memory, at most, can be used. This is partially true; at any instance, the programmer's view of storage is limited to a 65,536-byte region. But the programmer has the capability of moving this 65,536-byte region to any 16-byte boundary in the 1,048,576-byte space. This is done by manipulating the contents of a special register called a *segment register*.

The value loaded into the segment register is used to locate the 64K region in the 1M space that the 8088 instructions operate on. Because the segment register is also only 16 bits, it cannot by itself specify any boundary in the 1M space. To solve this problem, the 16-bit register can now specify 65,536 different byte regions, on any 16-byte boundary in the 1-megabyte space. The physical memory address is formed by shifting the contents of the segment register left 4 bits and adding it to the instruction-generated 16-bit address. Figure 3-3 illustrates the physical address generation.

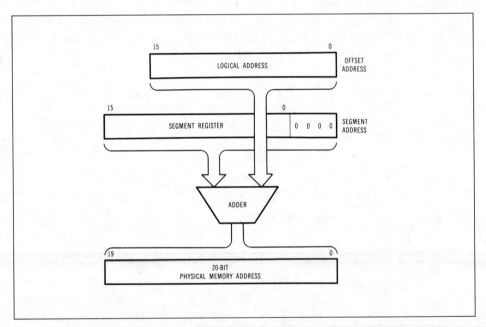

Figure 3-3. 8088 memory address generation. *(Courtesy Intel Corporation)*

There are four segment registers. One is used to address code, one is used to address data references by code, one is used to address data references in code through the stack, and one is an extra segment. The extra segment is typically used in data move operations when the operation takes place between two different 64K regions and there is a requirement for both a source segment register and a destination segment register.

These four segment registers can all point to different 64K regions in the 1-megabyte space. Thus, after the segment registers are set, the program instructions view a 64K code space. Anytime the program needs to reference outside these spaces, it must first manipulate the appropriate segment register. It should be noted that the segments can also overlap or all point to the same 64K space.

The segment's value is often referred to as the *base address*, and an address within a segment is called an *offset*. Thus, any address in the 1-megabyte address space can be identified by specifying a base and an offset. Note that many different base and offset combinations can be used to specify a memory address. Before we investigate addressing within a 64K segment (the offset), it is best to cover the register set of the 8088 microprocessor.

Registers

As mentioned, the 8088 has fourteen 16-bit registers. These registers can be further classified as follows: a data group of four registers, a pointer and an index group of four registers, four segment registers, an instruction pointer register, and a flag register. Figure 3-4 is a diagram of the 8088 register facilities.

Data Group Registers Four general-purpose, 16-bit registers are normally used by the instruction set to perform arithmetic and logical operations. These registers can be addressed also as eight 8-bit registers for byte operations of the instruction set.

The Pointer and Index Group The pointer and index group of four 16-bit registers is typically used to generate effective memory addresses as 16-bit values. These registers can be used also by the instruction set to perform arithmetic and logical operation.

In the 8088 instruction set, not all registers can be specified in each instruction. In many cases, an instruction can use only a specific register or register set to perform its function. For certain 8088 instructions performing specific operations, the registers have an implied usage, as shown in Table 3-4.

Segment Registers As previously discussed, the four 16-bit segment registers are used to place the 64K segments in the 1-megabyte address space. The segment register used with a specific memory reference is defined in Table 3-5. Note that a default segment register is selected by the 8088 microprocessor hardware. Further, in some cases, the programmer can override the default value and, by using a segment prefix instruction, specify a different segment register. See the previous section on memory addressing in this chapter for a description of the functions of these registers.

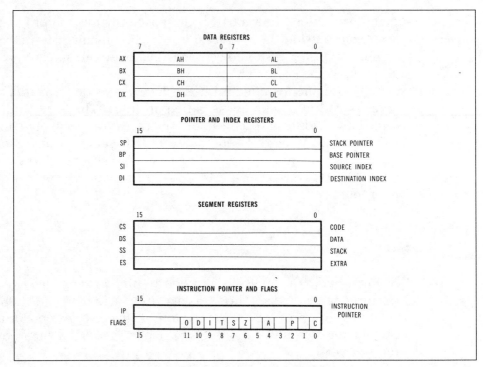

Figure 3-4. The 8088 register set. *(Courtesy Intel Corporation)*

Table 3-4.   Implicit Use of 8088 Registers

Register	Operations
AX	Word multiply, word divide, and word I/O
AL	Byte multiply, byte divide, byte I/O, translate, and decimal arithmetic
AH	Byte multiply and byte divide
BX	Translate
CX	String operations and loops
CL	Variable shift and rotate
DX	Word multiply, word divide, and indirect I/O
SP	Stack operations
SI	String operations
DI	String operations

The Instruction Pointer Register   The instruction pointer register contains the offset address of the next instruction from the current code-segment base value.

Table 3-5. Segment Register Use

Type of Memory Reference	Default Segment Base	Alternate Segment Base	Offset
Instruction fetch	CS	None	IP
Stack operation	SS	None	SP
Variable	DS	CS, ES, SS	Effective address
String source	DS	CS, ES, SS	SI
String destination	ES	None	DI
BP used as base register	SS	CS, DS, ES	Effective address

The Flag Register   The flag register is a 16-bit register, but only 9 bits are used. Of these bits, 6 are status bits that reflect the result of the instruction's arithmetic and logical operations and 3 are control bits. Figure 3-5 is a diagram of the flag bits. The following is a brief description of each flag:

AF   Auxiliary carry flag. It is set when there has been a carry out, a borrow from, or a borrow to a nibble in the decimal arithmetic instructions.

CF   Carry flag. This bit is set if there has been a carry out or a borrow to the high-order bit as a result of an arithmetic operation.

OF   Overflow flag. This bit is set if an arithmetic overflow has occurred. It indicates that the results are too large for the destination field.

SF   Sign flag. This bit indicates that the high-order bit of the result is set to a 1 and, thus, is a negative number.

PF   Parity flag. This bit is set when the results contain an even number of bits.

ZF   Zero flag. This bit is set when the result is zero.

DF   Direction flag. This bit is a control bit. When set, it causes string operations to be auto-decremented or processed from the high address to the low address. If this bit is set to zero, the string is processed in auto-increment mode.

IF   Interrupt-enable flag. This bit is a control bit. When set, it allows the 8088 processor to recognize external maskable interrupts.

TF   Trap flag. This bit is a control bit. When set, it puts the 8088
       microprocessor in single-step mode. After each instruction,
       an interrupt is automatically generated.

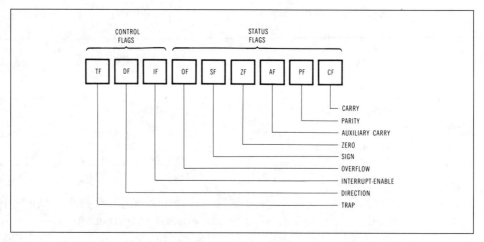

Figure 3-5. The 8088 flag bits. *(Courtesy Intel Corporation)*

Effective Memory Address Generation

Now that we have a good understanding of the resources in the 8088, we
can investigate how the instruction set addresses the memory within a
segment. As previously pointed out, a 20-bit address is physically made up
of two parts: a segment, or base, value and an offset, or effective-address,
value. The effective address is the sum of a displacement in the instruction, the contents of a base register, and the contents of an index register.
An 8088 instruction can specify any combination of these to create an effective address. Table 3-6 summarizes these addressing modes and the
registers available in each mode.

8086 Microprocessor

The 8086 microprocessor was identical to the 8088, with two exceptions.
First, the 8086 internal instruction queue was 6 bytes, versus the 4-byte
queue in the 8088. Second, it provided a 16-bit data bus, versus the 8-bit
data bus in the 8088. The 8086 was used in a number of compatible XT
class systems and later in the PS/2 models 25 and 30. It could run approximately 1.6 times faster than the 8088 at the same clock speeds. The 8086

offered no increased address space, no new instructions, and no new memory management features over the 8088.

Table 3-6. Effective Addressing Modes

Effective Address Mode	Registers Used
Displacement only	None
Base or Index only	BX, BP, SI, DI
Displacement + Base or Index	BX, BP, SI, DI
Base + Index	BP + DI, BX + SI BP + SI, BX + DI
Displacement + Base + Index	BP + DI + DISP BX + SI + DISP BX + DI + DISP

286 Microprocessor

The Intel 286 microprocessor, the first major enhancement to the 8086 architecture, was introduced in the PC AT systems. The 286 provided the following technical enhancements over the 8088/8086 processors:

- 24-bit memory addressing supporting 16 megabytes of attached memory
- Increased clock speeds (now up to 25 MHz)
- New instructions supporting multitasking environments
- Fewer clock cycles per instruction
- 16-bit data bus with a bus time of two clock cycles versus four clock cycles of the 8088
- New protected mode with an integrated memory management feature supporting:

  1 gigabyte virtual address space per task

Efficient task switching and access rights checking in a single instruction

Four-level memory protection scheme with segment descriptors defining the use and access rights to memory

- Support for older 8086 real-mode environment and the capability to switch from real mode to protected mode; unfortunately, switching from protected mode back to real mode was not as efficiently implemented

To users of the PC, the 286 only meant one thing, a high performance system. The full potential of 286 protected mode was never realized; few applications were developed for 286 protected mode because DOS couldn't support it. Access to extended memory (above 1 megabyte) while in DOS was very difficult; the use of extended memory was relegated to data applications such as RAM disks, print spoolers, and disk caches. DOS applications programmers who needed more program memory preferred to use the expanded memory schemes that mapped bus-attached memory to the 1M of real address space in the 286.

UNIX-like operating systems, which needed the features of 286 protected mode, were slow coming from IBM and others, further delaying efficient use of 286 protected mode. Today, several versions of UNIX and OS/2 and many lesser-known multitasking operating systems are ported to 286 protected mode.

Figure 3-6 is a block diagram of the 286 microprocessor. Figure 3-7 is a block diagram of protected mode memory addressing generation in the 286. Figure 3-8 illustrates the 286 user's register set. Figure 3-9 defines the data types supported by the 286 and its companion 287 numeric coprocessor.

386 Microprocessor

The introduction of the Intel 386 microprocessor provided the PC with a quantum leap in performance while retaining compatibility with existing software for the 8088 and 286 microprocessors. In addition, new protected modes of the 386 memory management hardware efficiently supported multiple operating system environments. The following is a summary of the 386 microprocessor's key technical improvements over the 286 microprocessor:

- Data and address buses were extended to 32 bits, supporting the attachment of 4 gigabytes of physical memory

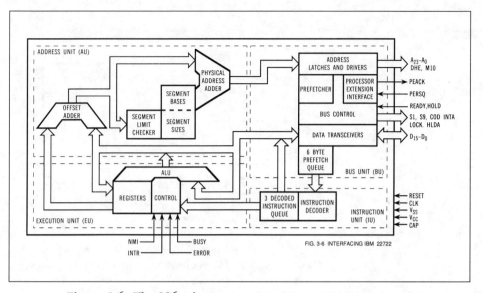

Figure 3-6. The 286 microprocessor. *(Courtesy Intel Corporation)*

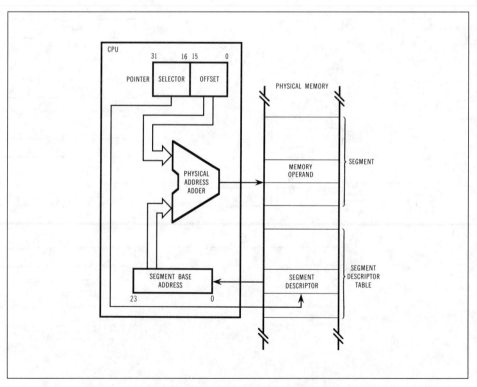

Figure 3-7. 286 memory addressing in protected mode.
(Courtesy Intel Corporation)

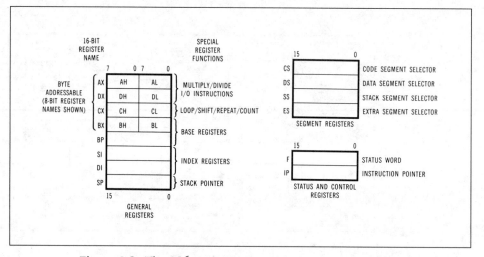

Figure 3-8. The 286 register set. *(Courtesy Intel Corporation)*

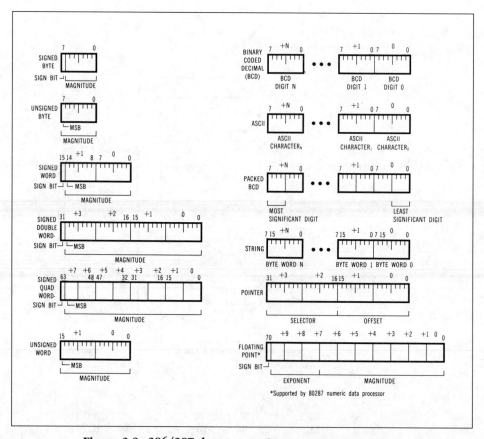

Figure 3-9. 286/287 data types. *(Courtesy Intel Corporation)*

- New instructions supported larger data types, larger address pointers, new functions, and memory management control
- Extended memory management features supported 64 terabytes of virtual memory per task, 32-bit linear address space mode, 8086 virtual protected mode, and page mode memory management
- Increased performance due to

    32-bit bus

    16-byte instruction queue

    New data types

    Fewer clocks per instruction

    New function instructions

    Faster memory management

    Higher clock speeds (16 to 33 MHz)

- Fully compatible with software for the 8088/8086 and 286 microprocessors

Aside from the 386's performance capabilities, the new 8086 protected mode is perhaps its most important new feature. In this mode, 8086 real mode applications can run in protected mode. This means that DOS and DOS applications can run as tasks under a protected mode operating system or supervisor. Environments can be created in which simultaneous DOS and DOS applications can be run on the 386. Using a window manager such as Windows 386 from Microsoft, a user can switch between several DOS applications running on the 386. You could effectively use extended memory above the 1-megabyte limit enforced by DOS, without modifying existing applications.

The 386 was complemented by a set of support chips that permitted efficient high-performance systems designs. Included with the 386 was the 387 numeric coprocessor and the 82380 integrated system support device providing 8 DMA channels, an interrupt controller, timer counters, DRAM refresh, and a wait-state generator. With the 80385 cache controller, the 386 could use low-cost DRAMs for system memory and still operate at peak performance. This four-chip set (386, 387, 82380, and 8038) provided a high performance, highly integrated central processor unit core.

Figure 3-10 is a block diagram of the 386 microprocessor. Figure 3-11 is a summary of the register architecture of the 386. Figure 3-12 is a block diagram of the address generation capabilities of the 386. Figure 3-13 is a summary of the data types supported by the 386 microprocessor and the 387 numeric coprocessor.

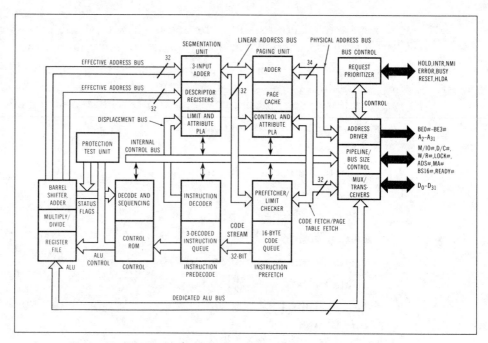

Figure 3-10. The 386 microprocessor. *(Courtesy Intel Corporation)*

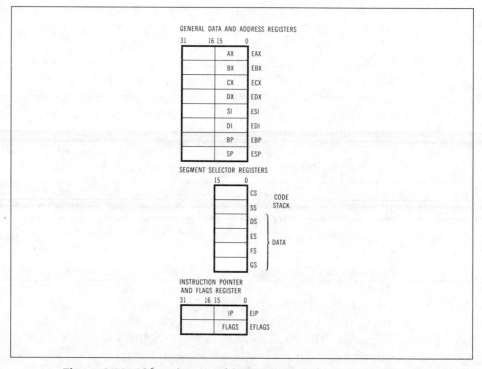

Figure 3-11. 386 register architecture. *(Courtesy Intel Corporation)*

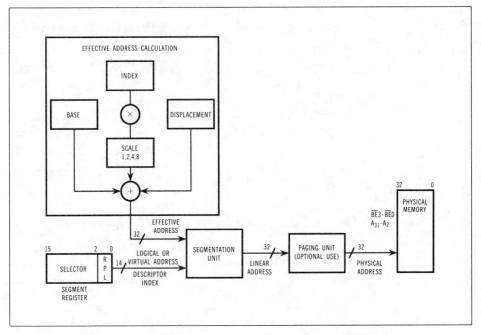

Figure 3-12. Memory address generation on the 386.
(Courtesy Intel Corporation)

386SX Microprocessor

The 386SX microprocessor is nearly identical to the 386. The one major difference is that the 386SX supports a 16-bit wide external data bus and a 24-bit address bus versus the 32-bit data bus and address bus of the 386. This permits the 386SX to be used in smaller, more cost-effective designs. Intel's intent was for designers to incorporate the 386SX when a 286 chip would normally be used. (Many AT bus systems are now available using the 386SX.) The 386SX chip is not a pin-for-pin replacement for the 286; therefore, upgrading 286 systems to 386SX in the field is not possible. As the clock rate for the 286 has increased, the viability of the 386SX has been questioned. The 286 high clock rate systems with zero wait-state memories outperform the 16-MHz 386SX system. The 386SX, however, has the advantage of supporting the 32-bit software capabilities of the 386 and its much enhanced memory management features. In other words, software for the 386 and 486 microprocessors will always run on the 386SX but may not run on the 286. If this is a concern, select a 386 or 386SX machine. IBM introduced the PS/2 model 55SX using the 386SX microprocessor as a low-end 386 system.

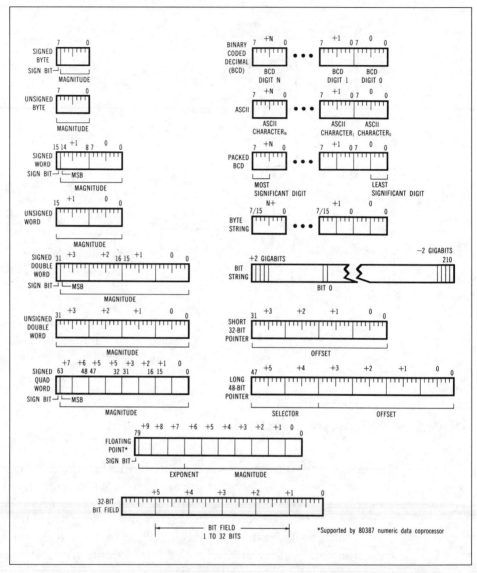

Figure 3-13. Data types supported by the 386 microprocessor and the 387 numeric coprocessor. *(Courtesy Intel Corporation)*

486 Microprocessor

The 486 is now the ultimate in 8086 and PC-compatible microprocessors offered by Intel. The 486 remains software compatible with the 386, adding only six new instructions. Other modifications were made to the system control registers to improve checking and support the management of the on-chip cache. The key features of the 486 are related not to new architecture capabilities but to dramatic performance improvements and the high level of silicon integration. The 486 contains the 387 numeric coprocessor and an 8K instruction and data cache system. The following is a summary of the key new features of the 486 chip:

- Addition of the 387 numeric coprocessor
- Addition of an 8K instruction and data cache system
- Modification of the bus interface to support single clock burst data transfers (16 bytes in five clock cycles)
- Support for a second-level cache
- Dramatic performance improvement (over 2 times that of the 386 at the same clock rate). The performance enhancements are attributed to the following 486 features:

  32-byte instruction queue

  Single clock cycle burst mode bus operation

  Integrated cache

  Significantly reduced number of clock cycles per instruction (many execute in a single clock cycle)

  Integrated numeric coprocessor

  Higher system clock speeds (25 MHz and 33 MHz now and rumored speeds of up to 50 MHz)

Figure 3-14 is a block diagram of the 486 microprocessor. Register architecture, memory addressing, and supported data types are identical to those presented previously for the 386 and 387. At present, the 486 is in the performance and price range of higher priced workstations. Over time, it will become the standard chip in PCs. Think of it: an improvement in performance more than 70 times greater than the computing power of the original PC!

Instruction Set Summary

The instructions in Table 3-7 are supported by all microprocessors described in the preceding sections: the 8088, 8086, 286, 386, 386SX, and 486. The 286, 386, and 486 microprocessors each added new instructions to support larger data types, more efficient data manipulation, and control of new memory management features.

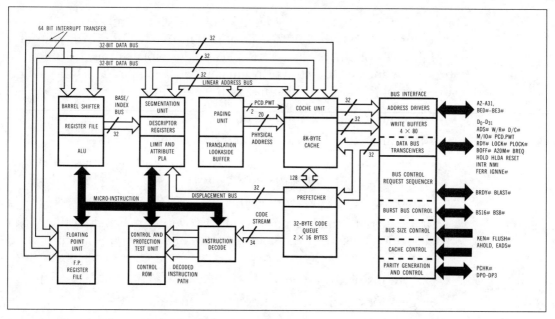

Figure 3-14. The 486 microprocessor. *(Courtesy Intel Corporation)*

Table 3-7.   Instruction Set Summary of the 8086 and 8088

Mnemonic and Description   Instruction Code

DATA TRANSFER

MOV = Move:

	76543210	76543210	76543210	76543210
Register/Memory to/from Register	100010dw	mod reg r/m		
Immediate to Register/Memory	1100011w	mod 0 0 0 r/m	data	data if w 1
Immediate to Register	1011 w reg	data	data if w 1	
Memory to Accumulator	1010000w	add-low	addr-high	
Accumulator to Memory	1010001w	addr-low	addr-high	
Register/Memory to Segment Register**	10001110	mod 0 reg r/m		
Segment Register to Register/Memory	10001100	mod 0 reg r/m		

PUSH = Push:

Register/Memory	11111111	mod 1 1 0 r/m
Register	01010 reg	
Segment Register	000 reg 110	

POP = Pop:

Register/Memory	10001111	mod 0 0 0 r/m
Register	01011 reg	
Segment Register	000 reg 111	

XCHG = Exchange:

Register/Memory with Register	1000011w	mod reg r/m
Register with Accumulator	10010 reg	

IN = Input from:

Fixed Port	1110010w	port
Variable Port	1110110w	

Table 3-7. *(cont.)*

Mnemonic and Description   Instruction Code

	76543210	76543210	76543210	76543210
OUT = Output to:				
Fixed Port	1110011w	port		
Variable Port	1110111w			
XLAT = Translate Byte to AL	11010111			
LEA = Load EA to Register	10001101	mod reg r/m		
LDS = Load Pointer to DS	11000101	mod reg r/m		
LES = Load Pointer to ES	11000100	mod reg r/m		
LAHF = Load AH with Flags	10011111			
SAHF = Store AH into Flags	10011110			
PUSHF = Push Flags	10011100			
POPF = Pop Flags	10011101			
ARITHMETIC				
ADD = Add:				
Reg./Memory with Register to Either	000000dw	mod reg r/m		
Immediate to Register/Memory	100000sw	mod 0 0 0 r/m	data	data if s:w = 01
Immediate to Accumulator	0000010w	data	data if w = 1	
ADC = Add with Carry:				
Reg./Memory with Register to Either	000100dw	mod reg r/m		
Immediate to Register/Memory	100000sw	mod 0 1 0 r/m	data	data if s:w = 01
Immediate to Accumulator	0001010w	data	data if w = 1	
INC = Increment:				
Register/Memory	1111111w	mod 0 0 0 r/m		
Register	01000 reg			
AAA = ASCII Adjust for Add	00110111			
DAA = Decimal Adjust for Add	00100111			
SUB = Subtract:				
Reg./Memory and Register to Either	001010dw	mod reg r/m		
Immediate from Register/Memory	100000sw	mod 1 0 1 r/m	data	data if s:w = 01
Immediate from Accumulator	0010110w	data	data if w = 1	
SBB = Subtract with Borrow				
Reg./Memory and Register to Either	000110dw	mod reg r/m		
Immediate from Register/Memory	100000sw	mod 0 1 1 r/m	data	data if s:w = 01
Immediate from Accumulator	0001110w	data	data if w = 1	
DEC = Decrement:				
Register/Memory	1111111w	mod 0 0 1 r/m		
Register	01001 reg			
NEG = Change Sign	1111011w	mod 0 1 1 r/m		
CMP = Compare:				
Register/Memory and Register	001110dw	mod reg r/m		
Immediate with Register/Memory	100000sw	mod 1 1 1 r/m	data	data if s:w = 01
Immediate with Accumulator	0011110w	data	data if w = 1	
AAS = ASCII Adjust for Subtract	00111111			
DAS = Decimal Adjust for Subtract	00101111			
MUL = Multiply (Unsigned)	1111011w	mod 1 0 0 r/m		
IMUL = Integer Multiply (Signed)	1111011w	mod 1 0 1 r/m		
AAM = ASCII Adjust for Multiply	11010100	00001010		
DIV = Divide (Unsigned)	1111011w	mod 1 1 0 r/m		

Table 3-7.   *(cont.)*

Mnemonic and Description	Instruction Code			
	76543210	76543210	76543210	76543210
IDIV = Integer Divide (Signed)	1111011w	mod 1 1 1 r/m		
AAD = ASCII Adjust for Divide	11010101	00001010		
CBW = Convert Byte to Word	10011000			
CWD = Convert Word to Double Word	10011001			
LOGIC				
NOT = Invert	1111011w	mod 0 1 0 r/m		
SHL/SAL = Shift Logical/Arithmetic Left	110100vw	mod 1 0 0 r/m		
SHR = Shift Logical Right	110100vw	mod 1 0 1 r/m		
SAR = Shift Arithmetic Right	110100vw	mod 1 1 1 r/m		
ROL = Rotate Left	110100vw	mod 0 0 0 r/m		
ROR = Rotate Right	110100vw	mod 0 0 1 r/m		
RCL = Rotate Through Carry Flag Left	110100vw	mod 0 1 0 r/m		
RCR = Rotate Through Carry Right	110100vw	mod 0 1 1 r/m		
AND = And:				
Reg./Memory and Register to Either	001000dw	mod reg r/m		
Immediate to Register/Memory	1000000w	mod 1 0 0 r/m	data	data if w = 1
Immediate to Accumulator	0010010w	data	data if w = 1	
TEST = And Function to Flags, No Result:				
Register/Memory and Register	1000010w	mod reg r/m		
Immediate Data and Register/Memory	1111011w	mod 0 0 0 r/m	data	data if w = 1
Immediate Data and Accumulator	1010100w	data	data if w = 1	
OR = Or:				
Reg./Memory and Register to Either	000010dw	mod reg r/m		
Immediate to Register/Memory	1000000w	mod 0 0 1 r/m	data	data if w = 1
Immediate to Accumulator	0000110w	data	data if w = 1	
XOR = Exclusive Or:				
Reg./Memory and Register to Either	001100dw	mod reg r/m		
Immediate to Register/Memory	1000000w	mod 1 1 0 r/m	data	data if w = 1
Immediate to Accumulator	0011010w	data	data if w = 1	
STRING MANIPULATION				
REP = Repeat	1111001z			
MOVS = Move Byte/Word	1010010w			
CMPS = Compare Byte/Word	1010011w			
SCAS = Scan Byte/Word	1010111w			
LODS = Load Byte/Wd to AL/AX	1010110w			
STOS = Stor Byte/Wd from AL/A	1010101w			
CONTROL TRANSFER				
CALL = Call:				
Direct Within Segment	11101000	disp-low	disp-high	
Indirect Within Segment	11111111	mod 0 1 0 r/m		
Direct Intersegment	10011010	offset-low	offset-high	
		seg-low	seg-high	
Indirect Intersegment	11111111	mod 0 1 1 r/m		

Table 3-7. *(cont.)*

Mnemonic and Description	Instruction Code		

JMP = Unconditional Jump:	7 6 5 4 3 2 1 0	7 6 5 4 3 2 1 0	7 6 5 4 3 2 1 0
Direct Within Segment	1 1 1 0 1 0 0 1	disp-low	disp-high
Direct Within Segment-Short	1 1 1 0 1 0 1 1	disp	
Indirect Within Segment	1 1 1 1 1 1 1 1	mod 1 0 0 r/m	
Direct Intersegment	1 1 1 0 1 0 1 0	offset-low	offset-high
		seg-low	seg-high
Indirect Intersegment	1 1 1 1 1 1 1 1	mod 1 0 1 r/m	

RET = Return from CALL:			
Within Segment	1 1 0 0 0 0 1 1		
Within Seg Adding Immed to SP	1 1 0 0 0 0 1 0	data-low	data-high
Intersegment	1 1 0 0 1 0 1 1		
Intersegment Adding Immediate to SP	1 1 0 0 1 0 1 0	data-low	data-high
JE/JZ = Jump on Equal/Zero	0 1 1 1 0 1 0 0	disp	
JL/JNGE = Jump on Less/Not Greater or Equal	0 1 1 1 1 1 0 0	disp	
JLE/JNG = Jump on Less or Equal/ Not Greater	0 1 1 1 1 1 1 0	disp	
JB/JNAE = Jump on Below/Not Above or Equal	0 1 1 1 0 0 1 0	disp	
JBE/JNA = Jump on Below or Equal/ Not Above	0 1 1 1 0 1 1 0	disp	
JP/JPE = Jump on Parity/Parity Even	0 1 1 1 1 0 1 0	disp	
JO = Jump on Overflow	0 1 1 1 0 0 0 0	disp	
JS = Jump on Sign	0 1 1 1 1 0 0 0	disp	
JNE/JNZ = Jump on Not Equal/Not Zero	0 1 1 1 0 1 0 1	disp	
JNL/JGE = Jump on Not Less/Greater or Equal	0 1 1 1 1 1 0 1	disp	
JNLE/JG = Jump on Not Less or Equal/ Greater	0 1 1 1 1 1 1 1	disp	
JNB/JAE = Jump on Not Below/Above or Equal	0 1 1 1 0 0 1 1	disp	
JNBE/JA = Jump on Not Below or Equal/Above	0 1 1 1 0 1 1 1	disp	
JNP/JPO = Jump on Not Par/Par Odd	0 1 1 1 1 0 1 1	disp	
JNO = Jump on Not Overflow	0 1 1 1 0 0 0 1	disp	
JNS = Jump on Not Sign	0 1 1 1 1 0 0 1	disp	
LOOP = Loop CX Times	1 1 1 0 0 0 1 0	disp	
LOOPZ/LOOPE = Loop While Zero/Equal	1 1 1 0 0 0 0 1	disp	
LOOPNZ/LOOPNE = Loop While Not Zero/Equal	1 1 1 0 0 0 0 0	disp	
JCXZ = Jump on CX Zero	1 1 1 0 0 0 1 1	disp	

INT = Interrupt			
Type Specified	1 1 0 0 1 1 0 1	type	
Type 3	1 1 0 0 1 1 0 0		
INTO = Interrupt on Overflow	1 1 0 0 1 1 1 0		
IRET = Interrupt Return	1 1 0 0 1 1 1 1		

PROCESSOR CONTROL	7 6 5 4 3 2 1 0	7 6 5 4 3 2 1 0
CLC = Clear Carry	1 1 1 1 1 0 0 0	
CMC = Complement Carry	1 1 1 1 0 1 0 1	
STC = Set Carry	1 1 1 1 1 0 0 1	
CLD = Clear Direction	1 1 1 1 1 1 0 0	
STD = Set Direction	1 1 1 1 1 1 0 1	

Table 3-7. *(cont.)*

Mnemonic and Description	Instruction Code

	76543210	76543210
CLI = Clear Interrupt	11111010	
STI = Set Interrupt	11111011	
HLT = Halt	11110100	
WAIT = Wait	10011011	
ESC = Escape (to External Device)	11011xxx	mod x x x r/m
LOCK = Bus Lock Prefix	11110000	

NOTES:
AL = 8-bit accumulator
AX = 16-bit accumulator
CX = Count register
DS = Data segment
ES = Extra segment
Above/below refers to unsigned value.
Greater = more positive;
Less = less positive (more negative) signed values
if d = 1 then "to" reg; if d = 0 then "from" reg
if w = 1 then word instruction; if w = 0 then byte instruction
if mod = 11 then r/m is treated as a REG field
if mod = 00 then DISP = 0*, disp-low and disp-high are absent
if mod = 01 then DISP = disp-low sign-extended to 16 bits, disp-high is absent
if mod = 10 then DISP = disp-high: disp-low
if r/m = 000 then EA = (BX) + (SI) + DISP
if r/m = 001 then EA = (BX) + (DI) + DISP
if r/m = 010 then EA = (BP) + (SI) + DISP
if r/m = 011 then EA = (BP) + (DI) + DISP
if r/m = 100 then EA = (SI) + DISP
if r/m = 101 then EA = (DI) + DISP
if r/m = 110 then EA = (BP) + DISP*
if r/m = 111 then EA = (BX) + DISP
DISP follows 2nd byte of instruction (before data if required)
  *except if mod = 00 and r/m = 110 then EA = disp-high: disp-low.
**MOV CS, REG/MEMORY not allowed.

if s:w = 01 then 16 bits of immediate data form the operand.
if s:w = 11 then an immediate data byte is sign extended to form the 16-bit operand.
if v = 0 then "count" = 1; if v = 1 then "count" in (CL)
x = don't care
z is used for string primitives for comparison with ZF FLAG.
SEGMENT OVERRIDE PREFIX

0 0 1 reg 1 1 0

REG is assigned according to the following table:

16-Bit (w = 1)		8-Bit (w = 0)		Segment	
000	AX	000	AL	00	ES
001	CX	001	CL	01	CS
010	DX	010	DL	10	SS
011	BX	011	BL	11	DS
100	SP	100	AH		
101	BP	101	CH		
110	SI	110	DH		
111	DI	111	BH		

Instructions which reference the flag register file as a 16-bit object use the symbol FLAGS to represent the file:
FLAGS =
X:X:X:X:(OF):(DF):(IF):(TF):(SF):(ZF):X:(AF):X:(PF):X:(CF)

PC Systems Performance and Bus Architectures

WHEN YOU WANT TO DETERMINE the suitability of a system to an application or purchase the best system at the lowest cost, system performance is a primary consideration. System performance is a complex issue that involves the capabilities of the hardware, operating system, and application software. The only completely true and accurate test of a system's performance is to measure the performance of the target system with the actual software environment and applications. This is often impractical and difficult to measure and interpret. A number of basic considerations, however, can provide useful information about the capabilities of specific systems.

This chapter investigates the key factors that contribute to system performance:

- Microprocessor type
- Microprocessor clock speed
- Wait states in bus cycles to memory and I/O
- Memory speed and location
- Memory system architecture
- Hard disk subsystem performance
- Display adapter subsystem performance
- ROM shadowing
- Communications subsystem performance
- LAN performance
- Numeric processor performance

Each of these is covered in detail later in the chapter. Also included in this chapter is a summary of the major PC bus expansion architectures.

Microprocessor Type

One of the most important factors in system performance is the type of microprocessor used in the system. PCs are built with several Intel or Intel compatible processors, from the low-end 8088 used in the original PC to the 32-bit 486. The performance of these microprocessors is differentiated by a number of key characteristics such as

- Bus width
- Clock speed and clocks per bus cycle
- Clocks per instruction
- New instructions and data type support

Bus width, clock speed, and clocks per bus cycle are interrelated and can be used to calculate the maximum bus bandwidth. The maximum bus bandwidth of a microprocessor is a good indication of its performance capability and is useful in comparing microprocessors. How effectively a microprocessor uses its bus bandwidth is also a factor. In the 8088 and 8086 microprocessors, the execution unit ran slower than the bus unit due to the high number of system clocks required to execute an instruction; the result was significant bus idle time. As the 286, 386, and 486 were introduced, fewer and fewer clocks were required to execute an instruction and the use of the available bus bandwidth became much higher. Thus, newer microprocessors are more efficient in their use of available bus bandwidth and benefit more from increased bus bandwidth capabilities.

Each new generation of microprocessor also introduced new instructions and data types, providing greater software efficiency and performance. To maintain compatibility with older software, however, few PC programs take advantage of the new instructions and data types of the newer processors. Because each microprocessor generation uses fewer clocks per instruction and new instructions allow better software efficiency, comparing bus bandwidth can be considered the minimum performance increase that can be expected. Table 4-1 is a summary of the bus bandwidth capabilities of the Intel microprocessor family at popular clock speeds with no wait states in the memory subsystem.

Most processor performance benchmark programs track the processor's performance relative to bus bandwidth. At the lower clock rate, benchmark tests follow bus bandwidth closely. At the higher clock rate (greater than 20 MHz), standard memory cannot keep up with the bus and special memory architectures are required. Because these architectures are not 100 percent efficient, processor benchmarks tend to be lower than that predicted by bus bandwidth at the higher clock rates. With the 32-bit

Table 4-1. Microprocessor Bus Bandwidth

Microprocessor Type	Bus Width	Clock Rate	Clocks/ Bus Cycle	Maximum Bus Bandwidth* (megabytes/sec)
8088	8 bit	4.77 MHz	4	1.19
8088	8 bit	8 MHz	4	2.0
8088	8 bit	10 MHz	4	2.5
8086	16 bit	8 MHz	4	4.0
8086	16 bit	10 MHz	4	5.0
286	16 bit	8 MHz	2	8.0
286	16 bit	10 MHz	2	10.0
286	16 bit	12 MHz	2	12.0
286	16 bit	16 MHz	2	16.0
286	16 bit	20 MHz	2	20.0
286	16 bit	25 MHz	2	25.0
386SX	16 bit	16 MHz	2	16.0
386SX	16 bit	20 MHz	2	20.0
386	32 bit	16 MHz	2	32.0
386	32 bit	20 MHz	2	40.0
386	32 bit	25 MHz	2	50.0
386	32 bit	33 MHz	2	66.0
486	32 bit	25 MHz	1.25	80.0
486	32 bit	33 MHz	1.25	105.6
486	32 bit	50 MHz	1.25	160.0

*In the bus bandwidth calculations, we assume no wait states on the local microprocessor bus and a five clock, 16-byte burst cycle on the 486.

bus interfaces used to execute 8-bit and 16-bit instructions and data transfers, the full efficiency of the 32-bit systems are not realized, resulting in benchmark results further reduced from those predicted by bus bandwidth comparisons.

Wait States

To keep down the cost of the memory subsystem, wait states often are inserted in the microprocessor's bus cycles. This has the obvious detrimental effect on processor performance, but the effect often is not as severe as one might predict. Wait states can be added to any type of bus cycle, including instruction fetch, data read/write, I/O, and DMA. Wait states in instruction fetch cycles are the most devastating to system performance because they represent 70 to 80 percent of all bus cycles in a typical application. Data read/write cycles are only 20 to 30 percent of the cycles, and I/O read/write cycles are 1 to 5 percent of a typical application.

The effect of wait states depends on the type of microprocessor. The 8088 and 8086 use four clocks per bus cycle; when one wait state is added, the bus cycle is five clocks, resulting in a 20 percent loss in system bus bandwidth. In the 286 and 386 family of processors, a bus cycle is two clocks. With one added wait state, the bus cycle is extended to three clocks, resulting in a 33 percent loss in bus bandwidth. In the 486, which uses a five clock burst for four bus cycles, addition of a single wait state can result in nearly a 50 percent reduction in bus bandwidth. In general, these types of performance penalties are not observed when wait states are added because the Intel processor has instruction queues that are filled at bus speed, which in general is faster than the processing time of the execution units. The queue size is 4 bytes in the 8088, 6 bytes in the 8086, 286 and 386, and 16 bytes in the 486. In the 386 and 486, wait states are more of a penalty because the execution units run nearly at bus speed. This is due to the execution of instructions in fewer clock cycles than in the earlier processors.

Wait states in DMA and I/O cycles are not much of a concern except in special applications that require high-speed I/O operation to keep up with an interface. In PC, XT, and AT systems, wait states are automatically inserted in the I/O bus cycles to attempt to maintain a constant bus cycle duration of approximately 1 microsecond. This ensures that PC adapter boards will work in any PC, XT, AT, and 386 AT bus systems at any clock rate. If faster I/O cycles are required on the AT bus, a signal can be activated that will remove all wait states from the I/O bus cycle. DMA cycles on the PC and AT are controlled by the clock input to the 8237 DMA controller chips on the system board. Wait states can be added also to these cycles using the READY line on the expansion bus slots. DMA cycles on AT bus class machines are typically slower than those on the PC because the processor clock is divided by two before it goes to the DMA chip. The DMA chip requires five clocks for a bus cycle. Thus, in an AT system ten processor clocks are required to execute a DMA cycle.

In general, a single wait state in an 8088 or 8086 system results in a 10 to 15 percent performance loss. A single wait state in a 286 or 386 system results in a 15 to 25 percent performance loss. In a 486, a single wait state results in a 20 to 35 percent loss of performance. The actual performance loss is highly dependent on the application software and could easily be outside these average ranges for specific applications.

To illustrate the effect of a single wait state on bus bandwidth, Table 4-2 records the bus bandwidth of selected microprocessors at various clock speeds. Comparing Tables 4-1 and 4-2 will give you an upper limit of the effect that inserting a wait state has on system performance.

Table 4-2. Microprocessor Bus Bandwidth with One Wait State

Microprocessor Type	Bus Width	Clock Rate	Clocks/Bus Cycle	Maximum Bus Bandwidth* (megabytes/sec)
8088	8 bit	4.77 MHz	5	0.995
8088	8 bit	8 MHz	5	1.6
8088	8 bit	10 MHz	5	2.0
8086	16 bit	8 MHz	5	3.2
8086	16 bit	10 MHz	5	4.0
286	16 bit	8 MHz	3	5.3
286	16 bit	10 MHz	3	6.6
286	16 bit	12 MHz	3	8.0
286	16 bit	16 MHz	3	10.7
286	16 bit	20 MHZ	3	13.3
286	16 bit	25 MHz	3	16.6
386SX	16 bit	16 MHz	3	10.7
386SX	16 bit	20 MHz	3	13.3
386	32 bit	16 MHz	3	21.4
386	32 bit	20 MHz	3	26.6
386	32 bit	25 MHz	3	33.3
386	32 bit	33 MHz	3	40.0
486	32 bit	25 MHz	2.5	40.0
486	32 bit	33 MHz	2.5	52.8
486	32 bit	50 MHz	2.5	80.0

*In the bus bandwidth calculations, we assume one wait state on the local microprocessor bus and a ten clock, 16-byte burst cycle on the 486.

Memory Speed and Location

The necessity to add wait states to a memory subsystem depends on the speed of the memory and its location. Memory must be fast enough to keep up with the microprocessor bus speed. Dynamic memory chips are available in a range of speeds typically with 150 ns to 80 ns access times. Unfortunately, dynamic memory chips require a per charge time at the end of each access, resulting in a minimum cycle time of 200 ns to 120 ns. At a significant cost premium, speeds as fast as 60 ns with 100 ns cycle times are available, if the bus cycles are assumed to be fully pipelined such that the memory cycle is synchronous with the processor bus cycle. Table 4-3 lists some bus cycle times for popular zero wait-state processors.

Table 4-3.   Bus Cycle Times for Zero Wait-State Microprocessors

Microprocessor	Bus Cycle Time
10 MHz 8088/8086	400 ns
12 MHz 286	167 ns
16 MHz 286/386	125 ns
20 MHz 286/386	100 ns
25 MHz 286/386	80 ns
33 MHz 386	67 ns
25 MHz 486	80/40 ns (first/next 3)
33 MHz 486	67/33 ns (first/next 3)
50 MHz 486	40/20 ns (first/next 3)

Thus, without special memory subsystem architectures, 286 and 386 machines can achieve cycle times in the 12 to 16 MHz range with no wait states. With some simple memory architecture tricks, the 386 can boost cycle times to the 20 to 25 MHz range.

Now that we have shown how memory and processor cycle times can be matched, we need to consider memory access time. In a processor memory cycle, the following items must be subtracted to obtain the memory access time requirements:

- Address/command skew delay
- Command and address decode delay
- Address multiplexer and buffer delays
- Data bus buffer delay
- Data valid setup time
- Capacitance delays on long address and data buses

If an aggressive 5 ns per item is used, 30 ns must be deducted from the bus cycle time for the required access time. If a more conservative

10 ns per item is used, 60 ns must be deducted. At the higher bus speeds, both access time and cycle time are critical parameters in zero wait-state memory design. To make maximum use of the memory's performance, it is desirable to minimize access time delays. For this reason, most new system designs place large amounts of system memory on the system board. If memory is attached directly to the microprocessor's local bus with no data and address buffers or only one set of data and address buffers, wait states can be avoided at higher clock rates. If memory expansion is added through the expansion bus slots, a minimum of two sets of data and address buffer delays are encountered (bus drivers on the system board and bus drivers on the adapter board). This can add from 30 to 50 ns of delays that must be made up in equivalent faster memory access times. Most memory adapter boards that are added to a higher clock rate system (greater than 10 MHz) require the insertion of a wait state.

To ensure maximum system performance, select a system that supports memory expansion on the system board because it will be less likely to require memory wait states. The IBM PS/2 systems illustrate this point well. Memory expansion boards on the Micro Channel bus slots typically require one additional processor clock on the bus for memory access to slot expanded memory.

Memory Subsystem Architecture

For 286, 386, and 486 systems at clock rates greater than 12 MHz, special memory architectures are required to use cost-effective dynamic RAMS with no wait states. The simplest approach is to use the page mode feature of the dynamic RAM device. In this mode, the first access to a block of RAM is at the normal speed and cycle time, but subsequent accesses within the block can be twice as fast as individual accesses. Because instruction and data accesses tend to be sequential, large blocks of instruction and data accesses often can take place at the higher page mode speed of the RAMs. This scheme will not eliminate wait states, but it can significantly reduce them in most typical applications.

The next most commonly used scheme is to use memory interleave. This scheme overcomes the problem of long RAM cycle times. Memory is designed as multiple subsystems with independent timing; this allows memory accesses to be overlapped and thus avoids the per charge time that increases cycle times. Sequential bus memory cycles are routed to different overlapping memory blocks to minimize the probability of back-to-back cycles in the same block of memory. Wait states are inserted only when back-to-back cycles are in the same block. The more blocks of independent memory (interleaves), the less wait states. Two-way and four-way interleave memories are typical.

Interleave memory designs are easy to do and are very effective in reducing wait states, but their effectiveness can depend on the application. Another problem with interleave memory systems is that they often require large amounts of memory to be effective. For example, if 1-mega-bit-by-1-bit dynamic memory chips are used in a 32-bit 386 design with 4-way memory interleave, the minimum memory size is 16M. If 256K-by-4-bit chips are used, the minimum 4-way interleave memory system is 4M. Systems are often designed to use 2-way interleave at lower memory sizes and 4-way interleave at larger memory sizes.

A very cost-effective and high-performance memory system architecture can be created by using both page mode and interleaved memory system designs. Most high clock rate 286 and 386 systems use this scheme for clock rates up to 25 MHz.

For 486 systems (the 486 supports an on-chip 8K cache) and for clock rates greater than 25 MHz, cache memory system designs are incorporated. The cache is a high-speed, zero wait-state memory that stores the most frequently used instructions and data. Because most programs execute loops and reference data in clusters, zero wait-state operation can be achieved after the cache is loaded. If the instruction and data are in the cache, it is called a *hit*. If it is not a hit, a standard memory cycle with wait states must be executed until the cache fills with the new data and instructions from main memory. The effectiveness of a cache design is determined by the hit ratio. For example, a hit ratio of 80 percent indicates that the instruction or data or both was in zero wait-state memory 80 percent of the time. The hit ratio depends on a number of items, including the following:

- Cache size, ranging from 32K to 128K (larger caches have better hit ratios)
- Does the cache support both instructions and data?
- Are write operations cached?
- Cache refill algorithm
- Cache refill speed and main memory speed

In general, a 32K cache will result in a typical hit ratio of 85 percent (85 percent of the time no wait states are added to bus cycles). Intel provides a companion chip for the 386 called the 80385 cache controller. This device supports a 32K cache and is used in many 386 designs at 25 MHz and 33 MHz clock rates. Even with a cache design, the system's main memory may still use page mode and interleave architectures to increase performance. The 486 supports an on-chip 8K cache with provisions for an external, second-level cache system.

ROM Shadowing

ROM shadowing is another memory architecture technique used to increase system performance. The PC's BIOS and adapter board ROMs are implemented in ROM or EPROM. This memory is in the upper 256K block of the PC's real mode 1M address space. ROM and EPROMS are much slower than dynamic RAM. System designs that support RAM in the ROM BIOS address space under program control can move the BIOS programs from ROM to shadow RAM, then execute them from the higher speed RAM. Software that uses BIOS calls can often see significant performance improvements by using shadow RAM.

PC display adapters and LAN controllers have ROM BIOS support on the adapters. This ROM can be moved to RAM to enhance performance. Adapter board ROM is often 8 bits wide to ensure compatibility with older PCs and XTs; when this ROM is moved to RAM, it is accessed as 16-bit or 32-bit instructions and data, and benefits by both wider bus width and faster RAM speed. This effect is particularly noticeable in display adapters such as the EGA.

Display Adapters

Display adapter performance can be enhanced by selecting one of the newer designs that supports the 16-bit bus of the AT class systems. Many EGA class adapters are designed with 8-bit bus interfaces. When these adapters are installed in newer AT class machines, access to the display memory is limited to 8 bits at a time. Further, BIOS support in ROM is also accessed and executed 8 bits at a time even though the AT bus supports 16-bit bus cycles. Most VGA adapters are designed with 16-bit bus interfaces to display RAM and ROM BIOS. For optimum performance in 16-bit AT bus systems, selection of a display adapter with 16-bit ROM and RAM interfaces significantly improves display performance. The PS/2 family incorporated the display adapter directly on the system board; this gave the display direct access to the 16- or 32-bit local memory bus of the system and thus provided excellent display performance.

Hard Disk Subsystem Performance

The performance of a hard disk subsystem is affected by two major components: the hard disk drive and the hard disk adapter. The most important attributes of the drive are its average access time and data transfer rate. Lower cost drives used on XT and early AT systems supported access times of 65 ms and data transfer rates of 5 megabits per second. The 20M to 30M drives in this performance range are available for $180 to $250. Drives in the 40M range with an average access time of less than 28 ms and data transfer rates greater than 10 megabits per second are available for about $300.

Newer high-performance drives use ESDI (Enhanced Small Device Interface) and require a hard drive adapter that supports this interface. The main attribute of ESDI is the capability to support data transfer rates up to 20 megabits per second. ESDI drives and adapters are used on the PS/2 family and are available for PC AT bus systems. Because most adapters provide sector buffering, the data transfer rate is not as important as average access time and the adapter interleave factor.

Some drives come with an integrated controller subsystem called SCSI (Small Computer Systems Interface), which requires a SCSI adapter in the PC. Because there is more intelligence in SCSI drives, they can often significantly reduce the processing required by the PC to support the detailed tasks of controlling the drive. SCSI drives often support sector buffering and file caching on the drive, which again relieves the PC from performing these tasks. In general, a SCSI drive with an ESDI hard disk interface to the SCSI subsystem on the drive provides the best performance but at a high cost.

The drive adapter can limit the capabilities of a high-performance drive. The key attributes of the drive adapter that affect system performance are

- Data transfer rate
- Interleave factor
- Sector buffers and size
- File caching capabilities

The adapter must be able to support the maximum data transfer rate of the attached drives. If you select a drive and an adapter separately, make sure that the data transfer rates are compatible.

The interleave factor of the drive adapter is essential to system hard disk performance. An interleave factor of 4 indicates that four revolutions of the drive disk are required to access all sectors on a specific track. Generally, the lower the interleave, the better the system performance. However, some applications perform better with a higher interleave factor. Most drive adapters support the formatting of a drive with alternate interleave factors.

Some newer adapters support large sector buffers and file caching. These adapters keep sectors and frequently used files in large areas of memory on the adapter; this significantly reduces file access times when the desired data is in the cache. These high-performance adapters are often used in systems that act as file servers on local area networks.

The adapters used to interface to the PC system bus can also affect performance. For maximum performance, adapters for AT class systems and above should have 16-bit bus interfaces to the sector buffers. Most hard disk adapters do not use DMA to transfer data from the adapter to the PC's system memory. This is because in 286 systems and above, the processor's string move instructions can transfer data from the sector buffers to system memory more efficiently than DMA transfers. These string move instructions support interruptable burst transfers at maximum bus bandwidth, while not tying up DMA channels.

Communications Performance

Most communications software uses the PC's asynchronous communications ports. These ports are typically built into the base system and are referred to as COM1 and COM2. Because communications software normally does not use BIOS support for asynchronous COM ports, the software interfaces to the ports directly.

The PC and XT systems used National Semiconductor's NS8250B UART, which supported a maximum asynchronous data rate of 57,600 baud. The NS8250B had a number of bugs that were programmed around in early PC communications software packages. In the PC AT, this part was replaced with the NS16450 device, which had a maximum data rate of 57,600 baud also. This device fixed many of the bugs in the original NS8250B. Most communications software can operate with either the NS8250B or the NS16450. The PS/2 and some newer AT bus systems use the NS16550 device. This device supports data rates up to 288K baud and has support for 16-byte transmit and receive FIFO and DMA.

Unfortunately, most PC designs still support a maximum data rate of only 57,600 and do not use the FIFO or DMA capability of the NS16550 device. Most communications software will support all three chips even though their hardware differs. The PC DOS MODE command allows the COM ports to be set to a maximum speed of only 9600 baud. The chips, however, can be set to a maximum data rate of 115,200 baud using custom programming. Although this setting violates the specifications of the driver and receiver chips, many applications use this setting to obtain the maximum data rate. This setting works on most systems if the interconnection cables are short and the processor is fast enough to keep up with the data rate. Many PC-to-PC file transfer packages and screen/keyboard sharing packages allow this setting using back-to-back PC connections through the COM ports.

LAN Performance

LAN performance is a complex issue involving a number of network parameters. Bottlenecks limiting network or user-perceived performance can occur at many points in a LAN. We shall concentrate on the performance effects associated with LAN adapters and system microprocessors in workstations and server PCs. Other factors that effect user-perceived performance on a LAN (such as LAN type, topology, access methods, LAN operating system extensions, number of servers, file organizations, and number and type of users) are beyond the scope of this book. A good source of information on PC local area networking is *Networking Personal Computers, Third Edition*, by Michael Durr and Mark Gibbs, published by Que Corporation.

Many attributes of LAN adapters that affect system performance are similar to the attributes of hard disk adapters that affect system performance. LAN adapters that have on-board microprocessors supporting layer 1 and 2 protocols can significantly offload processing in the PC and provide higher performance. LAN adapters typically have on-board ROM that is executed by the PC. A 16-bit interface to ROM and data buffers on the adapter will result in better system performance. 16-bit interface adapters with on-board microprocessors will provide the best system performance with the associated higher adapter cost. Often, nonintelligent adapters are used in client workstations, and higher performance adapters are used in systems acting as servers.

Workstation performance is typically limited by the processing power of the PC acting as a workstation on a LAN. This is particularly true if the PC is using a low-cost, nonintelligent adapter for LAN access. Experiments with XTs and ATs on 10-megabits-per-second Ethernet LANs with the same adapter indicate that data throughput with an AT is more than twice that with an XT.

Numeric Processor Performance

You can add a numeric coprocessor to the Intel family of microprocessors to enhance 8088, 8086, 286, and 386 processor performance in floating point, integer, and BDC arithmetic. Table 4-4 defines which numeric coprocessors are used with which microprocessors.

Table 4-4. Numeric Coprocessors for Intel Microprocessors

Microprocessor	Numeric Coprocessor
8088	8087
8086	8087
286	287
386	287 or 387
386SX	387SX
486	Integrated in 486

Applications that are arithmetic intensive can often see significant performance improvements. However, the software must be specifically designed to use the numeric coprocessor's instruction set enhancements. Numeric coprocessors add over 50 new instructions to the processor's instruction set. These new instructions support arithmetic on 16-, 32-, and 64-bit integers, 32-, 64-, and 80-bit floating point values, and exponential, logarithmic, and trigonometric functions.

In the 8087 numeric coprocessor, the interface to the 8088 and 8086 is tightly coupled and requires that the 8087 and the microprocessor operate at the same clock speed. The 287 numeric coprocessor is more loosely coupled and can operate on either the 286 or the 386 microprocessor and at different clock speeds. For maximum arithmetic processing performance, try to select a numeric coprocessor that operates at the same speed as the system's microprocessor.

Benchmark Evaluation of System Performance

The best way to determine system performance is to run your applications on each system and measure the results. But often this is simply not practical because access to the system and measurement techniques are difficult. The next best thing is to use a standard benchmark program to measure system performance. Benchmark programs can be simple or very complex, and are often the subject of arguments over their capability to truly reflect a system's performance. Most simple benchmark programs measure processor performance; complex benchmark programs measure processor performance, numeric coprocessor performance, hard disk subsystem performance, and display adapter performance. (When personal computing magazines review a new system, they often publish extensive benchmarking results.)

Two simple benchmark programs are often used to rate a system's processor performance. One is the Landmark CPU Speed Test, available from Landmark Software, 1141 Pomegranate Court, Sunnyvale, California, 94087. This program rates the system relative to a PC running at 4.77 MHz and relative to an equivalent clock speed for a 286 system. The second program is the System Information (SI) program from Peter Norton. This program calculates the system's performance relative to a PC XT running at 4.77 MHz. The SI program also calculates the hard disk subsystem's performance relative to a PC XT. Although the two benchmark programs often display different results on the same system, they are a good indicator of relative system performance and their results are often used in system advertisements to indicate processing power capabilities. Table 4-5 lists benchmark results advertised for various PCs and clock rates.

Table 4-5.   PC Benchmark Results*

PC System	Norton SI	Landmark AT Clock Speed
8088 4.77 MHz	1	2 MHz
8088 10 MHz	2.1	4.2 MHz
286 12 MHz	15.3	13.7 MHz
286 16 MHz	18.7	21.6 MHz
286 20 MHz	22.5	24 MHz
386SX 16 MHz	18	21.8 MHz
386SX 20 MHz	21	25 MHz
386 16 MHz	18.7	23 MHz
386 20 MHz	23	25 MHz
386 25 MHz	29	34.5 MHz
386 25 MHz with cache	36	43.5 MHz
386 33 MHz with cache	45.9	58.5 MHz

*These benchmark values are published in manufacturers' advertisements and are typical for these classes of systems. Actual benchmark performance may vary on different systems.

Bus Architectures

PC expansion slot bus architecture is split between three standards and systems. The first type of bus architecture is the PC/XT/AT bus, supporting both 8- and 16-bit data paths and 20- to 24-bit addressing with a crude multimaster bus capability. This bus is known as ISA, or Industry Standard Architecture.

The second bus architecture is the IBM MCA, or Micro Channel Architecture, introduced with the IBM PS/2 models 50 and above. Its main attributes are 32-bit address and data support, multimaster bus architecture, and asynchronous operation. It is incompatible with the ISA bus.

The industry countered the IBM MCA bus with the EISA bus. This bus maintained compatibility with the ISA bus and encompassed many of the features of the IBM MCA bus. The EISA bus architecture allows the use of existing PC adapter boards in EISA bus systems while supporting new adapters that take full advantage of the EISA bus's advanced features. The battle is now between ISA, EISA, and MCA bus systems.

There has been a tendency to believe that bus expansion slot architecture should be changed to support the increase in microprocessor speeds. Many systems manufacturers took a different approach to support new processor speeds. They simply designed a memory interface to the processor's local bus and installed large amounts of memory on the system board. With this approach, the system's performance could be increased without modifying the expansion bus slots.

Today, most ISA or AT bus architecture systems are actually two bus architecture systems. I/O devices are typically supported on the 8- or 16-bit ISA or AT bus, and memory is on a separate local processor synchronous bus. In this scheme, the AT bus can still be used in 32-bit 386 and 486 systems because the 32-bit memory is on a separate bus on the board and often has a custom 32-bit memory expansion slot.

The IBM PS/2 with an MCA bus uses the same approach to overcome the performance limitations of the MCA. System memory and display adapter memory are on a separate local bus and normally run one clock time faster than memory on the MCA bus. This brings into question the need for a high-performance expansion slot bus architecture in systems that support two bus architectures. High-speed devices such as memory expansion and display adapters would be on the system board's local buses, and slower devices such as LAN adapters, hard disk adapters, communications adapters, and printer ports could reside on a slower and lower cost peripheral bus. High-speed LAN and hard disk adapters that support data rates of 10 to 20 megabits per second and transfer rates of 8M to 10M are easily supported on the ISA bus architecture. This questions the need for high-cost and high-performance expansion slot bus architectures such as EISA and MCA. In most systems, these buses are used to support only low-speed, 8- or 16-bit peripheral devices with slow data rates. Memory is not normally attached on these buses, and adapter ROM can be shadowed in system RAM for increased performance.

The MCA bus architecture has other desirable features in addition to its increased address space and 32-bit data bus paths. MCA supports a scheme that eliminates the need for DIP switches and jumpers for adapter board configuration. It supports level-sensitive interrupts, which allow adapters to share interrupt levels. In addition, MCA supports a bus master architecture. Many of these same enhancements are also planned on the EISA bus implementations.

Table 4-6 is a summary of the performance levels possible using different PC bus architectures. Also included are proposed bus enhancements to these architectures. These enhancements take three basic forms. In the first, the bus width is extended; for example, the MCA will support a 64-bit data path by returning to a multiplexed address/data bus. The second performance enhancement scheme is to support a data streaming mode, in which blocks of bus data can be seen with only the starting address sent on the bus. This scheme is similar to the local bus mode of the 486 microprocessor and supports a bus transfer in a single clock cycle. The third approach is to reduce the bus cycle time.

Table 4-6.   Performance Levels of Bus Architectures

Bus Architecture	Performance Level (megabytes/sec)
PC AT 16-bit 0WS 10 MHz	10
PC AT 16-bit 0WS 12 MHz	12
PC AT 16-bit 0WS 16 MHz	16
MCA 16-bit 0WS 100 ns clocks	16
MCA 32-bit 0WS 100 ns clocks	20
MCA 32-bit 0WS data streaming 100 ns clocks	40 *
MCA 64-bit 0WS data streaming 50 ns clocks	160 *
EISA 32 bit	33
EISA 32 bit with data streaming	66 *

*Possible enhancements; not presently available.

In general, if the expansion bus slots are used to support standard peripheral devices and memory that are on the system board, MCA and EISA bus architectures offer little system performance improvement and will increase the systems cost.

Chapter 5

PC and XT Systems and Bus Architecture

THIS CHAPTER EXAMINES the systems architecture and expansion slot bus of PC and PC XT class systems and the PS/2 models 25 and 30. These systems generally are implemented using the system architecture illustrated in Figure 5-1. Some systems use 8088, 8086, or NEC V series microprocessors. The processor clock rates vary from 4.77 MHz (in the original PC) to greater than 10 MHz. To use the vast amount of PC software on the market, all these systems have maintained hardware compatibility. Further, to ensure the compatibility of expansion boards for the PC family, expansion bus compatibility has been maintained. This chapter describes expansion bus operation, general timing and loading design guidelines, and mechanical considerations for adapter board design.

Note: An important feature of the PC AT bus is its compatibility with the PC and PC XT. In general, adapter boards designed for the PC and PC XT bus will operate in a PC AT. Thus, if your expansion adapter is designed for 8-bit bus interfacing applications using PC and PC XT bus specifications, it will probably operate in a PC AT class system.

PC/XT Expansion Bus Description

Most interfacing applications attach to the PC through one system-bus expansion card slot. On the system bus, data is transferred during a bus cycle. This chapter describes the types of bus cycles and how they are used to transfer information between memory, I/O, and the 8088 microprocessor.

The two general classifications of bus cycle are the 8088-driven bus cycle and the DMA-driven bus cycle. When the 8088 microprocessor

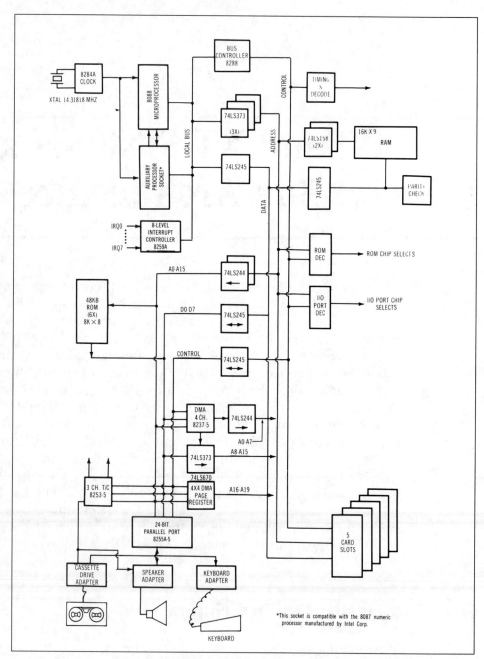

Figure 5-1. PC and XT system architecture.

generates a bus cycle, it drives the bus with the system address of a memory location or an I/O port, controls the direction of data flow, and is either the source or destination for the data. When the 8088 drives the bus, one of five different bus cycle types are generated:

Memory-read bus cycle

Memory-write bus cycle

I/O-port-read bus cycle

I/O-port-write bus cycle

Interrupt-acknowledge bus cycle

The interrupt-acknowledge bus cycle is not covered here because it occurs only on the local bus system and is not present on the system bus.

The second general classification of bus cycles are those driven by the DMA controller (the 8237-5 chip). During direct memory access (DMA) operations, the 8088 microprocessor is removed from the system bus and the 8237-5 DMA controller drives the bus cycles. The DMA controller drives a memory address onto the bus and controls the flow of data between an interface adapter and memory. Note that in the DMA bus cycles, the DMA controller does not handle the data directly. Data is transferred directly between the interface adapter and memory. When the DMA controller drives the system bus, two types of bus cycles are generated. The first type is a cycle that reads data from an interface adapter and writes the data into a memory location specified by the address from the DMA controller. The second type of bus cycle reads data from a memory location specified by the DMA controller, then writes that data into an interface adapter.

Table 5-1 is a summary of the types of bus cycles generated on the system unit's bus. The next section details the operation of each of these bus cycles.

Table 5-1. Summary of Bus Cycle Types

Bus Cycle	Purpose	Direction of Data Flow
Memory read	8088 data or an instruction fetch	Memory to 8088
Memory write	8088 data write	8088 to memory
I/O port read	8088 data fetch from I/O	I/O port to 8088
I/O port write	8088 sends data to I/O	8088 to I/O port
Interrupt acknowledge	Send interrupt data to 8088	8259-A to 8088
DMA write I/O	Send data from memory to I/O interface adapter	Memory to I/O
DMA read I/O	Send data from I/O interface adapter to memory	I/O to memory

Memory-Read Bus Cycle

The memory-read bus cycle is used to fetch instructions and data for the system's memory. This memory may be on the system board, in the system-bus card slots, in ROM, or in RAM. The memory-read bus cycle is driven from the 8088 microprocessor. All bus cycles consist of a minimum of four processor clocks. Each clock is approximately 210 ns, 125 ns, or 100 ns, depending on the 8088's clocks speeds of 4.77 MHz, 8 MHz, or 10 MHz, respectively. Thus, a minimum length for a memory-read bus cycle is 840 ns, 500 ns, or 400 ns, again depending on the processor clock speed.

The length of the bus cycle can be extended when a memory adapter board in the system-bus card slots lowers a bus interface line called READY. The memory adapter must perform this action; otherwise, the bus cycle will be four clocks in length. (The timing and control of the READY signal is covered later.) Active bus signals are driven from the 8088 micro-processor and its signal-buffering circuits. The one exception is the data bus, which is driven with the data from the address of a memory location on the adapter.

Figure 5-2 illustrates the basic timing and signals used on the system bus to execute a memory-read bus cycle. The memory-read cycle begins during the T1 clock with the ALE signal becoming active. The back edge of this signal indicates that the address bus contains a valid memory address. Next, at approximately T2, the $\overline{\text{MEMR}}$ bus signal is activated. This indicates to the memory adapters attached to the bus that the cycle is a memory-read cycle. It also indicates that if the adapter contains memory with an address corresponding to the one on the address bus, the adapter should drive the data bus with its memory contents. All memory devices on the adapter must decode the address on the bus and, thus, determine if it should respond. At the beginning of the T4 clock, the 8088 micro-processor captures the data from the data bus. Shortly after the beginning of the T4 clock, the $\overline{\text{MEMR}}$ bus signal is deactivated; at the end of the T4 clock, the bus cycle ends.

Memory-Write Bus Cycle

The memory-write bus cycle is used any time an instruction in an 8088 program writes data to a memory location. As in the memory-read bus cycle, the 8088 and its bus buffers drive onto the system bus the address of the memory location that should accept the data. In addition to driving the

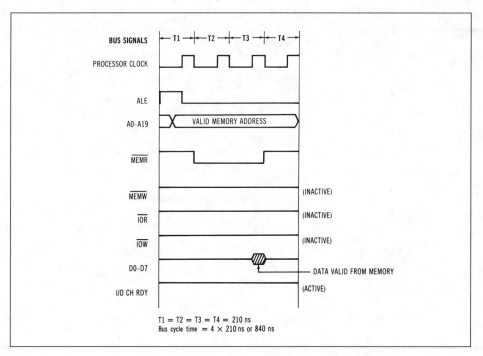

Figure 5-2. Memory-read bus cycle.

address bus and the control signals, the 8088 drives the data bus with the data to be written in the selected memory location.

Figure 5-3 illustrates the basic timing of the memory-write bus cycle. During clock time T1, the ALE bus signal is activated, which indicates that the address bus contains a valid memory address. Next, at approximately T2, the $\overline{\text{MEMW}}$ bus signal is activated, which indicates that the bus cycle is a memory-write cycle. Shortly after the $\overline{\text{MEMW}}$ signal is activated, the 8088 processor drives the system data bus with the data to be written into the selected memory location. At T4, the $\overline{\text{MEMW}}$ bus signal is deactivated; at the end of T4, the bus cycle is completed.

I/O-Port-Read Bus Cycle

The I/O-port-read bus cycle is initiated each time an 8088 microprocessor IN instruction is executed. This bus cycle is similar to the memory-read bus cycle. Its purpose is to fetch data from one of the I/O port addresses in the I/O port address space. In the PC design, the bus cycle is always a minimum of five clocks, or approximately 1.05 microseconds. An I/O

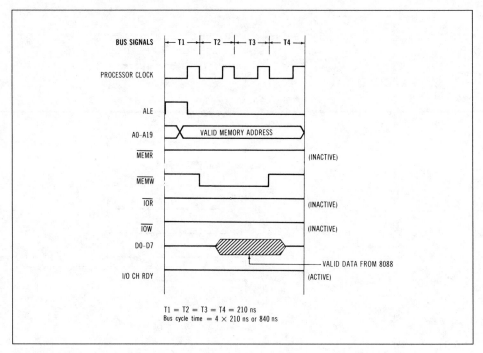

Figure 5-3. Memory-write bus cycle.

port device may extend the length of the bus cycle by deactivating the READY bus signal.

During an I/O-port-read bus cycle, the 8088 microprocessor drives a 16-bit port address onto the system address bus. Note that during this bus cycle, the high-order 4 bits of the address bus are never activated. Figure 5-4 illustrates the basic timing of an I/O-port-read cycle.

I/O-Port-Write Bus Cycle

An I/O-port-write bus cycle is initiated each time the 8088 microprocessor OUT instruction is executed. This bus cycle writes data from the 8088 to a specific I/O port address in the I/O address space of the 8088 microprocessor. The bus cycle is normally four clocks in length, but the PC design automatically inserts an extra wait-state clock called a TW clock. Thus, in the PC, all I/O-port-write bus cycles are a minimum of five clocks, or approximately 1.05 microseconds in a 4.77-MHz machine. In higher clock rate PCs or XTs, additional wait states are typically added to maintain the approximately 1 microsecond cycle. This insures that adapter board designs for systems with a 4.77-MHz clock speed will still

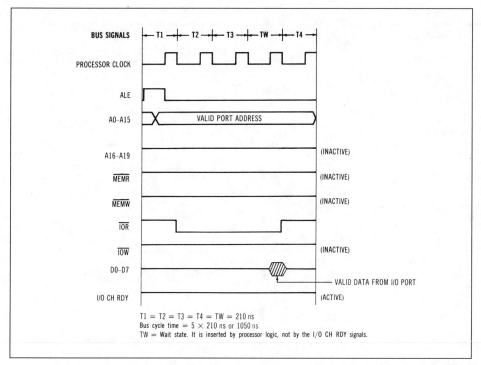

Figure 5-4. I/O-port-read bus cycle.

operate in the higher clock rate systems. The bus cycle can be further extended through the use of the READY signal on the system bus.

Only bits 0–15 of the address bus are used to address the I/O ports. Thus, address bits 16–19 are not activated during the bus cycle. Figure 5-5 illustrates the basic timing of an I/O-port-write bus cycle. As with the other bus cycles, during the T1 clock time, the ALE bus signal is activated, which indicates that the address bus contains a valid port address. Next, at clock time T2, the $\overline{IOW}$ bus control signal is activated, which indicates that the bus cycle is an I/O-port-write cycle and that the selected port address should take data from the data bus. Shortly after the T2 clock time, the 8088 microprocessor drives the data bus with the data for the port address. At the beginning of the T4 clock time, the $\overline{IOW}$ bus control signal is deactivated. At the end of the T4 clock, the bus cycle is completed.

DMA Bus Cycle

DMA bus cycles are more complicated because read and write functions are both performed in the same cycle. In addition, the bus is driven not from the 8088 microprocessor but from the DMA controller and its

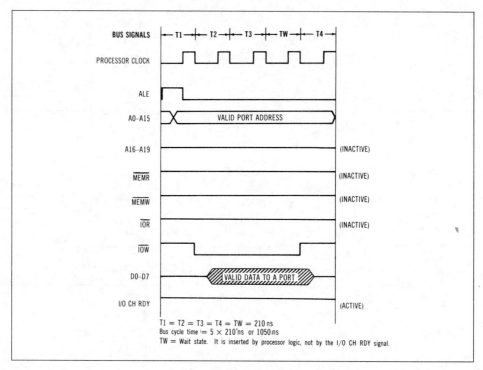

BUS SIGNALS |← T1 →|← T2 →|← T3 →|← TW →|← T4 →|

PROCESSOR CLOCK

ALE

A0–A15   VALID PORT ADDRESS

A16–A19   (INACTIVE)

MEMR   (INACTIVE)

MEMW   (INACTIVE)

IOR   (INACTIVE)

IOW

D0–D7   VALID DATA TO A PORT

I/O CH RDY   (ACTIVE)

T1 = T2 = T3 = T4 = TW = 210 ns
Bus cycle time = 5 × 210 ns or 1050 ns
TW = Wait state. It is inserted by processor logic, not by the I/O CH RDY signal.

Figure 5-5. I/O-port-write bus cycle.

support circuits. The cycles are not initiated by the 8088 microprocessor or the DMA controller; they are initiated by a request from an interface adapter. A set of bus activities precedes the actual DMA bus cycle. (This activity is covered in Chapter 10, which details the DMA capabilities of the PC.)

A DMA bus cycle can be initiated from the system bus by raising any of three system-bus signal lines: DRQ1, DRQ2, or DRQ3. The first indication on the system bus that a request has been granted and that the DMA bus cycle has started is when the bus is signaled by the activation of the AEN bus signal. Shortly after the AEN signal is activated, one of four signals—DACK0, DACK1, DACK2, or DACK3—is activated. These signals indicate to the interface adapter which DMA request or channel is being serviced by this DMA bus cycle.

A normal DMA bus cycle takes five processor clock times to execute. In the PC design, an extra clock time is added, lengthening the DMA cycle to six clocks, or approximately 1.26 microseconds when a 4.77-MHz processor clock is used. In higher clock rate PCs and XTs, the processor clocks are normally divided by two, then used to run the DMA chips. Thus, an 8-MHz or 10-MHz system will actually run the DMA cycles at 4 MHz or

5 MHz, respectively, because the 8237 DMA chips are not available at the 8-MHz and 10-MHz clock rate performance levels.

When the DMA controller has control of the system bus, its timing signals will be generated from the same clock signal that the 8088 processor uses or from a divide-by-two processor clock at higher 8088 clock rates. Because the DMA controller generates slightly different bus timings than those from the microprocessor, DMA clocks are called S clocks. The S clock times indicate the state of the DMA controller, just as the T clocks indicate the state of the 8088 microprocessor.

When the DMA controller is not executing a DMA cycle, it is in an *idle state*, continually executing an SI clock state while looking for requests from the system. (SI clocks are idle bus cycle clocks.) When a request is detected, the controller sends a signal to the 8088 processor telling it to get off the bus at the next convenient time. The controller goes to the S0 clock state, which continually looks for the 8088 microprocessor response that the bus has been given up and that it is free to begin a DMA cycle.

When the controller receives the HLDA (hold acknowledge) signal from the 8088 processor, it enters the S1 clock state, signaling the beginning of the DMA cycle. The DMA controller then proceeds through the six clocks states of the bus cycle. Figure 5-6 illustrates the bus timing of these six clock states for a DMA cycle that reads data from the requesting interface adapter and then writes the data into the memory location specified by the DMA controller.

DMA Memory-Write Cycle

The purpose of a DMA memory-write bus cycle is to fetch data from an interface adapter and write that data into the memory location specified by the DMA controller. After the DMA cycle is initiated on the bus, the controller and its support circuits drive the system address bus with the address of the target memory location. Next, the $\overline{\text{IOR}}$ bus signal is activated, which indicates that the interface adapter that requested the DMA cycle should drive the system data bus with its data. Next, the $\overline{\text{MEMW}}$ bus signal is activated; this indicates that the memory addressed earlier in the cycle should take the interface adapter's data and write it into memory. Note that the data from the interface adapter is not buffered anywhere. It is the responsibility of the interface adapter to maintain valid data until the memory can perform the write operation. Figure 5-6 illustrates the basic bus signal timing used in this bus cycle.

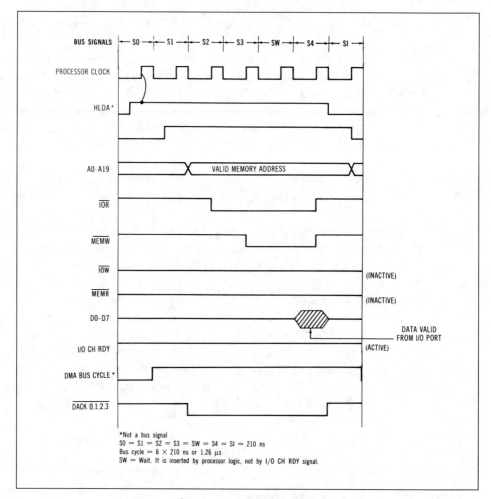

Figure 5-6. DMA memory-write bus cycle.

DMA Memory-Read Cycle

The DMA memory-read cycle is used to transfer data from system memory to an interface adapter. After the DMA cycle is initiated on the system bus, the DMA controller and its support circuits drive the system address bus with a memory address. Next, the controller activates the $\overline{\text{MEMR}}$ bus signal, thereby indicating to the memory that it should drive the system data bus with its contents. Next, the controller activates the $\overline{\text{IOW}}$ bus signal. This indicates to the interface adapter that it should take the data from memory. Figure 5-7 illustrates the basic signal and bus timings used in a DMA memory-read cycle.

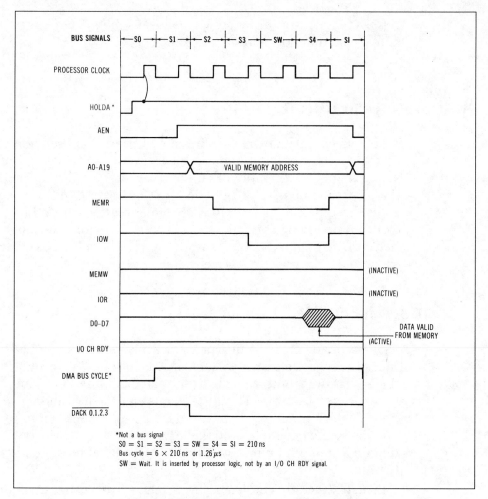

Figure 5-7. DMA memory-read bus cycle.

Memory-Refresh DMA Cycle

DMA memory-read bus cycles are used by the system to refresh the dynamic memory of the system. The system hardware automatically generates a dummy DMA memory-read bus cycle every 72 processor clocks, or approximately every 15.12 microseconds. The DMA controller is programmed to continuously increment the memory address with each cycle, thus providing the refresh address required by dynamic memory. Because the data read during these cycles is not used, the DMA cycle is shortened and, thus, the bus bandwidth used to refresh memory is reduced. These DMA cycles occur only on DMA channel 0 and are five clocks in length. Thus, 5 out of every 72 processor or bus clocks are used to support the refresh function in the system. This means the system bus is used 7 percent of the time for memory refresh.

Wait-State Generation

When attaching interfaces to the bus of the PC, a common problem is matching the speed of the bus cycles with the speed of the interface design. It is not uncommon for an interface to operate at a data rate slower than what the bus cycles provide for. The PC system bus is designed to solve these problems. The READY signal on the system bus, when controlled properly by a bus-attached adapter, can extend the length of the PC bus cycle to match that of a slower interface or halt a bus cycle until it is synchronized with an interface cycle.

8088 Wait-State Generation

As mentioned, all 8088 microprocessor bus cycles are normally four clock times in length and are described as T1 through T4. In some bus cycles, the PC hardware automatically inserts an extra idle clock time, called TW time, in the bus cycle. The READY bus signal line can be used to insert new or additional wait states. Because the 8088 memory-read and memory-write bus cycles and the I/O-read and I/O-write bus cycles have different timing requirements, the READY signal must be controlled differently.

Wait-State Generation in Memory Bus Cycles   The PC hardware does not insert any wait states in the 8088 memory-read or memory-write bus cycles; thus, they are four clock cycles in length. (The "regen" memory buffers on the display adapter request wait states for synchronization. This is done using the READY signal and is generated by the adapter and not by the system card's logic.) Figure 5-8 illustrates the bus signal timings necessary to generate a wait state for an 8088 memory-read or memory-write bus cycle.

The system board circuits sample the status of the READY bus signal at the rising edge of the T2 bus clock time. Because there is a setup time requirement and the delay of a 74LS74A latch circuit, the bus signal must be valid (active high) 75 nanoseconds prior to the rising edge of the T2 bus clock to generate a no wait state. If a wait state is required, the READY bus signal must be valid (inactive low) 60 nanoseconds prior to the rising edge of the T2 bus clock. If the READY signal is held low (inactive) until the rising edge of the next clock, an additional wait state is inserted. Again

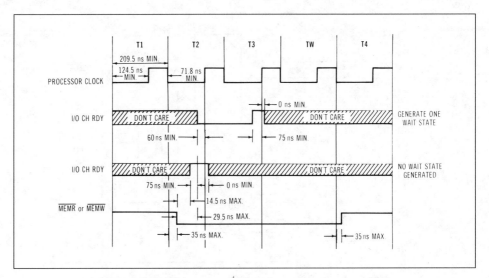

**Figure 5-8. Wait-state timing for a memory-read or
memory-write bus cycle.**

due to setup time and circuit delays, READY must go active high 75 ns before the rising edge of the next clock time; otherwise, an additional wait state is generated. These timings are based on worst-case setup and the delay timings of the circuits used in the READY circuit path.

The circuit shown in Figure 5-9 can be used to generate from one to six wait states in the 8088 memory-read or memory-write bus cycle. The first part of the circuit decodes the block of memory for which a wait state will be generated. This is done by simply decoding from the address bus the significant bits that define the address range for which a wait state will be generated. The output of the decoder is then sampled by the falling edge of the $\overline{\text{MEMR}}$ or $\overline{\text{MEMW}}$ bus signal. Note that if wait states are required only on a read operation, the $\overline{\text{MEMW}}$ signal can be removed from the OR operation. Similarly, if wait states are required only on the memory-write cycles, the $\overline{\text{MEMR}}$ signal is removed from the OR operation.

When the SN74S74 latch is set, the READY signal on the bus is deactivated. The circuit's timings are such that it will meet the setup and delay timings required to grant a wait state. The shift register circuit, generated using the SN74LS174 device, counts the number of clocks and, thus, the wait states generated before READY is activated by clearing the SN74S74 latch. The number of wait states is thus selected by jumpering the appropriate output of the SN74LS174 to clear the SN74S74 latch.

Wait-State Generation in I/O Bus Cycles   I/O-read or I/O-write cycles for the 8088 are normally four clocks in length, but in the PC design, an extra wait state is automatically generated by the system board circuits indepen-

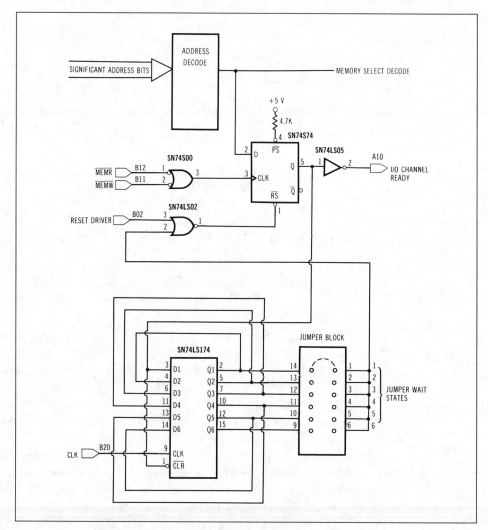

Figure 5-9. Wait-state generation for a memory-read or memory-write bus cycle.

dent of the READY bus signal. The READY signal can still be used to generate additional wait states. Figure 5-10 illustrates the bus signals and timings used to generate additional wait states on the I/O-read and I/O-write bus cycles. In general, the timings are the same as those used for the 8088 memory-read and memory-write bus cycles, except that READY is sampled with the rising edge of the T3 clock, not the T2 clock. To insert an additional wait state, READY must go active 60 nanoseconds prior to the rising edge of the T3 clock. To ensure that an additional wait state is not inserted, READY must go active 75 nanoseconds prior to the rising edge of the T3 clock.

Figure 5-11 illustrates a circuit that can be used to generate from one

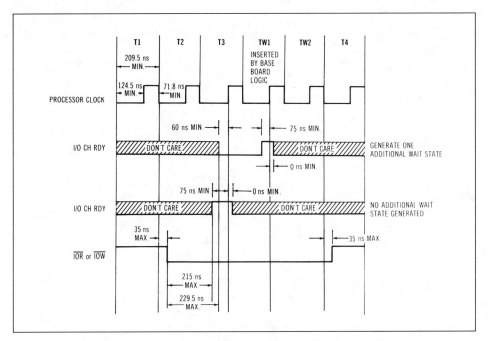

**Figure 5-10. Wait-state timing for an I/O-port-read or
I/O-port-write bus cycle.**

to five additional wait states in the 8088 I/O-read or I/O-write bus cycle. In
this circuit, the significant address bits are decoded to determine the I/O
address range for which extra wait states will be generated. The falling edge
of the $\overline{IOR}$ or $\overline{IOW}$ bus signal is used to sample the decoder output and set
the SN74LS74 latch. After this latch is set, it deactivates the READY signal on
the bus. The SN74LS174 device, acting as a shift register, counts the clocks
and, thus, the wait states generated before its output is used to clear the
SN74LS74 latch. When the latch is cleared, READY becomes active and the
bus cycle ends. If wait states are required only in I/O-read cycles, the $\overline{IOW}$
signal is not used to sample the decoder output. Similarly, if wait states are
required only in I/O-write cycles, the $\overline{IOR}$ signal is not used.

Note that the first stage of the shift register output is not used to generate a wait state. This is because the system board has already generated
the first wait state. This circuit counts the wait states; it does not generate
them. This circuit only generates wait states beyond that which is generated by the system board.

Wait-State Generation in DMA Bus Cycles

Wait-state generation in DMA (direct memory access) bus cycles and in mi-
croprocessor-generated bus cycles is different because a DMA bus cycle

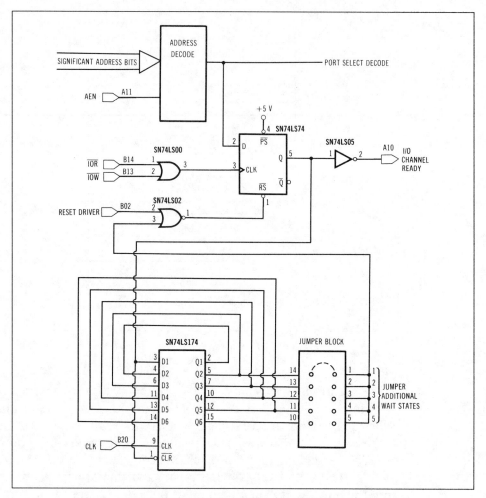

**Figure 5-11. Wait-state generation for an I/O-port-read or
I/O-port-write bus cycle.**

contains both read and write operations. There are two types of DMA cycles.
The first type reads from memory and writes to an I/O device or adapter.
The second one reads from an I/O device or adapter and writes to memory.
Signal timings are different on DMA cycles because the DMA controller samples the READY signal on the opposite edge of the processor clock. In addition, the PC automatically inserts a wait state in all DMA cycles on channels
1, 2, and 3. No wait states are inserted on channel 0; it is used only to support
memory refresh and is not available for normal DMA functions. Figure 5-12
illustrates the timings of the bus during DMA cycles.

The DMA controller uses the processor clock to generate the bus
timing and control lines that are driven from the DMA controller. These

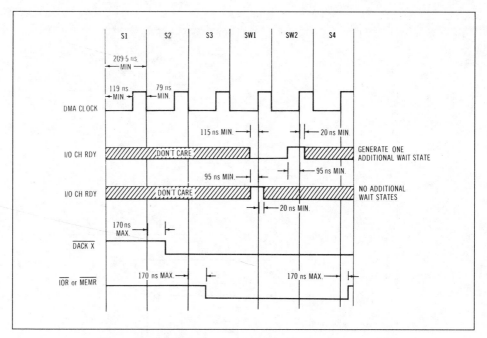

Figure 5-12. Wait-state timing for a DMA bus cycle.

bus clocks are called S clocks, rather than T clocks. The activation of the AEN bus signal indicates that the present bus cycle is a DMA cycle. To ensure that an additional wait state is inserted in a DMA cycle, the READY signal must be deactivated 135 nanoseconds prior to the falling edge of the bus clock's SW1 state. To ensure that an additional wait state is not taken, READY must be deactivated 115 nanoseconds prior to the falling edge of the next S clock.

Additional wait states can be generated under three different conditions: first, when a specific channel requests a DMA cycle; second, when the DMA transfer is pointed to a specific block of memory; and third, when a DMA transfer both takes place on a specific channel and is pointed to a specific block of memory. Figure 5-13 illustrates a circuit that can be used to insert up to four additional wait states in a DMA cycle when requested on a specific channel. The DACK signal sets a latch that drops the READY bus signal. The SN74LS174 device counts the bus clocks and resets the not ready latch when the desired number of wait states has been inserted. The first and second stages of the shift register are not used because the READY signal is sampled one clock time later in DMA cycles, and one wait state has already been inserted by the system board.

Figure 5-14 illustrates a circuit that inserts one to four additional wait states in a DMA bus cycle only when it decodes a specific memory address

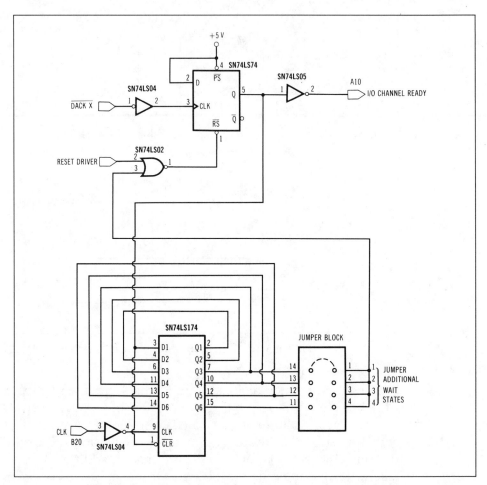

Figure 5-13. Wait-state generation for a DMA bus cycle.

block. This circuit can be used to also generate wait states in DMA bus cycles for a specific DMA channel and a specific decoded range of memory addresses. The generation of wait states on a specific DMA channel is accomplished by including in the SN74LS10 OR circuit each of those DMA channels' DACKs that requires wait states.

The insertion of extra wait cycles in a DMA cycle may not increase the read access time portion of the cycle. This is particularly true if the cycle is a read from I/O and a write to dynamic system memory. The memory-write function is triggered from the leading edge of the $\overline{\text{MEMW}}$ bus signal. Thus, delaying the trailing edge has no effect on the timing requirement for data from the I/O device because inserting wait states in DMA cycles does not change the relationship of the leading edge of the read bus signal to the leading edge of the write bus signal. Also, if a memory or I/O device needs wait states generated for both 8088-initiated

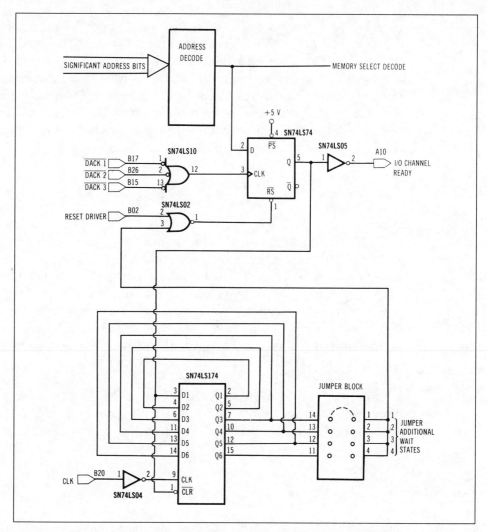

Figure 5-14. DMA wait-state generation on a specific channel and memory block.

cycles and DMA bus cycles, both circuits are required. The READY outputs of each circuit can be simply tied together.

System-Bus Signal Descriptions

The PC system bus is available for the attachment of adapter devices and unique interfacing projects at five to eight different 62-pin card slots on the processor card. All the card slots are bused with identical signals on each pin. All signals are at TTL-logic levels, except the signals provided in the connectors for the power and ground buses. The bus is a demultiplexed and repowered superset of the 8088 microprocessor bus. The 8088 bus signals are augmented by signals to support direct memory access, interrupts, timings, and control I/O read, I/O write, memory read, memory write, wait-state generation, memory refresh, and error detection. The following series of definitions gives detailed functional descriptions of all 62 signals in the bus slot connectors.

OSC

The OSC (oscillator) signal is an output-only signal with a frequency of 14.31818 MHz and a period of approximately 70 ns. It has a duty cycle of approximately 50 percent. The frequency of the OSC signal, which has the highest frequency on the bus, can be adjusted and trimmed using a variable capacitor that is typically on the system motherboard. On systems with clock rates different than the 4.77-MHz 8088 clock rates, there is no timing relationship between this OSC signal and the 8088 oscillator and clock.

The OSC signal can be divided by four to give the 3.58-MHz frequency required for TV color burst information. Care should be taken when this signal is used to clock other bus signals because bus delays effectively desynchronize this signal with respect to other bus signals. Thus, specific timing relationships cannot be guaranteed.

CLK

The CLK (clock) signal is derived from the OSC signal used to drive the 8088 microprocessor. (In a 4.77-MHz system, it is derived from the OSC signal described in the preceding section.) It is an output-only signal. The CLK signal is obtained by dividing the 8088 OSC input signal by three, which gives a frequency of 4.77 MHz for a 4.77-MHz system, 8 MHz for 8-MHz systems, and 10 MHz for 10-MHz systems. The OSC signal is not symmetric; it has a one-third/two-thirds duty cycle. Its period is 210 ns with a high time of 70 ns and a low time of 140 ns for a 4.77-MHz system, 83 high and 42 low for an 8-MHz system, and 66 high and 33 low for a 10-MHz system. This signal is well synchronized with respect to memory-read and memory-write control, and it can be used to generate system-bus wait states. If the 8088 is replaced with a NEC V20 microprocessor, the CLK signal may create error conditions because the V20 series requires a symmetric clock input.

RESET DRV

RESET DRV (reset driver) is an output-only signal that is held active high during system power-on sequences. It remains active until all levels have reached their specified operating range; then it goes inactive. In addition, the RESET DRV line is brought active high if any power level falls outside its specified operating range after power on. This signal is generally used to provide a power-on reset for bus-attached interface logic to I/O devices to bring them to a known state before operation by the system. This signal is set active and inactive on the falling edge of the microprocessor's OSC input signal. Due to logic delays, this synchronization should not be relied on for any attachment design.

A0–19

Address bits A0 through A19 are output-only signals used to address system-bus attached memory and I/O. (A0 is the least significant bit, and A19 is the most significant bit.) These twenty signal lines are driven by the 8088 microprocessor during system-bus cycles for memory read, memory write, I/O read, and I/O write. They are driven by the direct memory access logic feature during DMA cycles.

With 20 address lines, it is possible to address 1M of system memory, but not all address space is available in the system bus. Base system memory resides on the system board, and this address space cannot be addressed on the system bus. Similarly, the system processor board contains address space for BIOS ROM, which resides at the top of the 1M address space. This, again, cannot be addressed on the system bus. The processor, through the use of the IN and OUT instructions, can address I/O devices using lines A0 through A15 on the address bus. Lines A16 through A19 are not used and are held inactive during I/O port bus cycles. On the PC, however, only address lines A0 through A9 are used for addressing the I/O ports. In addition, only I/O port addresses in the range 0200 to 03FF hex are valid on the system bus. Exceptions to this rule are explained in later chapters.

D0–7

Lines D0 through D7 are bidirectional data lines used to transmit data between the 8088 microprocessor, memory, and I/O ports. (D0 is the least significant bit and D7 is the most significant bit.) During the 8088-

initiated write bus cycles, data is valid slightly before the back rising edge of the $\overline{IOW}$ or $\overline{MEMW}$ control signal. Usually, the rising edge of the $\overline{IOW}$ signal is used to clock the data on the data bus into the I/O port registers; the rising edge of $\overline{MEMW}$ clocks the data into memory. During the 8088-initiated read bus cycles, the addressed memory (or I/O port register) must place its data on the data bus before the rising edge of the $\overline{MEMR}$ (or $\overline{IOR}$) control signal.

During direct memory access cycles, the data bus is used to transfer data directly between an I/O port and memory without the intervention of the microprocessor. During the DMA cycles, the processor is disconnected from the bus and the direct memory access control device, 8237-5, controls the bus transfer.

ALE

The ALE (address latch enable) signal is an output-only signal driven from the 8288 bus controller. It is used to indicate that the address bus is now valid, enabling the beginning of a bus cycle. This signal goes active high prior to the address bus being valid and falls to inactive low after the address bus is valid. The signal is used to latch address information from the local address/data bus of the 8088 microprocessor. The system's data bus does not contain address information; thus, ALE cannot be used to demultiplex addresses from the data bus. The ALE signal is a good synchronization point when looking at 8088-initiated bus cycles because it starts at the beginning of each bus cycle. ALE is not active during direct memory access cycles.

I/O CH CK

The I/O CH CK (I/O channel check) signal is a low-level, input-only signal used to report error conditions on bus-attached interface cards. When this signal is set low, it generates a nonmaskable interrupt (NMI) to the 8088 microprocessor. The NMI is masked by an I/O register port bit and must be enabled before the interrupt can be received by the 8088 processor. The I/O CH CK signal is also masked by an I/O register port bit and must be enabled before it can cause an NMI. In addition, if the line is not masked, its state can be read in an I/O register port bit. Because there is more than one source for an NMI, the software must determine the source by checking the status of the I/O CH CK line in the I/O port register status bit. (See Chapter 12 for a discussion of I/O port address and bit assignments.) In the system, this line is used to report parity error conditions on bus-attached memory cards.

I/O CH RDY

The I/O CH RDY (I/O channel ready) signal is an input-only signal used to extend the length of bus cycles so that memory or I/O ports that are not fast enough to respond to a normal bus cycle of four clocks can still be attached to the system bus. If a memory port or an I/O port wants to extend the bus cycle, it forces the I/O CH RDY line low when it decodes its address and receives a $\overline{\text{MEMR}}$, $\overline{\text{MEMW}}$, $\overline{\text{IOR}}$, or $\overline{\text{IOW}}$ command. The I/O CH RDY signal should be carefully controlled so that only required additional wait states are added to the bus cycle. By holding this line inactive, additional wait states can extend the bus cycle in increments of one processor clock cycle to a maximum of ten clock cycles. This signal should be driven with an open-collector driver because it is ORed with other I/O CH RDY signals from other bus-attached interface cards.

IRQ2–7

IRQ2 through IRQ7 (interrupt requests 2 through 7) are six input-only signals used by the system bus to generate interrupt requests to the 8088 microprocessor. These signals go directly to the 8259A interrupt controller of the processor card. The BIOS programs of the ROM initialize the 8259A controller such that IRQ2 is the highest priority signal and IRQ7 is the lowest. If the level is not masked, a rising-edge signal will generate an interrupt request to the 8088 microprocessor. After a rising-edge request occurs, it must remain active until the 8088 processor issues an INTA (interrupt acknowledge) signal. The INTA signal is not present on the system bus; thus, the request is usually reset with an I/O register port bit using the OUT command issued in the interrupt-service routine. If the interrupt request is not held active until the INTA signal time, a level-7 interrupt is generated regardless of the priority of the level. The operating characteristics of these lines can be changed by reprogramming the initialization parameter in the 8259A controller.

$\overline{\text{IOR}}$

The $\overline{\text{IOR}}$ (I/O read) signal is an output-only signal from the 8288 bus controller. It is used to indicate to the I/O ports that the 8088-initiated bus cycle is an I/O-port-read cycle and the address on the address bus is an I/O port address. The I/O port address should respond by placing its read data on the system data bus. Because the $\overline{\text{IOR}}$ signal is active low, the I/O port should place its data on the bus approximately 30 nanoseconds prior to the rising edge of the signal to ensure that the processor gets valid data. When a direct access occurs, the $\overline{\text{IOR}}$ signal is driven from the direct memory access (DMA) controller on the processor board, an 8237-5 device. In this case, the address bus does not contain an I/O port address; it contains the memory address where the port's read data will be written. The I/O port is selected not by an address but by the active DACK signal from the 8237-5 controller.

$\overline{\text{IOW}}$

The $\overline{\text{IOW}}$ (I/O write) signal is an active low-level output-only signal. It is driven from the 8288 bus controller during 8088-initiated bus cycles and indicates that the address bus contains an I/O port address and the data bus contains data to be written into the I/O port. When the $\overline{\text{IOW}}$ signal goes active low, the data bus may not be valid; thus, port data should be clocked or latched using the rising edge of this signal. When a DMA bus cycle occurs, this signal is driven from the 8237-5 DMA controller. The $\overline{\text{IOW}}$ signal is then used to write data from memory, which is now on the data bus, to the DACK-selected I/O port. Again, data may not be valid on the leading active low edge of this signal; thus, the data should be clocked into the I/O port using the rising edge of the signal.

$\overline{\text{MEMW}}$

$\overline{\text{MEMW}}$ (memory write) is a low-level active signal used to write data from the system bus into memory. This signal is driven from the 8288 bus controller during 8088-initiated bus cycles and indicates that the address bus contains the address of a memory location to which the data on the data bus is to be written. Data may not be valid on the data bus when $\overline{\text{MEMW}}$ first goes active low, but the data is valid prior to the rising edge of the signal. During DMA cycles, this signal is driven from the 8237-5 DMA controller and is used to write data on the bus from an I/O port into memory. Be careful when using this signal to initiate a dynamic memory-write cycle because the write data may not be valid as it goes active. Dynamic RAM memories may have to be designed to use the "late write," or "CAS write," feature.

MEMR

The $\overline{\text{MEMR}}$ (memory read) signal is a low-level output-only signal used to request read data from memory. This signal is driven from the 8288 bus controller on 8088-initiated bus cycles. It indicates that the address bus contains a valid memory-read address and that the specified memory location should drive the system data bus with its read data. As with the $\overline{\text{IOR}}$ signal, memory must drive valid data onto the data bus approximately 30 nanoseconds before the rising edge of the $\overline{\text{MEMR}}$ signal to ensure that the processor receives valid data. During DMA cycles, this signal is driven from the 8237-5 DMA controller and indicates that the address memory location should respond by driving the data bus with its read data so that it can be written into the DACK-selected I/O port.

DRQ1–3

Lines DRQ1 through DRQ3 (direct memory access request 1 through 3) are active-high input-only lines used by the interface to request data cycles. If a device or interface logic wants to transfer data between itself and memory without intervention of the 8088 microprocessor, the request is initiated by raising a DRQ line. These lines go directly to the 8237-5 DMA controller on the processor system card, where they are prioritized with other DMA requests before the DMA cycle is granted.

The ROM BIOS of the PC initializes the DMA controller such that DRQ0 is the highest priority. But DRQ0 is not available on the system bus; it is used on the processor card to refresh the system's dynamic memory. Depending on the mode programmed in the DMA controller, care must be taken when controlling DRQ lines. If the DRQ is held active-high too long, more than one cycle may be taken. Typically, the DRQ is reset by its corresponding DACK signal. See Chapter 10 for a detailed discussion of the direct memory access function.

DACK0–3

Signals DACK0 through DACK3 (direct memory access acknowledge 0 through 3) are active low-level output-only signals issued by the 8237-5 DMA controller. They indicate that the corresponding DRQ has been honored and the DMA controller will take the bus and proceed with the requested DMA cycle. There is no corresponding DRQ0 on the system bus; thus, DACK0 indicates that the present DMA cycle is a dummy read cycle that can be used to refresh system dynamic memory. During the DACK0 memory-read cycle, the address bus contains valid incrementing refresh addresses. DACK0 refresh cycles occur every 15.12 microseconds.

AEN

The AEN (address enable) signal is an output-only active-high signal issued by the DMA control logic. It indicates that a DMA bus cycle is in progress. On the processor card, this signal is used to disable the 8088 microprocessor's address, data, and control buses from the system bus and enable the address and control bus from the DMA controller. On the system bus, the AEN signal disables I/O port address decodes during DMA cycles so that DMA memory addresses are not used as I/O port addresses. This is possible because $\overline{IOW}$ and $\overline{IOR}$ may be active with memory addresses on the address bus during DMA cycles.

TC

The TC (terminal count) signal is an output-only active-high signal issued by the 8237-5 DMA controller. It indicates that one of the DMA channels has reached its preprogrammed number of transfer cycles. This signal is typically used to terminate a DMA block transfer. Because the TC signal is issued when any of the four DMA channels reaches its terminal count, it is necessary to condition this signal with the appropriate DACK signal. Thus, the interface logic should AND the TC with the DACK to get the TC for the specific channel. A TC signal can be used as an interface timing signal because it occurs every 990.804 ms. This is how long it takes the refresh cycle to address the first 65,536 memory addresses, after which the TC is reached and the cycle is restarted.

Bus Power and Ground

Figure 5-15 illustrates the signals present on the system bus. In addition to the previously discussed signals, the system contains the following power levels:

+5 Vdc   The +5-volt direct current power level is available on two pins of the card-edge connectors on the bus. It is regulated to ±5% (+4.75 to +5.25 volts dc).

+12 Vdc   The +12-volt dc power level is available at one pin of the card-edge connectors on the bus. It is regulated to ±5% (+11.4 to +12.6 volts dc).

−5 Vdc   The −5-volt dc power level is available on one pin of the card-edge connectors on the bus. It is regulated to ±10% (−4.5 to −5.5 volts dc).

−12 Vdc   The −12-volt dc power level is available on one pin of the card-edge connectors on the bus. It is regulated to ±10% (−10.8 to −13.2 volts dc).

System dc and frame ground are provided at three pins on the card-edge connectors of the bus.

System-Bus Timings

The key to the design of any system-bus attached interface is an understanding of its timing compatibility with the system bus. (For example, you need to know how fast data must be presented after memory or a register is accessed by the 8088 microprocessor.) This section presents detailed timing information for each type of bus cycle on the system bus.

Timing information is presented as maximum and minimum worst-case data for the IBM PC XT with a 4.77-MHz processor clock speed. Thus, the timing information is valid for all conditions of bus loading and power levels. When the original source of information did not list a worst-case minimum delay, I used one-half of the typical specification. In general, this will provide a sufficient design margin. No typical timing information is used in maximum worst-case delay-timing calculations; this ensures that designs based on this data will have no difficulty operating on the system bus.

This data is based on timing information in the *1982 Intel Component Data Catalog* and Texas Instruments' *1981 TTL Data Book for Design Engineers*. Also, data discussed here represents system-bus timings as they appear at the expansion-card slots on the system board, and as they are defined by the PC system unit board logic schematics published in the *IBM Technical Reference Manual*. Except for data taken from the *IBM Technical Reference Manual*, timing data presented here does not necessarily represent information endorsed or supported by IBM.

As mentioned, timings are provided for the bus cycles of an IBM PC XT at a 4.77-MHz clock speed. Naturally, timings will vary for systems that operate at high clock speeds, such as 8 MHz and 10 MHz. Due to the use of custom integrated circuits that replace TTL devices and the use of higher

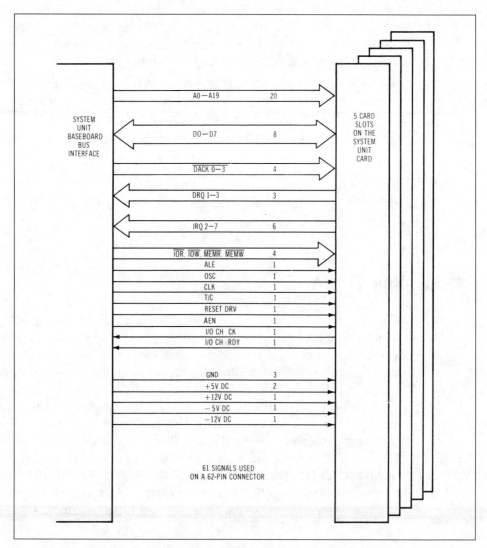

Figure 5-15. Connection of the system unit bus to five feature-card slots.

clock rate 8088, 8086, and NEC V series microprocessors, it is nearly impossible to calculate all the variations in bus timings. A good rule is to scale these timing values to the clock speed of the target system. For example, t1, t2, and t3 values for 8-MHz and 10-MHz systems would be as follows:

8-MHz system   t1 = 125 ns, t2 = 83 ns, t3 = 42 ns

10-MHz system   t1 = 100 ns, t2 = 67 ns, t3 = 33 ns

In general, timings from clock edge to signal will be valid independent of the processor clock speed. For DMA and I/O cycles, higher clock speed systems normally insert additional wait states to maintain the standard PC 4.77-MHz bus operation cycle time. For DMA operation at high clock speeds, the DMA cycle's S clocks are normally one-half the processor's clock speeds. In these cases, the t1, t2, and t3 times for 8-MHz and 10-MHz systems are as follows:

8-MHz system   t1 = 250 ns, t2 = 167 ns, t3 = 83 ns

10-MHz system   t1 = 200 ns, t2 = 125 ns, t3 = 75 ns

It is likely that the actual timings of the system bus will be better than the values presented in the tables. A design should not count on this, however, because worst-case conditions will occur. (In many cases, the problem will be intermittent and very difficult to diagnose.) Also note that the timing information will be affected by improper power levels and grounding and by very high capacitive or dc loads. Figures 5-16 through 5-21 illustrate the signal timing relationships of the different bus cycles.

System-Bus Loading and Driving Capabilities

When attaching a design to the system bus, important considerations are bus signal driving capability and bus loading. For bus output signals, you have to determine if there is sufficient signal drive to support your design. If not, signal repowering is needed. For input bus signals, you need to determine if your design has sufficient capability to drive the system bus.

The bus loading and driving specifications presented here are derived from an inspection of the logic schematics for the IBM PC XT system that were published in the *IBM Technical Reference Manual* and from data in the *1982 Component Data Catalog* and Texas Instruments' *1981 TTL Data Book for Design Engineers*. Compatible systems and newer systems designed with custom integrated circuits will have slightly different driving capabilities and loading characteristics; in general, the driving capabilities are better and the loading is less.

System-Bus Drive Capability

Two specifications on the bus output signals are of interest: IOL and IOH. IOL refers to the maximum current that can be sinked into the output driver at the low logic level. IOH is the maximum current that can be

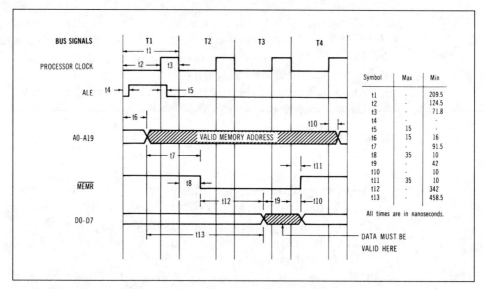

Figure 5-16. Signal timing of 8088-initiated memory-read bus cycle.

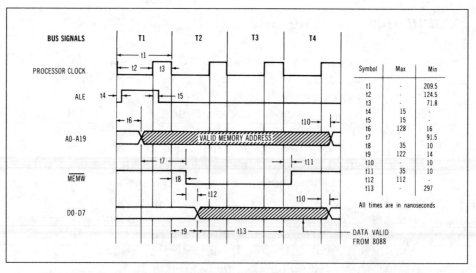

Figure 5-17. Signal timing of 8088-initiated memory-write bus cycle.

sourced from the driver at the high logic level. Table 5-2 lists the capability of the output drivers in the bus expansion card slots. Note that some bus signals are used on the system board before being driven to the card slots. Because Table 5-2 takes into account the use of these loads, it re-

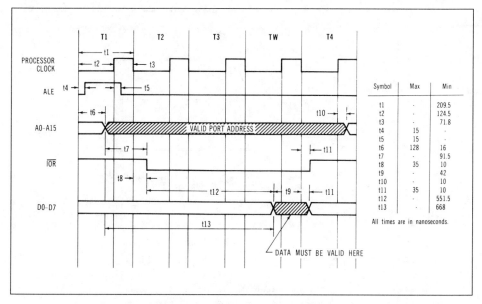

Figure 5-18. Signal timing of 8088-initiated I/O-port-read bus cycle.

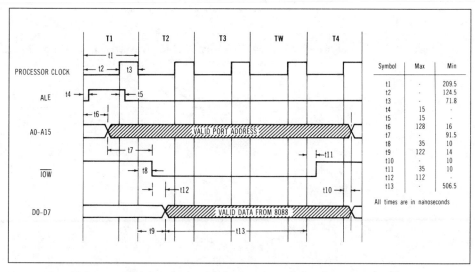

Figure 5-19. Signal timing of 8088-initiated I/O-port-write bus cycle.

flects the true drive available in the five I/O system-bus card slots. The actual drive available for a specific design is the difference between the values given in the table and the values taken by the other cards in the remaining card slots.

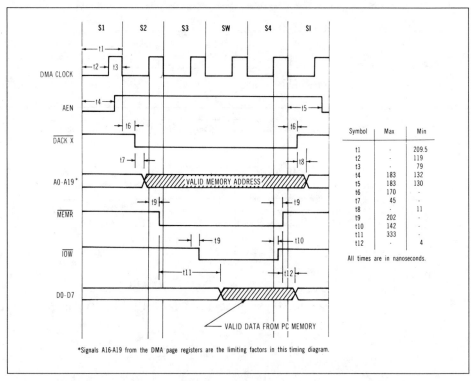

The table embedded in the timing diagram:

Symbol	Max	Min
t1	.	209.5
t2	.	119
t3	.	79
t4	183	132
t5	183	130
t6	170	.
t7	45	.
t8	.	11
t9	202	.
t10	142	.
t11	333	.
t12	.	4

All times are in nanoseconds.

*Signals A16-A19 from the DMA page registers are the limiting factors in this timing diagram.

Figure 5-20. Signal timing of DMA-initiated read-from-memory, write-to-I/O bus cycle.

Table 5-2. System-Bus Drive Capability

Bus Output Signal	IOL (mA)	IOH (mA)
D0–D7	23.6	−14.96
A19–A16	7.2	−2.46
A14, A15	21.2	−2.51
A13	23.2	−2.56
A0–A12	23.4	−2.56
IOR, IOW, MEMR, MEMW	23.8	−4.98
CLK	23.2	−14.96
AEN, DACK0	24.0	−15.00
DACK1	3.2	−0.20
DACK2, DACK3	2.8	−0.18
ALE	14.8	−0.94
RESET DRV, T/C	8.0	−0.40
OSC	5.0	−1.00

Note: Table values are adjusted for loads taken on the system board. Values are worst-case instances of the 8088 bus drive or the DMA bus drive.

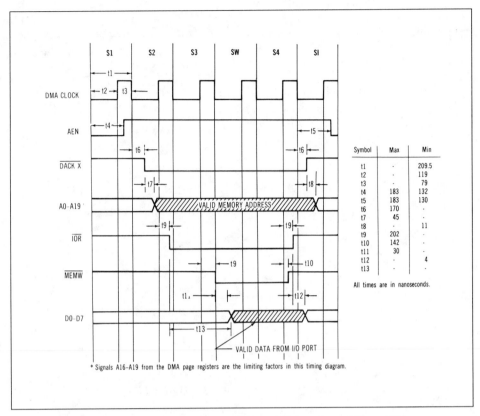

Figure 5-21. Signal timing of DMA-initiated read-from-I/O, write-to-memory bus cycle.

Table 5-3 reflects the output drive loads taken by some popular IBM PC cards. To determine the available load, sum the values in the tables for the cards in your system, then subtract that value from the values for the IBM monochrome display and parallel printer adapter.

System-Bus Load in Card Slots

The system-bus input signal presents a load to the cards in the expansion bus card slots. This load is the low-level input current, or IIL, required from the driver to establish a good low-level logic signal. The driving circuit must provide current in the upper level to the bus-receiving circuit. This is called the high-level input current, or IIH. The IIL and IIH load values for the bus input signal are listed in Table 5-4.

Table 5-3. Bus Loading

	Bus Signal	Load Taken From IOL (mA)	IOH (mA)
IBM Monochrome Display and Parallel Printer Adapter	D0–D7	−0.2	0.020
	A0–A3	−0.2	0.020
	A4–A9	−0.8	0.040
	A10–A19	−0.4	0.020
	AEN	−0.4	0.020
	MEMW	−0.8	0.040
	IOR	−0.4	0.020
	IOW	−0.4	0.020
	MEMR	−0.4	0.020
	RESET DRV	−0.4	0.020
	CLK	−2.0	0.050
IBM Color Graphics Monitor Adapter	D0–D7	−0.2	0.020
	OSC	−0.4	0.020
	RESET DRV	−0.8	0.040
	CLK	−0.4	0.020
	AEN	−0.8	0.040
	MEMR	−0.8	0.040
	MEMW	−0.8	0.040
	IOR	−0.8	0.040
	IOW	−0.41	0.050
	A0	−0.2	0.020
	A1, A2	−0.8	0.040
	A3	−1.2	0.060
	A4–A9	−0.8	0.040
	A10–A19	−0.4	0.020
IBM Parallel Printer Adapter	D0–D7	−0.2	0.020
	A3–A7, A9	−0.4	0.020
	A8	−0.8	0.040
	RESET DRV	−0.4	0.020
	IOR	−0.4	0.020
	IOW	−0.4	0.020

Table 5-3. *(cont.)*

	Bus Signal	Load Taken From IOL (mA)	IOH (mA)
IBM Diskette Drive Adapter	D0–D7	−0.2	0.020
	A0–A9	−0.4	0.020
	AEN	−0.4	0.020
	$\overline{\text{IOR}}$	−0.4	0.020
	$\overline{\text{IOW}}$	−0.4	0.020
	DACK2	−0.4	0.020
	RESET DRV	−0.4	0.020
IBM 64K RAM Card	D0–D7	−0.2	0.020
	A0–A13	−0.4	0.020
	A14	−4.0	0.100
	A15	−2.4	0.070
	A16–A19	−6.0	0.150
	DACK0	−0.8	0.040
	$\overline{\text{MEMR}}$	−2.4	0.070
	$\overline{\text{MEMW}}$	−2.4	0.070
IBM Game Control Adapter	D0–D7	−0.2	0.020
	A0–A9	−0.4	0.020
	AEN	−0.4	0.020
	$\overline{\text{IOR}}$	−0.4	0.020
	$\overline{\text{IOW}}$	−0.4	0.020

Table 5-4. Load Presented to the Bus Input Signals

Bus Signal	Load Taken From IOL (mA)	IOH (mA)
D0–D7	−0.4	0.040
I/0 CH CK	−0.4	0.020
I/0 CH RDY	−0.4	0.020
IRQ2–IRQ7	−0.010	0.010
DRQ1–DRQ3	−0.010	0.010

Capacitive Bus Loading

Another concern when designing for attachment to the system bus is capacitive loading on the output bus signals. As each load is added, the capacitance that the driver circuit sees is increased. As the capacitance increases, the signal becomes distorted and delayed. Each load adds from 10 to 20 picofarads of capacitance to the bus. Thus, with 10 loads, the capacitance is from 100 to 200 picofarads. In general, signal capacitance values greater than 200 picofarads will affect the bus signals to the extent that unreliable operation may occur.

General Rules

In general, a loading calculation will not be required if a few simple rules are followed. First, do not attach an NMOS LSI device directly to the system bus. Typically, these devices have a very low drive capability and are not tolerant to negative undershoot that may exist on the system bus. Second, do not present more than two LS device loads to any bus signal. Third, decouple bus drivers and transceivers with a 0.1 microfarad capacitor between the +5 volt and ground leads. Last, do not run the bus signal for long distances on the attachment card because this will add excessive capacitance and will distort and delay the bus signal. Diagonal buffer circuits should be placed near the bus connector. If these simple rules are followed, you should not have to go through a detailed bus loading calculation.

System-Bus Mechanical and Power Characteristics

Most interface designs will be done on cards that must fit in one of the system unit's card slots. This section provides information relative to the mechanical aspects of the system unit and to the card size that will fit in the card slots. The power-supply capabilities of the system unit are covered also. This provides the interface designer with needed information on the voltage levels, power, and tolerances of power available to implement a design.

System-Bus Card Slots

The original PC provided five system-bus expansion slots. With the introduction of the PX XT, this was increased to eight slots. Most compatibles provide eight slots. Slots 7 and 8 sometimes have mechanical restrictions that limit the length of the adapter boards permitted in these slots.

The connectors are capable of supporting 62 signal connectors to a card, 31 on each side of the card. The connection tabs are spaced on 100-mil centers, or one-tenth of an inch apart. Each card slot is capable of accepting a card, with components and wiring area, of approximately 4.1 inches by 13 inches (10.42 cm by 33.02 cm). The card slots in the original PC are spaced 1 inch apart; in the PC XT, the spacing was reduced to .75 inch.

Cards are retained by attaching an L bracket to the back end of the card; the bracket, in turn, attaches to the top of the system unit's bulkhead. Cables may be attached to the rear of the card and can extend through the L bracket and through the slots cut in the rear of the bulkhead of the system unit. This scheme allows cards to be nearly any length or height up to the maximum size specified earlier. In addition, a connector may be attached to the rear of the card and extended through the bulkhead slots; this eliminates the need for an internal cable from the card to the bulkhead.

Figure 5-22 shows signal and slot labeling conventions. Figure 5-23 shows the arrangement of the card slots on the system unit's logic board for a PC; three additional slots would be added for a PC XT. Adapter boards designed mechanically for the PC and PC XT will fit in a PC AT system-bus expansion slot even though the slot will also accept a larger AT size board.

PC Card Size

Figure 5-24 presents the maximum dimensions of cards that will fit in a system unit card slot. The card should be constructed of a material with a minimum thickness of 0.06 inch to ensure good contact in the connectors. In addition, the card-edge signal tabs should be plated with gold to ensure a positive, long lasting, and reliable contact.

Several manufacturers provide excellent prototyping cards that can be used to wire wrap a design so that you can run it in a system. The following manufacturers offer a family of wire-wrapped prototyping boards for all members of the PC and PS/2 family.

Vector Electronic Co., Inc.
12460 Gladstone Avenue
Sylmar, CA 91342

On Target Associates
3000 Scott Boulevard, #113
Santa Clara, CA 95054

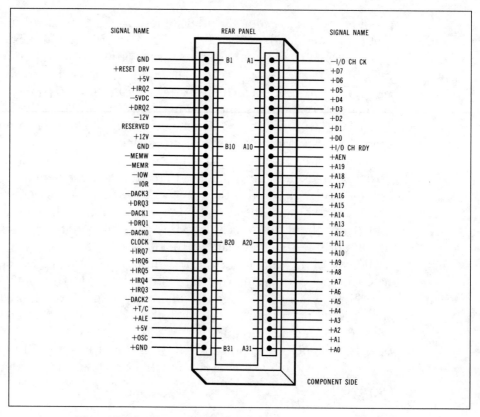

Figure 5-22. Pin and signal definitions for the card slots.

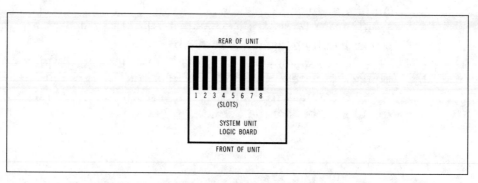

Figure 5-23. Arrangement and location of the card slots in the system unit.

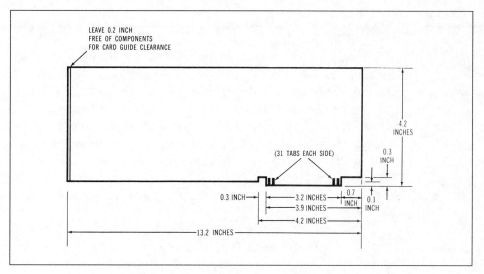

Figure 5-24. Dimensions of PC cards.

The L brackets used to mount the adapter board to the PC rear bulkhead are available with connector cutouts for most types of interconnections from

Globe Manufacturing Sales Inc.
1159 US Route 22
Mountainside, NJ 07092-2896

System Unit Power and Power Decoupling

Four power levels are available on the signal tabs in each card slot. Table 5-5 summarizes these levels, the total power from the power supply, its tolerances, and the total wattage.

Table 5-5. PC Power Supply

DC Power (Vdc)	Max (Vdc)	Min (Vdc)	Current (Amps)	Power (Watts)	Typical Current/ Slot (Amps)
+5.0	5.25	4.80	7.0	35.0	0.7
−5.0	5.50	4.60	0.3	1.5	0.03
+12.0	12.6	11.52	2.0	24.0	0.10
−12.0	13.2	10.92	0.25	3.0	0.05

Common problems in circuit designs are improper power distribution and decoupling. Because most electronic devices have highly variable power requirements that are often dependent on the operation occurring at an instant in time, they require a decoupling device. A decoupling device supplies the short-term power requirements of a device so that the power does not have to come directly from the system's power supply. The wiring and cables in the system's power supply add inductance to the power source; thus, the power supply cannot respond quickly to high transient power requirements. To solve this problem, decoupling capacitors are typically added at key points in the design so that transient power can be drawn from the capacitors and not directly from the power supply.

For large, slow power fluctuations, a bulk capacitor is used to store the power requirements. These bulk-type decoupling capacitors are typically tantalum capacitors having capacitances of 8 to 20 microfarads. These devices should be tied across the power level and ground at the card-edge connector and at the extreme end and top of card. It is particularly important to decouple the +5-volt power level because it will likely draw the most power in a typical design.

For high-frequency transient power requirements, smaller high-frequency decoupling capacitors must be used. These devices are typically ceramic capacitors in the range of 0.1 to 0.01 microfarad. These devices are normally placed across the ground and power leads of high transient-current devices. Devices that typically require a high-frequency decoupling capacitor are bus drivers, bus transceivers, S-type TTL devices, LSI devices, and any high-current, high-switching-speed device.

Chapter 6

PC and XT Interrupts, DMA, and Timer Counters

THIS CHAPTER PRESENTS ways of using and extending the capabilities of PC system interrupts, DMA (direct memory access), and timer-counter support functions. These support functions are present on all versions of the PC, from the original PC to the newer PS/2 systems. For reasons of software compatibility, these functions are viewed by PC systems software as nearly identical across all PC family members. Each new version of the PC system, however, has introduced enhancements and minor changes in interrupts, DMA, and timer-counter functions. This chapter presents these functions in the PC and XT systems. The programming interface and the theory of operation for these functions are presented in detail and are not repeated for the PC AT and PS/2 systems. The equivalent chapters on the PC AT and PS/2 systems (Chapters 11 and 13, respectively) present enhancements and changes to these functions. Therefore, I suggest that this chapter be read prior to consulting the chapters on PC AT and PS/2 interrupts, DMA, and timer counters.

System Interrupts

Interrupts are useful and often necessary functions when interfacing a design to a microprocessor system. Their major advantage is the capability to get the attention of the microprocessor to service a function, without requiring the processor to be constantly polling an interface for work requests. This leaves the processor free to do other things until it is required by the interface.

A good example of the use of interrupts is the servicing of the PC keyboard. Each keystroke generates at least one interrupt to the 8088 microprocessor. As the microprocessor is executing its program, it cannot also be in a loop waiting for the user to press a key because the full attention of the processor would be devoted to looking for the next keystroke and the program would never get executed. A simple solution is to have the program that is being executed stop periodically and look at the keyboard interface to see if a key has been pressed. However, the application program must know when to look and how often; otherwise, much of the processing time would be used in nonproductive polling of the keyboard interface. The interrupt function of the PC solves this problem. It automatically stops the program at some convenient point (the next instruction boundary), then points the processor to the program needed to service the keyboard each time a key is pressed. After the keyboard program has serviced the keypress, the hardware automatically returns control to the next sequential instruction in the program that was executing.

The interrupt function is often used in interfacing applications that require synchronization with external events or when error or status conditions require the attention of the processor or the program. Because many interface conditions may require service, and possibly all at the same time, the PC's interrupt functions provide nine interrupt levels or request ports. These nine request ports are prioritized such that when multiple requests are active at the same time, they are serviced in a sequential, predescribed order.

PC Interrupt System

The 8088 microprocessor has two interrupt input ports: a maskable-interrupt input port and a non-maskable-interrupt (NMI) input port. Attached to the NMI are three possible sources for the NMI: a baseboard RAM parity error, an auxiliary processor-socket interrupt request, and an I/O-channel check request.

Because the NMI is not masked internally in the 8088 microprocessor, logic on the baseboard uses an I/O-register port bit to mask and unmask the NMI. An 8259A interrupt controller is attached to the maskable-interrupt 8088 port. The 8259A controller extends the 8088 port to eight prioritized interrupt request level ports. Thus, a total of nine interrupt level requests are available for interfacing applications. Some are used by the system's integrated I/O and the system-bus attached adapters. Table 6-1 is a brief summary of the interrupt levels and their present use on a PC XT system. Figure 6-1 is a graphic representation of the PC and XT interrupt system.

Table 6-1. Summary of Interrupt Levels

Interrupt Level		Usage
Highest Level	NMI	Baseboard RAM parity, I/O channel check, numeric processor
	IRQ0	System timer output 8253-5 channel 0
	IRQ1	Keyboard scan code interrupt
Available in	IRQ2	Not used at present
System Bus	IRQ3	Not used at present
	IRQ4	RS232-C serial port
	IRQ5	Not used at present
	IRQ6	Diskette DRV status
	IRQ7	Parallel PRT port (not used in BIOS)

The Interrupt Controller

The 8259A interrupt controller expands the 8088 microprocessor's maskable-interrupt input port to eight prioritized interrupt input ports. Figure 6-2 is a block diagram of the key elements of an 8259A interrupt controller. The logic in the controller captures interrupt requests in a bank of eight latches called the interrupt request register (IRR). The IRR can be programmed to be set by either an edge-sensitive signal or a level-sensitive signal. An 8-bit interrupt mask register (IMR) can be programmed to enable or disable any interrupt requests to the controller.

After interrupt requests are set in the IRR, they are fed through priority-resolving logic. The results of the priority logic are then fed to another 8-bit register called an in-service register (ISR). This register reflects the interrupt level presently being serviced by the 8088 microprocessor. The controller can be programmed to support a variety of interrupt prioritization modes by setting mode bits during the controller's initialization. These modes are covered later in the chapter. In addition, the controller allows the masking and clearing of the interrupt request during system operation by programming a set of command control registers. During operation of the controller, you can also read the status of many of the controller's internal registers.

The 8259A controller is used also on the PC AT and PS/2. On these systems, two 8259A controllers are cascaded to create fifteen 8259A equivalent interrupts. On newer systems, the functions of the 8259A are implemented in custom LSI silicon chips. (The PC system design does not

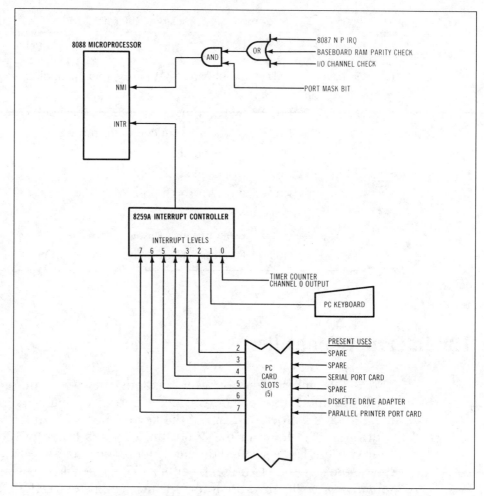

Figure 6-1. Block diagram of an interrupt system.

support cascade mode because the cascade interface lines do not exist on the system bus.)

Sequence of Events in an Interrupt

When an interrupt request occurs in the system, a sequence of events directs the request to the proper program needed to service the request. Before this can occur, however, some system initialization is required. This section describes the event sequence that occurs when an interrupt is activated. Let us assume that the interrupt initialization sequence has been done and that the interrupt request is not masked.

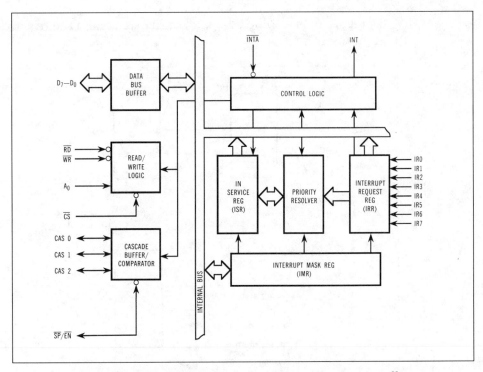

Figure 6-2. Block diagram of an 8259A interrupt controller.
(Courtesy Intel Corporation)

1. The interface logic activates an interrupt-request line on the system bus interface.

2. The interrupt controller (8259A) receives the request and prioritizes it with other requests that may be coming or pending.

3. If the request is the only one or is the next highest level pending at the end of the higher-level service, an interrupt request is sent to the 8088 microprocessor.

4. The 8088 MPU sends two INTA response pulses to the 8259A interrupt controller. The first freezes the priority and sets the levels in the service latch. The second INTA requests an 8-bit pointer value.

5. The 8088 processor receives the 8-bit pointer value. It is used to index into a low memory table, which contains the IP and the offset value of the interrupt-service routine for the level being serviced.

6. The 8088 microprocessor fetches the IP and code segment value, pushes its present IP, code segment, and flags onto the system stack, then branches to the newly fetched IP and code segment value. The interrupt-service program will now begin execution.

Figure 6-3 is a block diagram of the signal and the data flow during a system interrupt.

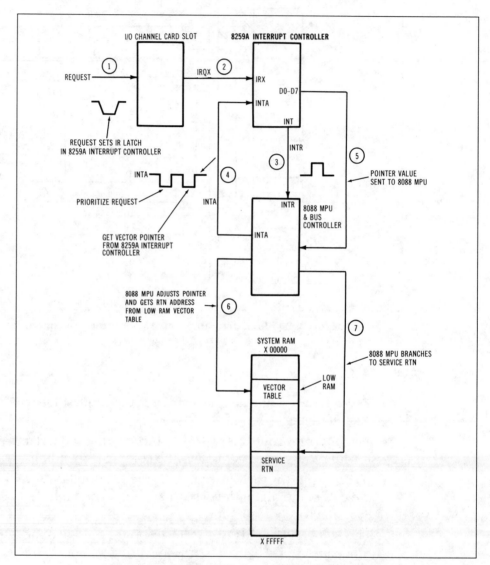

Figure 6-3. Diagram of the interrupt signal flow.

Interrupt Housekeeping

After the interrupt-service routine begins execution, a few housekeeping chores need to be done before the routine is executed. First, if the routine uses part of the 8088 register (which is highly likely), it should push the present register values onto the system stack so that the values will not be altered and can be returned at the end of the routine. Second, you may want to reset the interrupt request itself and reset the in-service latch by issuing an EOI (end of interrupt) to the 8259A interrupt controller. This will allow additional interrupts to be received by the 8259A controller.

Additional requests from the 8259A controller to the 8088 microprocessor are still masked. This occurs automatically when the interrupt is serviced. It can be enabled by changing the status bit in the flag register or by POPing the old status from the stack during the RTN instruction at the end of the routine. If it is enabled before the end of the routine, a higher level of interrupt request may interrupt the present level. This may not be bad, but study the consequences carefully.

Now, the interrupt-service routine may finally be executed. Again, at the end of the routine, a bit more housekeeping is required. First, the registers saved on the system stack must be restored from the interrupted program. This is done by POPing them off the stack, restoring the system flags to their old values, and executing an interrupt RTN instruction, which POPs the old IP and code segment from the stack and then branches to the address contained in the OP and code segment registers.

System Initialization for Interrupts

In the preceding descriptions, we have assumed that the interrupt controller stack pointer and interrupt vector tables have been initialized to support the desired results when an interrupt occurs. The following is a summary of the events in a interrupt sequence, including the required initialization sequence.

1. Initialize the stack pointer to the status and register-save restore area in system RAM.

2. Initialize the low RAM addresses in 8088 memory with the addresses of the interrupt-service routines. The first 1024 bytes of the 8088 address space are reserved for a four-byte pointer to any of 256 possible interrupts. The four-byte value consists of an IP (instruction pointer) value and a CS (code segment) value. BIOS does this only for interrupts that it is using.

3. Initialize the 8259A-5 interrupt controller chip by initializing the ICWs (interrupt command words) and the OCWs (operation control words). This means unmask the interrupt levels.

4. Unmask the system interrupt in the 8088 MPU by setting the status bit in the flag register.

5. The interface generates an interrupt request.

6. The 8259A interrupt controller gets the request, then sets the request latch.

7. The 8259A controller sets the INTR request to the 8088 microprocessor.

8. The 8088 MPU responds with an INTA pulse, which prioritizes the request and sets the request in the service latch of the 8259A controller.

9. The 8088 MPU sends a second INTA pulse. The 8259A controller responds with the level's pointer value, which is used to index into 8088 low storage to obtain the level's service address.

10. Next, the 8088 MPU masks the interrupt, pushes its flags onto the stack, pushes the next instruction address (IP and CS values) onto the stack, fetches the new IP and CS values using the pointer value, and branches to the new IP and CS address value.

11. The interrupt-service routine pushes registers that it will use and could destroy onto the stack.

12. To allow additional interrupt levels, the interrupt routine issues an EOI (end of interrupt) instruction to the 8259A controller.

13. The interrupt-service routine is executed.

14. Upon completion of the service routine, the register and status are restored by POPing them from the stack.

15. Last, the service routine executes an interrupt-return instruction, which unmasks the interrupts, pops the old CS and IP values from the stack, branches to these values, and picks up execution from where it was interrupted.

Interrupt Initialization

Now that we have a good understanding of how interrupts operate in the PC, it is time to consider the details of the system initialization in order to use interrupts. The initialization (outlined in the interrupt-sequence summary) is directed at both the memory of the 8088 microprocessor and the 8259A-5 interrupt controller chips. Let us first consider the initialization of the low RAM memory of the 8088 MPU, which contains the interrupt vector table.

Interrupt Vector Table Initialization

The first 1024 bytes of memory in an 8088, 286, 386, or 486 microprocessor system are devoted to the interrupt function in the processor system. The 8088 MPU architecture supports a maximum of 256 interrupts. The low RAM area is used to store the addresses of each of the 256 possible interrupt-service routines. Each address is made up of two 16-bit values: an instruction pointer (IP) and a code segment (CS) value. When an interrupt occurs, the interrupt vector table is accessed, and the associated CS and IP values are used to branch to the correct interrupt-service routine. The interrupts of an 8088 MPU can be generated in a variety of ways, including internally, by software, and externally. Figure 6-4 illustrates the use of the low RAM area for all types of 8088 MPU interrupts.

As previously discussed, an 8-bit pointer is passed to the 8088 processor on the second INTA pulse of an interrupt cycle. This pointer is used to develop a 10-bit address for addressing the RAM vector table in the first 1024 bytes of 8088 memory. The 10-bit pointer has the following address value:

A9 A8 A7 A6 A5 L3 L2 L1 0 0

The two least significant bits are set to zero by the 8088 microprocessor so that each vector has a four-byte space reserved for the IP and the CS. The L1 L2 L3 field is added by the 8259A controller hardware and represents the encoded level values being serviced. This value is transferred to the 8088 MPU as the three least significant bits in the second INTA bus cycle byte. Fields A5 through A9 come from the 8259A interrupt controller as the remaining bits of the second INTA bus cycle byte. This field (A5–A9) is programmed into the 8259A controller in initialization command word 2 (ICW2) data. The A5–A9 value locates the position of the 32-byte area in the low 1024 memory address space, which contains the address pointers for the eight interrupt levels supported by the 8259A interrupt controller.

The PC BIOS initializes the A9 through A5 value to 00001. Thus, the vector table of the 8259A controller is located in low PC RAM at hex address 00020. The interrupt vector pointer for level 0 is located at hex address 00020, and the level-4 vector pointer is located at hex address 00030. Figure 6-5 shows the memory map for the interrupt vector table, as initialized by BIOS. Note that the four-byte pointer in the table is stored with the IP value in the two lowest addresses and CS in the two highest addresses. In addition, the least significant byte of the addresses of the IP and CS are stored in the least significant byte of their two-byte fields. It is possible to move the vector table location of the 8259A controller by

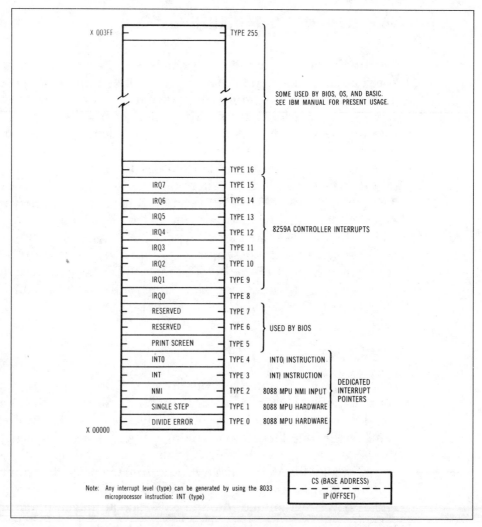

Figure 6-4. Vector pointers of the 8259A interrupt controller in the PC's low memory.

changing the A9 through A5 field in ICW2. But the consequences of doing this should be carefully considered because the PC BIOS expects the table to be at hex address 00020.

8259A Interrupt Controller Initialization

Now that we know how to initialize the interrupt vector table so that it will point interrupts to the desired service routine, we must consider the ini-

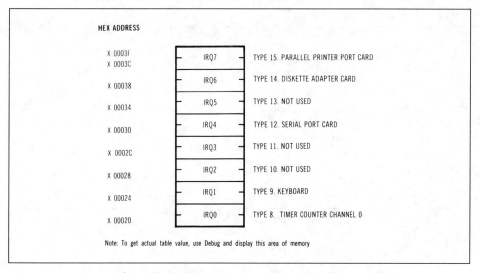

HEX ADDRESS

X 0003F	IRQ7	TYPE 15. PARALLEL PRINTER PORT CARD
X 0003C		
X 00038	IRQ6	TYPE 14. DISKETTE ADAPTER CARD
X 00034	IRQ5	TYPE 13. NOT USED
X 00030	IRQ4	TYPE 12. SERIAL PORT CARD
X 0002C	IRQ3	TYPE 11. NOT USED
X 00028	IRQ2	TYPE 10. NOT USED
X 00024	IRQ1	TYPE 9. KEYBOARD
X 00020	IRQ0	TYPE 8. TIMER COUNTER CHANNEL 0

Note: To get actual table value, use Debug and display this area of memory

Figure 6-5. The 8259A interrupt controller vector table.

tialization and operation of the 8259A interrupt controller. The controller can be addressed through I/O port addresses 0020 and 0021 hex. A quick look at the register set that needs to be initialized reveals that there are more registers than the two I/O address ports can support. The 8259A controller overcomes this problem by first using the I/O port addresses in initialization mode. Then it reuses the addresses in an operation command mode that is automatically entered after the initialization mode is completed.

Initialization mode can be entered at any time by writing to port address 0020 hex with data bit 4 set to one. This byte of data contains other information to be defined later and is called initialization command word one (ICW1). Up to three additional initialization command words must follow ICW1 before the operation command mode is entered. These ICWs are written to I/O port address 0021 hex and are pushed on an internal register stack in the 8259A interrupt controller. They must be written in sequence.

After the last ICW is written to the 8259A controller, it enters operation control mode. Writing to I/O port address 0021 hex sets operation control word one (OCW1). OCW2 is addressed by writing to I/O port address 0020 hex with data bits 3 and 4 set to zero. OCW3 is addressed by writing to I/O port address 0020 hex with data bit 3 set to one and data bit 4 set to zero. There are only three OCWs; their bit definitions are covered later. Table 6-2 summarizes the addressing structure of the 8259A interrupt controller.

Table 6-2. ICW and OCW Addresses of the 8259A Interrupt Controller

Port Address (Hex)	Register
0020	ICW1
0021	ICW2
0021	ICW3*
0021	ICW4
0021	OCW1
0020	OCW2
0020	OCW3

*Skipped in PC initialization
Note: These addresses are valid only if executed in the order shown.

Initialization Command Words

When initialization command word one (ICW1) is written to the 8259A, the following initialization sequence starts:

1. Edge-sensitive mode is reset, which means, following initialization, an interrupt-input request must make a low-to-high transition to generate an interrupt.
2. The interrupt mask is cleared.
3. Interrupt-input 7 is assigned the lowest priority.
4. The slave mode address is set to 7.
5. If IC4 equals zero, all functions selected in ICW4 are set to zero.

Figure 6-6 is a summary of the ICWs within the 8259A interrupt controller. The following section describes the meaning of each bit and bit field in the 8259A's four initialization command words (ICWs).

ICW1 Bit Definitions

D0 (IC4)   This bit is set to one if the initialization sequences will include an ICW4. For the first initialization sequences in the PC, ICW4 must be set.

D1 (SNGL)   This bit indicates that more than one 8259A interrupt controller is in the system. The PC initializes this bit to one, indicating that only one 8259A controller is in the system.

D2 (ADI)   This bit is not used in 8088 mode; the PC sets it to zero.

D3 (LTIM)	This bit indicates that interrupt requests will be generated on either an input level or an input edge. A one indicates that level-triggered mode is set, and a zero indicates that level-sensitive mode is set. The PC sets this bit to zero for edge-triggered mode.
D4	This bit *must* be set to one.
D5–D7	These bits are not used in 8088 mode; they are set to zero by the PC.

In summary, the PC BIOS sets ICW1 to a hex value of 13.

ICW2 Bit Definitions

| D0–D2 | These bits are not used when the 8259A controller is in 8088 mode; they are set to zero by the PC. |
| D3–D7 | These are the high-order bits of the 8-bit pointer. They are sent on the second INTA bus cycle and are used to locate the interrupt vector pointer table in low PC memory. |

In summary, the PC BIOS sets ICW2 to a hex value of 08.

ICW3 Definition   ICW3 is not used in the PC system because it does not allow multiple 8259A interrupt controllers in the system. Because bit 1 in ICW1 is set to one, which indicates that only one 8259A controller is in the system, the third I/O port write goes not to ICW3 but to ICW4. Thus, only three ICWs are written to an 8259A interrupt controller in the PC system.

ICW4 Bit Definition

| D0 (uPM) | This bit indicates that the 8259A controller is in 8085 or 8088 mode. It is set to one in the PC to indicate 8088 mode. |
| D1 (AEI0) | This bit enables the automatic resetting of the interrupt request in the in-service register (ISR) as soon as the 8088 MPU honors the interrupt request. This happens on the second INTA pulse sent by the 8088 processor. As soon as the ISR bit is reset, the controller can send another higher-level request to the 8088 microprocessor. This may or may not be desirable depending on the function of the first interrupt-service routine. Normally, the service routine performs its function, then issues an EOI command allowing further interrupts. The PC BIOS sets this bit to zero, which indicates that the service routine must send an EOI command to clear the ISR bit and enable additional interrupts. |

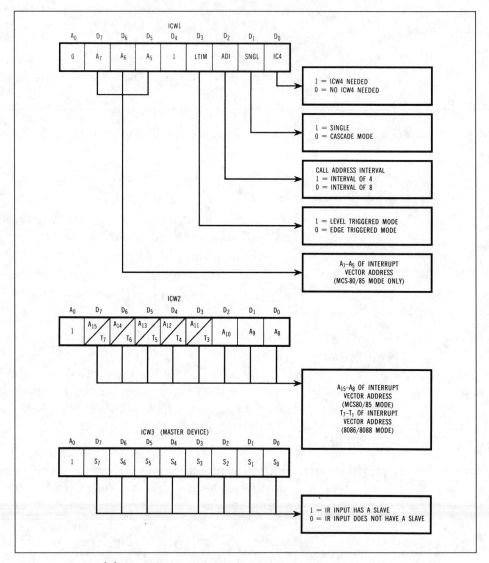

Figure 6-6. Summary of the ICW format. *(Courtesy Intel Corporation)*

D2 (M/S)	This bit indicates to the controller that it is a master controller or a slave controller in a multiple controller system. The PC design supports only a single controller. The PC BIOS sets this bit to one, indicating master mode.
D3 (BUF)	This bit indicates to the controller that it is in a buffered data bus system and that it should generate a control signal to enable the bus buffer during

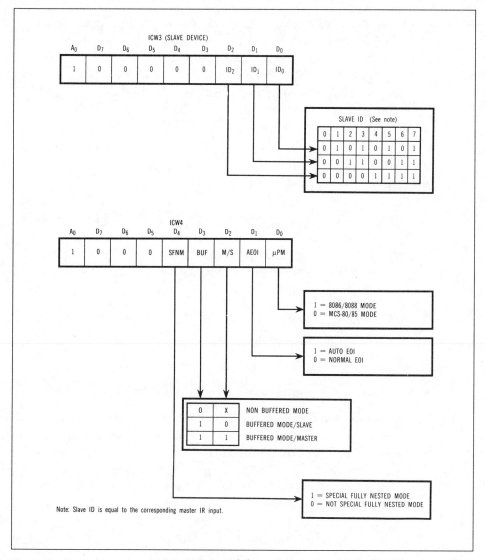

Figure 6-6. *(cont.)*

interrupts. Because the PC is a buffered data bus system, this bit is set to one.

D4 (SFNM)   This bit indicates to the controller that it is in a multiple controller system and it must use a fully nested mode of interrupt prioritization that will establish a priority between controllers. Because the PC is a single controller system, this function is not used in the PC and this bit is set to zero.

D5–D7   These bits are not used and are set to zero.

In summary, the PC BIOS sets ICW4 to a hex value of 09.

Now the 8259A controller is initialized and is ready to accept interrupt requests at its inputs. During the operation of the controller, it may be necessary to change the mode of operation or obtain the status of interrupts pending in the controller. To enable these functions, the controller goes into a new mode after initialization, in which it accepts commands called operation control words (OCWs).

Operation Control Words

In operation control mode, I/O addresses and register bit values change meaning, and the writing to I/O port addresses 0020 and 0021 hex is changed to writing to operation control word (OCW) registers. The three OCW registers are written to as follows:

OCW1   Port address 0021 hex

OCW2   Port address 0020 hex with data bits 3 and 4 set to zero

OCW3   Port address 0020 hex with data bit 4 set to zero and data bit 3 set to one

Figure 6-7 is a summary of the bit definitions in OCWs.

OCW1 Bit Definitions   The bits in OCW1 are used to set and clear the masking of interrupts at the input to the controller. Thus, an interrupt source can be enabled or disabled by writing data to this register. Bit 0 masks (enables or disables) level 0, bit 1 controls level 1, and so on in order such that all eight bits control all eight interrupt levels. A zero written to a bit in the OCW1 mask register resets the mask and enables the corresponding interrupt level. Thus, a one written to a bit sets the mask and disables the corresponding interrupt level. The present value of this register can be obtained by reading the I/O port register address 0021 hex while in operation mode.

OCW2 Bit Definitions   OCW2 is used to rotate and change the priority of the interrupt requests and to select the end of the interrupt mode to be used.

D0–D2   These bits indicate to the controller the specific level that will be acted on by the other commands specified in OCW2. This field is an encoded value in which binary value 000 indicates level 0, 001 indicates level 1, and so on through binary value 111, which indicates level 7.

D3 and D4   These bits are not used and are set to zero.

D5–D7   These three bits are encoded and represent eight
            possible commands to the controller. D5, the EOI bit,
            indicates that the command is an end-of-interrupt
            mode command. D6, the SL bit, indicates that the
            command uses the encoded-level select field
            specified in bits D0–D2. D7, the R bit, indicates that
            the level-priority rotate function will be set.

Following is a description of all the combinations of commands defined by this 3-bit field:

001   A hex value of 1 in the field defines a nonspecific end-of-
      interrupt command. If the automatic end-of-interrupt mode
      is not set in ICW4 during initialization, as is the case in the
      PC, the interrupt request set that is in the in-service register
      (ISR) must be reset using an end-of-interrupt (EOI)
      command. This command is issued in the interrupt-service
      routine and resets the highest level in the IS register.

011   A hex value of 3 in this field defines a specific EOI
      command. In this case, the level specified in the D0–D2
      field is reset in the IS register.

101   A hex value of 5 in this field causes a nonspecific EOI
      command, which resets the highest IS register request to the
      lowest priority and moves all other levels up one position in
      priority.

100   A hex value of 4 in this field sets an automatic priority
      rotation mode, such that each time an automatic EOI occurs,
      the priorities are rotated. Because the PC is initialized in
      nonautomatic EOI mode, this command is not normally
      used.

000   A hex value of 0 in this field clears the automatic priority
      rotation mode in the automatic EOI mode.

111   A hex value of 7 in this field causes a rotation of priority and
      a specific EOI command, where the level reset in the IS
      register is specified in the D0–D2 field.

110   A hex value of 6 in this field causes a set priority command.

The D0–D2 field contains the level that will have the lowest priority, thus
fixing all other priorities. Therefore, if the lowest priority is set to level 5,
level 6 will have the highest priority.

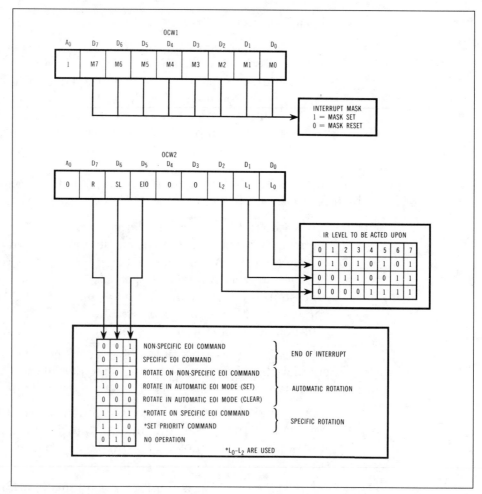

Figure 6-7. Summary of the OCW format. *(Courtesy Intel Corporation)*

OCW3 Bit Definitions

D0 (RIS) and
D1 (RR):

These bits are encoded and are used to select a status read mode. A hex value of 0 or 1 in this field causes no action. A hex value of 2 allows the reading of the value in the controller's interrupt request register (IRR) on the next read command issued to the controller. The read command may be issued by I/O port address 0020 or 0021 hex. A hex value of 3 in this field allows the reading of the contents of the in-service (IS) register on the next read command issued to the controller.

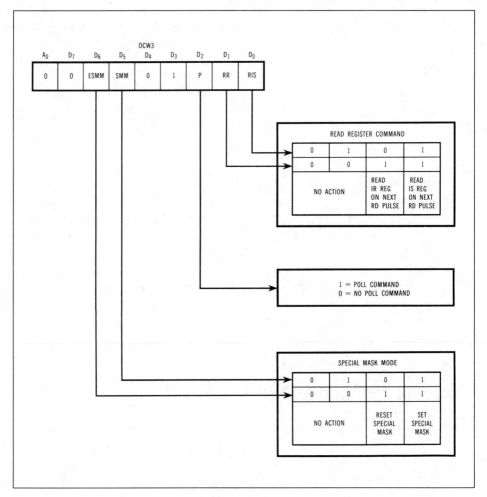

Figure 6-7. *(cont.)*

D2 (P)   This bit issues a special command to the
                controller that is similar in function to the first
                INTA pulse issued on a hardware interrupt
                response. (It sets the highest requesting level in
                the IS register.) On the next read command
                issued to the controller, the returned data has the
                encoded value in D0–D2 of the interrupt request.
                This mode is not used in PC BIOS.

D3   This bit is not used but must be set to one.

D4   This bit is not used but must be set to zero.

D5 (SMM) and   These bits allow the mask register to be used in a
D6 (ESMM)   special way. When an interrupt is set in the in-

service register and is not reset with an EOI, all higher and lower levels that are not masked can still be serviced while interrupts on the original level are inhibited. This mode is selected by setting bits D5 and D6 to one; it is reset by setting bit D5 to zero and bit D6 to one. This mode is not used in PC BIOS.

Impact of Changing ICWs and OCWs

As can be seen from the multitude of initialization and operation modes available in the 8259A interrupt controller, it is a complex device that has significant control over the operation of the PC. If care is not taken, a change in these modes can impact the operation of the PC and its software to the extent that much of the BIOS and application software will not function properly. Thus, it is recommended that your applications use the initialization modes and operation modes selected by BIOS.

Interrupt Performance

In many applications, the time it takes for the processor to begin servicing an interrupt request—from the initial interrupt request on the I/O bus—is critical. This time, typically called the *interrupt latency time*, is made up of several items. The following is a list of the items that should be considered:

1. The 8088 MPU hardware processing time. This is the time it takes the 8088 microprocessor to receive the interrupt from the 8259A interrupt controller, get the level and pointer value from the 8259A controller, punch the flags and present program address onto the stack, and branch to the interrupt-service routine. This time is 61 processor clocks. At 210 nanoseconds per clock in the PC, the 8088 MPU processing time is 12.81 microseconds.

2. Interrupts are only serviced at the end of each 8088 instruction. (Thus, if an interrupt request occurs at the beginning of an instruction, it will not be serviced until the end of that instruction.) Because most instructions are not long, this time is typically in the range of 1 to 5 microseconds. But in the 8088's instruction set, the multiply and divide instructions are quite long and may require analysis if your application is very time dependent. Some 8088 instructions will not

allow an interrupt until the execution of the next instruction. The repeat, lock, and segment override prefixes are considered part of the instruction that they prefix and no interrupts are allowed between the prefix and the instruction. The move to segment register instructions and POP segment register instructions do not allow interrupts to be recognized until after the following instruction.

3. If your application is on a low level, it must wait for interrupt-service routines on a higher level to complete. Thus, the execution time of active interrupt-service routines must be added to your interrupt latency time. A simple solution to this problem is to go to a higher level or mask interrupts on higher levels. However, do not mask an interrupt source that BIOS needs to operate. This is particularly important if you are using BIOS functions requiring interrupts.

4. Any 8088 registers that will be used by your interrupt-service routine must be saved at the beginning of the service routine. Saving a large number or all of the processor's registers can take a significant amount of time. A technique that is sometimes helpful is to save only those registers that are needed to perform the critical task in the beginning of the routine. Later, save the remaining registers used in the routine.

Due to the variables in any interrupt latency calculation, no specific value can be used as a general rule. Each application must be analyzed to arrive at a latency value.

Circuit for Interfacing to an I/O Bus Interrupt-Request Line

Figure 6-8 illustrates a circuit that can be used to interface to the system's I/O bus interrupt-request lines. In this circuit, a positive-going edge from your application sets the SN74LS74 D latch. The output of the latch is fed to the input of an SN74LS125A tristate buffer; the tristate buffer's output is attached to the system-bus interrupt-request line. Both the clear on the D latch and the enable on the tristate buffer are controlled though programmable I/O port bits.

The D latch holds the request active so that it is seen by the second INTA pulse from the 8088 microprocessor. The latch can then be reset by an OUT instruction in the interrupt-service routine. The programmable I/O port bit on the clear signal input to the D latch can be used also to inhibit an interrupt request from occurring without using the mask register in the 8259A interrupt controller. The tristate buffer and its I/O port bit

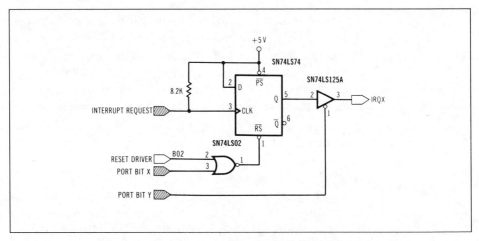

Figure 6-8. Interrupt-request circuit for the PC bus interface.

allow the source to be enabled or disabled from the bus interface. Thus, the interrupt-request line on the bus can be used by other features or applications when it is disabled from your source.

Expanding Interrupts on the PC

The PC system bus provides for only six interrupt sources. Many of these interrupt levels are used to support the basic I/O functions and adapters of the system. Thus, if an interface design requires a large number of interrupt levels, it may be difficult to implement on the PC. This section describes a solution to this problem. The method described allows each of the six interrupt levels on the system bus to be expanded to eight fully prioritized sublevels. Thus, for each system-bus interrupt level that is not used, you can provide eight additional interrupts. For example, if all six levels are not used, they could be expanded to a total of 48 interrupt levels.

As mentioned, the cascade function of the 8259A interrupt controller on the system board is not supported because the bus does not provide the required signal lines. The 8259A interrupt controller can still be used in an interface design to expand the number of interrupt sources and priority levels. In a specific design, the 8259A interrupt controller would be attached to the system bus and given an I/O port address. Further, it would be initialized similar to the 8259A controller on the system unit baseboard.

After initialization, the 8259A controller will accept and prioritize interrupts that it receives and will activate the INT output signal. The INT signal is then used to request an interrupt, using one of the system-bus interrupt-request signals. In the interrupt-service routine for that level, the

8259A controller in the interface design is issued an operation control word three (OCW3) command with bit 2 active, which indicates poll mode.

After poll mode is set, the 8259A controller does not expect an INTA response signal from the 8088 microprocessor. (This signal is not available on the system bus.) The 8259A controller treats the next read command as an interrupt acknowledge. The read command contains the encoded value of the level that generated the request. Figure 6-9 illustrates the format of the read data.

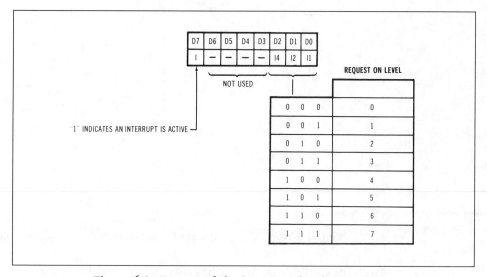

Figure 6-9. Format of the interrupt-level status byte.

The interrupt-service routine for the baseboard's 8259A controller interrupt level can now use the read data to branch to the service routine for the specified sublevel. In the 8259A controller on the interrupt expansion interface designs, the interrupts are frozen between the issuing of poll mode and the reading of the interrupt level. Figure 6-10 is a block diagram of how the 8259A controller is connected in the system. Figure 6-11 is an illustration of the connections required on the system bus for an 8259A interrupt controller acting as an interrupt-expansion device.

Initialization of the Expansion 8259A Device

The expansion 8259A device does not have to operate using the same modes as that of the controller on the baseboard. This gives the interface designer greater freedom to select modes of operation best suited for the application. Some modes must be selected, however, for the expansion 8259A to operate properly. For example, during initialization, the expan-

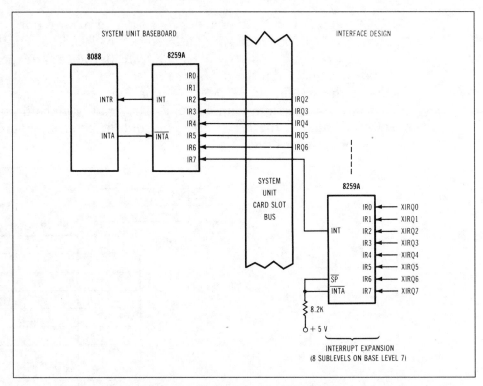

Figure 6-10. Block diagram of an interrupt-expansion circuit.

sion 8259A must operate in master mode and 8085 mode. Figure 6-12 shows a chart and a flowchart that initialize the expansion 8259A to operate in a fully nested mode with edge-triggered interrupt-request inputs and a normal end-of-interrupt mode.

Software Service Routine for Expansion Interrupts

Interrupts generated as inputs to the expansion 8259A controller cause interrupt requests on the system baseboard's 8259A controller. Thus, a special interrupt-service routine must be written to handle expansion interrupts. Figure 6-13 is a flowchart of one possible service routine for handling and directing the expansion interrupts to the proper software support program.

Further Interrupt-Level Expansion

This concept can be further expanded by adding 8259A devices to the first expansion 8259A device. You can add up to eight additional 8259A con-

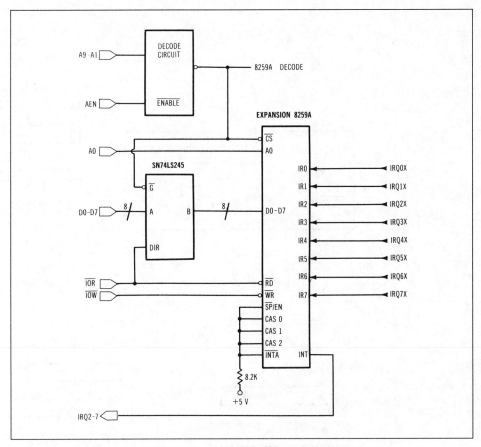

**Figure 6-11. The bus connections for an 8259A controller
expansion device.**

trollers to an 8259A controller attached to one of the bus interrupt levels.
This would allow eight 8259A devices, for a total of 64 interrupt levels on a
single bus-input interrupt-request input. The software would have to first
poll the expansion 8259A device to determine which of the additional
eight devices requested service. Second, the device that requested service
would be polled to determine which of its eight inputs generated the input request. Figure 6-14 is a block diagram of this two-tiered 8259A implementation.

System Direct Memory Access

In many interfacing applications, you need to accept data from or transmit
data to an interface at rates higher than those possible with a simple I/O

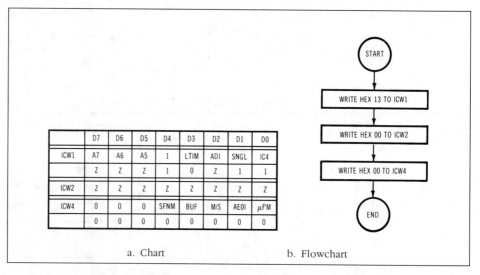

	D7	D6	D5	D4	D3	D2	D1	D0
ICW1	A7	A6	A5	1	LTIM	ADI	SNGL	IC4
	Z	Z	Z	1	0	Z	1	1
ICW2	Z	Z	Z	Z	Z	Z	Z	Z
ICW4	0	0	0	SFNM	BUF	M/S	AEOI	μPM
	0	0	0	0	0	0	0	0

a. Chart   b. Flowchart

Figure 6-12. Initialization of the expansion 8259A device.

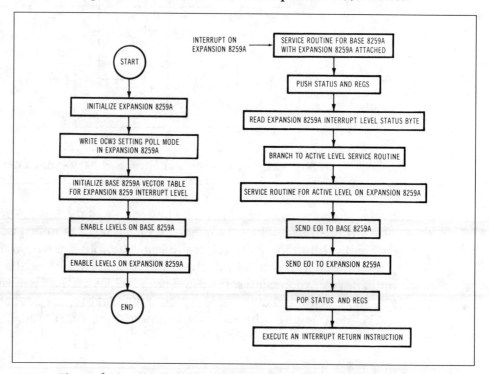

Figure 6-13. Initialization and service routine for the expansion 8259A device.

loop that uses IN and OUT instructions. A good example of this problem is the data transmitted to and received from the PC's diskette drives. The data rate to and from the diskette drive adapter is high enough to make it

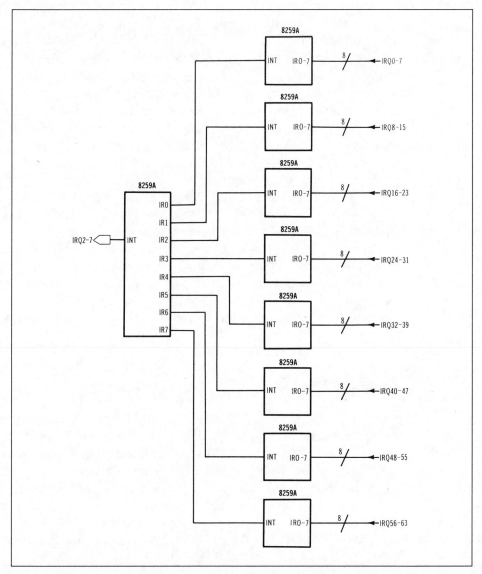

Figure 6-14. Block diagram of 64 interrupt levels on one system-bus request level.

difficult for the 8088 processor to keep up with the data transfer and still service other devices, such as the keyboard. To solve these high data-rate transfer problems in the PC design, a special function called direct memory access (DMA) is provided. A DMA controller device allows an interface or adapter to read data from memory or write data to memory without using the 8088 microprocessor. In the PC design, this device is an Intel 8237-5 DMA controller chip.

During normal program execution, the 8088 microprocessor provides address and control information by driving the system bus, and is the source or destination of data. When an interface wants to transfer data using the DMA facility, it sends a request signal to the DMA controller. The controller prioritizes this request and sends a hold request signal to the 8088 microprocessor. At the end of the current bus cycle, the 8088 MPU removes itself from the system bus and sends a hold acknowledge signal to the DMA controller, indicating that the bus is now free.

The DMA controller then attaches itself to the system bus and drives the address bus and control bus, executing a data-transfer cycle between the requesting interface (or adapter) and memory. The interface (or adapter) is notified of this action by the DMA controller sending a DMA acknowledge signal to the interface or adapter. The DMA controller can be thought of as a third party that, when requested, takes over as the system-bus master and directs the transfer of data between memory and the adapters or interfaces. During DMA operations, the DMA controller does not handle the bus; data is transmitted directly between memory and the interface or adapter. Figure 6-15 is a block diagram of DMA data transfer in the PC system.

DMA Usage in the PC

The 8237-5 DMA controller chip in the PC has four DMA channels. Two of these channels are used in the PC design. Channel 0 is used by the system unit's dynamic memory refresh function, and channel 2 is used to transfer data between the diskette drive adapter and memory. Channels 1 and 3 are not used at present. Channels 1, 2, and 3 are available on the system bus for use by features or interfaces installed in the bus card slots. The PC BIOS initializes the DMA controller so that channel 0 has the highest priority and channel 3 has the lowest. The following list summarizes the priority and use of the four PC DMA channels:

Highest priority	Channel 0	Supports memory refresh
	Channel 1	Not used at present
	Channel 2	Supports diskette drive adapter
Lowest priority	Channel 3	Not used at present

DMA Operation

The following is a step-by-step description of the actions taken by the PC during a DMA operational cycle.

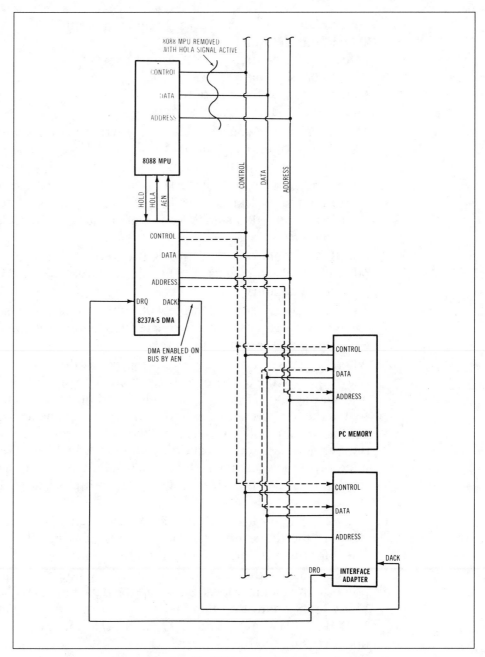

Figure 6-15. Flow diagram of DMA operations.

1. Before a DMA operation can occur, the 8237-5 controller must be initialized to perform the proper type of cycle. The following items require specification at initialization.

Select read-to-memory or write-from-memory function
Type of transfer: burst or single byte
Byte count to be transferred
Priority of channels
Memory address for start of transfer
Enable the channel's request signal

This initialization is accomplished by writing control words to the 8237-5 controller using the I/O port OUT instructions of the 8088 microprocessor. Initialization is covered later in this chapter.

2. The interface adapter sends a DRQ signal to the 8237-5 controller, indicating that a data transfer is requested on a specified channel. There are three DRQ signals (one signal each for channels 1, 2, and 3) on the system bus.

3. The 8237-5 controller prioritizes this request with requests from other channels and sends an HRQ signal to the 8088 MPU wait-state generation circuitry.

4. The wait-state circuits scan the 8088 microprocessor's status lines and look for a processor-passive state (which means no bus activity or a bus cycle that is almost finished).

5. When a passive state is detected, the controller logic sends a not ready signal to the 8088 processor, causing it to put the 8088 MPU in a wait state at time 3T of the next cycle. In addition, a HOLDA signal is sent to the 8237-5 controller, indicating that at the next clock, the bus will be free and a DMA cycle can take place. Signals are sent also to the bus address, control, and data buffers, which remove the 8088 microprocessor from the system bus. It should be noted that the 8088 MPU still proceeds with the bus cycle until clock time T3, then it suspends the cycle.

6. The 8237-5 controller detects the HOLDA signal and sends a DACK signal to the requesting interface adapter. This signal acts as a chip select for the adapter, enabling it on the system bus.

7. The 8237-5 controller now drives onto the system bus an address that points to the memory location where the data transfer will take place. The 8237-5 controller also takes control of the bus control lines ($\overline{\text{MEMR}}$, $\overline{\text{MEMW}}$, $\overline{\text{IOR}}$, and $\overline{\text{IOW}}$) and performs the read and write operations on the bus.

8. After receiving the DACK signal, the interface or adapter drops the DRQ signal to the controller. When the controller completes the cycle, it drops the HRQ signal to the wait-state control logic. The wait-state circuits then drop the HOLDA signal to the controller, indicating that the 8088 microprocessor will again take over the bus. Finally, the wait-state circuits drop the not ready condition to the 8088 proc-

essor and reenable its bus buffers. The bus cycle that was suspended at clock time T3 is restarted and continues normal bus-cycle operation. When the bus cycle is restarted, two extra clock times are inserted in the cycle to give it sufficient access time.

These operations are performed on every DMA cycle. The DMA function is done in this manner so that the 8088 microprocessor can operate in maximum mode and still support the auxiliary processor socket. In maximum mode, the 8088 processor does not support hold and hold-acknowledge protocols; thus, the function is simulated using the wait-state control circuitry on the baseboard. This scheme seems at first to be inefficient, but it does allow overlapping of the 8088 MPU bus cycle with a DMA cycle because the 8088 processor executes the suspended bus cycle up to clock time T3.

Initialization of the 8237-5 Controller

The 8237-5 DMA controller has 16 read/write I/O port register addresses that contain both initialization data and device status. Note that not all 16 port addresses can be both read and write. The PC decodes the 8237-5 device so that the port addresses reside in the I/O port address range 0000 to 000F hex. In the 8237-5 controller, the port addresses are divided into two groups. Addresses 0000 to 0007 hex are read/write registers that contain DMA starting memory addresses for each channel, the current memory address for the next DMA cycle on each channel, and the current byte count of each channel. (Addresses 0000 to 0007 are covered in the "Address and Count Register" section in this chapter.) The second group of I/O port addresses, at 0008 to 000F hex, contain control and status registers that define the operation of each channel.

Control and Status Register Definitions

Table 6-3 defines the functions of each of the addresses in the range 0008 to 000F hex. Note that functions are different on a read than they are on a write. Thus, it is typically not possible to read the contents of write-only registers. The definitions of the write registers are covered first.

Command Register   The command register is loaded by writing to I/O port address 0008 hex. The definitions of the register bits are summarized next and are defined in Figure 6-16.

Table 6-3. Control and Status Register Addresses

I/O Port Read Address (Hex)	Function
0008	Read status register
0009	Not used
000A	Not used
000B	Not used
000C	Not used
000D	Read temporary register
000E	Not used
000F	Not used

I/O Port Write Address (Hex)	Function
0008	Write command register
0009	Write request register
000A	Write single-mask bit register
000B	Write mode register
000C	Clear byte pointer flip-flop
000D	Master clear
000E	Clear mask register
000F	Write all mask-register bits

Bit 0 Enables or disables the memory-to-memory move function of the controller. When this function is selected, channels 0 and 1 are used to point to two different blocks of memory and can be used to transfer data between the two blocks. This function cannot be used in the PC because channel 0 is dedicated to the memory refresh function.

Bit 1 Valid only when the memory-to-memory move function is selected. It disables the address incrementing or decrementing function on channel 0, allowing a fixed pattern to be written into a block of memory. Again, this function is not used in the PC.

Bit 2 Enables or disables the DMA controller.

Bit 3 Selects a special compressed DMA bus cycle. In this mode, only three clocks are used to generate the DMA bus cycle. This mode should not be selected in the PC because it would reduce the memory and I/O port addresses' access time below their specified limits and would cause an invalid operation.

Bit 4   Selects a special rotating priority mode. This function should not be selected in the PC because the memory refresh on channel 0 must always have the highest priority.

Bit 5   Selects the timing of the bus cycle's write signal. The PC selects a late-write mode. This should not be changed because the system's dynamic memory cycles are triggered from the leading edge of the write signal; if it comes earlier in the DMA cycle, the data would not be valid, resulting in an invalid data-write operation.

Bit 6   Selects the active level of the DRQ signals coming to the controller. The PC selects the high level as active.

Bit 7   Selects the active level of the DACK signals sent by the controller. The PC selects the low level as active.

The PC BIOS initializes the command register with a hex value of 00.

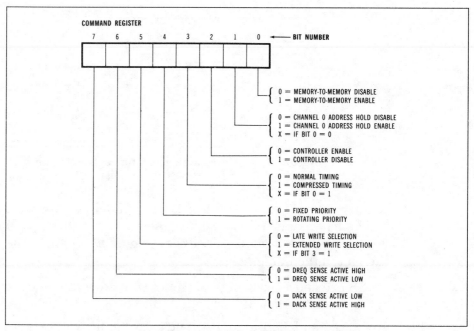

Figure 6-16. Command register bit definitions.
(Courtesy Intel Corporation)

Write Request Register   The write request register can be loaded by writing to I/O port address 0009 hex. This register can be used to generate a DMA request under software control. The bit definitions of the write request are defined in Figure 6-17.

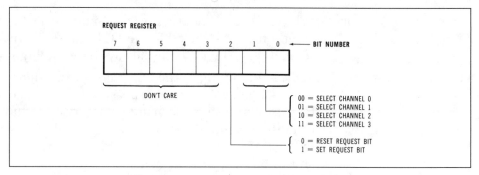

Figure 6-17. Write request register bit definitions.
(Courtesy Intel Corporation)

Write Single-Mask Bit Register   Writing to the write single-mask bit register, hex address 000A, allows individual DMA channels to be masked off or on. Figure 6-18 defines the bit's functions in this register.

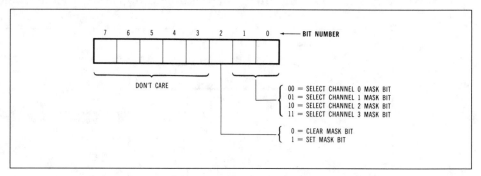

Figure 6-18. Write single-mask bit register definitions.
(Courtesy Intel Corporation)

Mode Register   The mode register is a write-only register that defines several modes of operation for each of the four DMA channels. It is loaded by writing to I/O port address 000B hex. Figure 6-19 defines the functions of each bit in the mode register.

Bits 0 and 1	Select the DMA channel that the mode command will be applied to.
Bits 2 and 3	Define the type of cycle that will be performed on the specified channel. There are three operations available: (1) a verify operation that performs a bus cycle without a read or write operation, (2) a write operation that takes data from an interface or adapter and writes it into memory, and (3) a read operation that takes data from memory and writes it into the interface or adapter.

Bit 4   Enables or disables an auto-initialization mode on a specified channel. When this mode is selected, it reinitializes the DMA channel's current address register and current count register with the values in the base address and the count register. This happens when the current count register reaches zero and the terminal count signal is issued from the controller. This function allows the controller to be automatically set up to accept more DMA requests after an earlier DMA function has been completed.

Bit 5   Selects an increment or decrement function on the current DMA address register.

Bits 6 and 7   Select the type of DMA operations permitted on the selected channel. Four basic modes of operation are available:

- In single-byte transfer mode, the DRQ signal must be raised for each byte transferred. If the DRQ is held active, the controller allows one 8088 MPU bus cycle after each DMA cycle, thus ensuring that the processor is never completely locked from the bus due to a hung DMA request.

- In block transfer mode, only one DRQ signal initiates the transfer of an entire block of data. The block transfer is stopped when the terminal count is reached. The 8088 MPU is blocked from the bus during the block transfer. This mode of operation should not be selected in the PC because is could block DMA cycles that are required to support the memory refresh function and diskette-drive data transfers, thus causing an overrun condition. In addition, the memory precharge timing specification is violated when back-to-back DMA cycles are allowed.

- In demand transfer mode, data is transferred as long as the terminal count has not been reached and the DRQ signal is active. This mode of operation can be used if the DRQ signal is dropped after each DMA cycle; otherwise, the same problems as those in block transfer mode are present.

- Cascade mode is the fourth method of operation. The PC programs all DMA channels for single-byte transfer mode operation.

The PC BIOS initializes channels 1 and 3 (the two channels not used by the PC) with the hex values of 41 and 43, respectively.

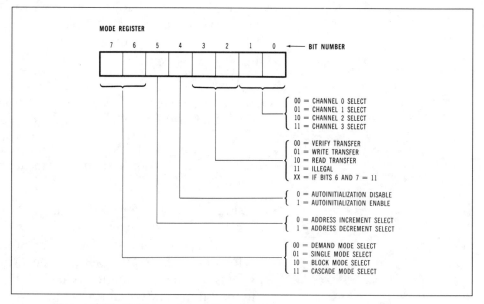

Figure 6-19. Mode register bit definitions. *(Courtesy Intel Corporation)*

Clear Byte Pointer Flip-Flop   No data is associated with the write operation to the PC I/O port address labeled clear byte pointer flip-flop. A write-to-port hex address 000C clears an internal flip-flop used to point to the high or low byte of 16-bit word values, which are loaded and read from port addresses 0000 to 0007 hex. When the flip-flop is cleared, the next read or write operation at the port address loads or reads the low-order bits of the 16-bit value. The read or write operation toggles the flip-flop so that the next read or write operation points to the high-order 8 bits of the 16-bit value. This technique conserves register decodes in the controller. This function is used to read and write the contents of the current address register for each channel, the base address register for each channel, the current count register for each channel, and the base count register for each channel. Each of these registers is 16 bits but has only an 8-bit port address.

Master Clear   When you write to the I/O port address at 000D hex, called master clear, it performs a clear function on the controller. The controller requires initialization after a master clear command is sent. No data is associated with this command.

Clear Mask Register   The clear mask register is at I/O port address 000E hex. Writing to this PC I/O port address resets all the DMA channel mask-register bits, thus enabling all four channels.

Write All Mask-Register Bits   The write all mask-register bits register is written to by addressing PC port address 000F hex. It is used to both individually and simultaneously control the DMA channel's mask-register bits. Figure 6-20 defines the bits in this register.

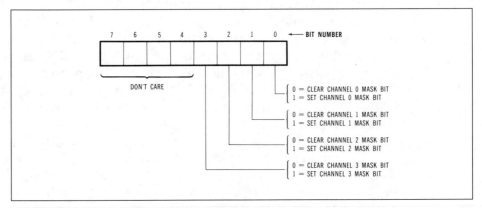

Figure 6-20. Write all mask-register bits definitions.
(Courtesy Intel Corporation)

Status Register   The controller's status can be obtained by reading PC I/O port address 0008 hex. The status register contains status bits that indicate if a channel has reached its terminal count and thus has completed the DMA transfer. The register also contains status bits that indicate if a channel has a DMA request pending. Figure 6-21 defines the bits in the status register.

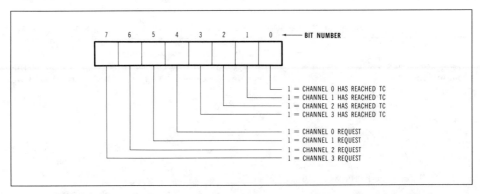

Figure 6-21. Status register bit definitions. *(Courtesy Intel Corporation)*

Temporary Register   After a memory-to-memory transfer operation, the value of the last byte transferred can be obtained by reading the temporary register at PC I/O port address 000D hex. Because the memory-to-memory transfer cannot be used in the PC design, the register is not used.

Address and Count Registers

Each DMA channel has four 16-bit registers that are used to point to the memory location for the transfer, maintain a transfer length count, and terminate the transfer. The starting address of a DMA operation is loaded into a base register in the controller by writing to a PC I/O port address. A second address register, called the current address register, contains the address to be used on the next DMA cycle. When data is written to the base address for a specific channel, the current address register is automatically loaded with the same value. There is a base register and current address register pair for each of the four DMA channels.

The number of bytes to be transferred, before the operation is terminated or reinitialized by the auto-initialization function, is controlled by the contents of the base count and current word count registers. Each of these registers is 16 bits, and there is a set for each of the four DMA channels. The base count register is loaded with the number of bytes that will be transferred. The current word count register contains the count value left to be transferred before the operation is terminated or reinitialized. Note again that loading the base count register automatically loads the same value into the current count register.

All of these registers are read and written to using the PC port addresses in the range 0000 to 0007 hex and the function of the byte pointer flip-flop described previously. Table 6-4 describes the PC I/O port addressing for the address and count registers in the 8237-5 controller.

Table 6-4.   Port Addresses for the PC Address and Count Registers

Channel	Register	Operation	CS	IOR*	IOW†	A3‡	A2‡	A1‡	A0‡	Internal Flip-Flop	Data Bus DB0–DB7
0	Base and current address	Write	0	1	0	0	0	0	0	0	A0–A7
			0	1	0	0	0	0	0	1	A8–A15
	Current Address	Read	0	0	1	0	0	0	0	0	A0–A7
			0	0	1	0	0	0	0	1	A8–A15
	Base and current word count	Write	0	1	0	0	0	0	1	0	W0–W7
			0	1	0	0	0	0	1	1	W8–W15
	Current word count	Read	0	0	1	0	0	0	1	0	W0–W7
			0	0	1	0	0	0	1	1	W8–W15
1	Base and current address	Write	0	1	0	0	0	1	0	0	A0–A7

Table 6-4. *(cont.)*

Channel	Register	Operation	CS	IOR*	IOW†	A3‡	A2‡	A1‡	A0‡	Internal Flip-Flop	Data Bus DB0–DB7
			0	1	0	0	0	1	0	1	A8–A15
	Current address	Read	0	0	1	0	0	1	0	0	A0–A7
			0	0	1	0	0	1	0	1	A8–A15
	Base and current word count	Write	0	1	0	0	0	1	1	0	W0–W7
			0	1	0	0	0	1	1	1	W8–W15
	Current word count	Read	0	0	1	0	0	1	1	0	W0–W7
			0	0	1	0	0	1	1	1	W8–W15
2	Base and current address	Write	0	1	0	0	1	0	0	0	A0–A7
			0	1	0	0	1	0	0	1	A8–A15
	Current address	Read	0	0	1	0	1	0	0	0	A0–A7
			0	0	1	0	1	0	0	1	A8–A15
	Base and current word count	Write	0	1	0	0	1	0	1	0	W0–W7
			0	1	0	0	1	0	1	1	W8–W15
	Current word count	Read	0	0	1	0	1	0	1	0	W0–W7
			0	0	1	0	1	0	1	1	W8–W15
3	Base and current address	Write	0	1	0	0	1	1	0	0	A0–A7
			0	1	0	0	1	1	0	1	A8–A15
	Current address	Read	0	0	1	0	1	1	0	0	A0–A7
			0	0	1	0	1	1	0	1	A8–A15
	Base and current word count	Write	0	1	0	0	1	1	1	0	W0–W7
			0	1	0	0	1	1	1	1	W8–W15
	Current word count	Read	0	0	1	0	1	1	1	0	W0–W7
			0	0	1	0	1	1	1	1	W8–W15

*0 = read CMD; †0 = write CMD; ‡Hex PC port address 000x; (Courtesy Intel Corporation)

DMA Page Registers

The 8237-5 DMA controller chip supports only 16 bits of addressing and transfers lengths of only 65,536 bytes. The PC's 8088 microprocessor supports a full 1M of system memory. Thus, the controller cannot perform DMA operations using the full 1M address space of the system. To overcome this problem, the system unit's base logic board provides a set of 4-bit page registers. There is a 4-bit page register for channels 1, 2, and 3. The contents of these registers can be loaded and read using the I/O port addresses of the PC.

When a DMA cycle takes place, the contents of the appropriate page register are gated onto the system's address bus and become the high-order 4 bits of the DMA address used to access memory. Thus, a unique 20-bit address is generated for each transfer on each DMA channel. This allows a DMA operation to take place in every 64K block of the 1M space of the system. This page register scheme does not allow a DMA operation to cross a 64K-formed boundary. Figure 6-22 illustrates how the DMA transfer address is formed using the page registers.

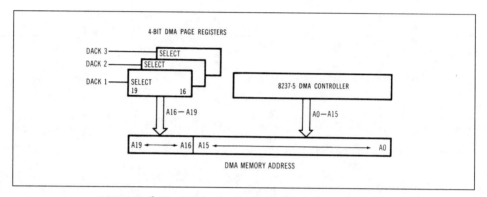

Figure 6-22. DMA memory address generation.

The page registers can be loaded and read using the following PC I/O port addresses:

DMA Channel	PC I/O Port Addresses
1	0083 hex
2	0081 hex
3	0082 hex

DMA Performance

If your interfacing design uses DMA and requires a high data rate or a very low latency time to the first byte transferred, this section will be of interest.

Maximum DMA Transfer Rate   Each DMA cycle takes five processor clock times, but in the PC design, the baseboard logic automatically inserts one extra clock as a wait state to ensure a long enough access time from memory and I/O ports. Thus, in the PC, each DMA transfer takes six clocks. Because each clock is approximately 210 nanoseconds, the total cycle time is 1.26 microseconds.

The PC design also requires that the DMA controller be run in single-byte transfer mode. This means that an 8088 MPU bus cycle must be between each DMA cycle. Because the 8088 processor bus cycles are four clocks long, or 840 nanoseconds, this time must be added to the DMA cycle time. Thus, the minimum time between DMA cycles is 2.1 microseconds. This gives the PC a maximum DMA data rate of 476K per second. If any other devices or memory inserts a wait state in other 8088 MPU bus cycles, this will further reduce the maximum data rate.

DMA Latency   Often an important requirement of a design is not the data rate, but how quickly the first byte can be transferred. This frequently determines if a byte buffer is required between the interface and the PC bus. In the PC design, after a DMA request is raised, it may take up to seven processor clocks before the cycle begins. This time can be extended if wait states are inserted in the 8088 processor bus cycles.

Reusing a DMA Channel

The use of a DMA channel by an interface or adapter does not preclude it from being used again on a different interface design. Obviously, both interfaces cannot use the same channel at once, but if there is no requirement to run both interfaces at the same time, you can share the DMA channels.

A good example of how this can be accomplished is in the PC's diskette adapter design. A programmable I/O port bit is used to enable and disable the DMA DRQ2 request signal and the DACK2 signal. If a zero is written to bit 3 of PC I/O port 03F2 hex, the diskette adapter disconnects from the bus signals and they are free to be used by a different adapter. Figure 6-23 illustrates how this can be accomplished in an interface design.

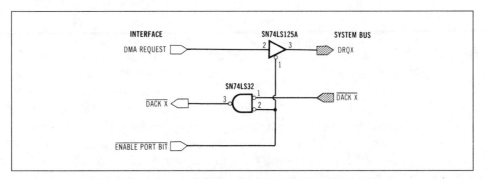

**Figure 6-23. Circuit for enable and disable programming
of a DMA channel.**

Terminal Count Signal

The 8237-5 controller generates an output control signal each time any of four DMA channels reaches a terminal count condition (that is, each time the transfer byte counter decrements to zero). This signal is typically used by the interface to terminate further DMA requests on a specific channel. Because the terminal count signal is activated on any channel's terminal count condition, it must be conditioned, or ANDed, with each DACK signal so that a specific channel's ending condition can be detected. The terminal count signal is available on the system bus.

High-Speed Data Transfer

A key consideration in many types of interfacing applications is high-speed data transfer between the PC and an adapter or a device. In this section, we will discuss high-speed data-transfer techniques and their performance capabilities. It is important to determine the PC's data-transfer capabilities using several different techniques because your design should use the method that meets the performance requirements of your application. The techniques discussed include programmed I/O data transfer in both BASIC and assembly language, the use of the PC's DMA function, and the special buffering techniques needed for very high-speed data-transfer requirements.

Programmed I/O Data Transfer

The technique used most often to transfer data between the PC and a device or an adapter is simple programmed I/O. The data transfer is done entirely under program control. A typical data-transfer loop is shown in Figure 6-24. The data is being transferred from a memory buffer in the PC to an I/O port address. The loop has several different functions to perform beyond the simple sending of data. First, it must maintain a memory address pointing to the buffer, then increment this address on each transfer. Second, the loop must maintain a count of the desired number of bytes of data to be transferred and test the loop count for an ending condition. Third, if the I/O port cannot accept the data as fast as the loop can provide data, provision must be added to the loop for testing for a READY or data taken signal.

BASIC Data Transfer   In many cases, the data-transfer function will be slow enough to do in BASIC. The following is an example of a data-transfer loop written in BASIC:

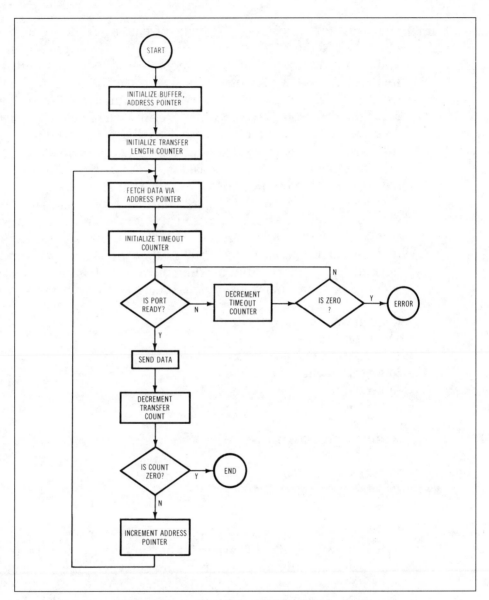

Figure 6-24. Typical data-transfer loop program.

```
10 DIM BUF(100)
20 FOR CNT=0 TP 1000
30 WAIT &H3BC,&H01
40 BUF(CNT)=INP(&H3BD)
50 OUT &H3BC,0
60 NEXT
70 END
```

This loop transfers 1000 bytes of data from the input port address 03BD hex to the BUF array. Statements 10 and 20 dimension the buffer and set up the loop count. Statement 30 causes a wait until bit zero of input address 03BC hex becomes active. This bit is used to indicate that the data input port contains valid data that can now be read. Statement 40 reads the data from the port and places the data in a buffer. Statement 50 resets the data-ready bit in hex register 03BC, indicating to the adapter that the data has been read and the new data can be loaded into the input port. Statement 60 repeats the data-transfer function for 1000 cycles, then passes control to the next BASIC statement.

Following are two BASIC data-transfer loops that have been timed. One loop reads data from a port and puts it in an array. The other reads the data from an array and writes it to an I/O port. In both cases, it is assumed that the data is always available so that interlock control signals are needed. In both loops, the maximum data rate measured was 4.75 milliseconds per byte transfer, or approximately 210 bytes per second.

Read from port loop

```
10 DIM BUF(1000)
20 FOR CNT=0 TO 1000
30 BUF(CNT)=INP(&H3BD)
40 NEXT
50 END
```

Write to port loop

```
10 DIM BUF(1000)
20 FOR CNT=0 TO 1000
30 OUT &H3BC,BUF(CNT)
40 NEXT
50 END
```

Assembly Language Data Transfer   Programmed data-transfer performance can be dramatically improved by using 8088 assembly language. Following is an example of an assembly language data-transfer loop. In this loop, data is transferred from a memory buffer to an I/O port. The loop manages the memory addresses and maintains a byte count that is tested during each transfer cycle. In this loop, we assume that the data is accepted as fast as it can be sent.

```
START MOV DX,PORT   Load DX reg with port address
      MOV BX,BUFFER Load BX reg with buffer address
      MOV CX,COUNT   Load CX reg with loop count
LOOP  MOV AL[BX]   Load AL reg with data from buffer
      OUTB DX     Write AL reg data to port
```

```
INC BX      Increment buffer address
DEC CX      Decrement loop count
JNZ LOOP    Loop if count not equal to zero
WAIT
```

This data-transfer loop transferred data at a rate of 11.5 microseconds per byte, or 86.95 kilobytes per second. This is more than 400 times faster than the equivalent BASIC data-transfer loop. Using higher clock rate PCs, 286 systems, or 386 systems, much higher programmed data-transfer rates can be addressed. Refer to Chapter 4 to scale these performance numbers to other systems and clock rates.

DMA Data Transfer

The DMA function of the PC is specifically designed to aid in high-speed data transfer. Using the DMA facility, it is possible to transfer data at a maximum rate of 476 kilobytes per second. At this rate, approximately one half of the system-bus bandwidth is used. This will slow the execution of any program to half speed when the maximum DMA data rate is in operation. The DMA facility is designed such that the microprocessor cannot be locked out.

Figure 6-25 is a diagram of a circuit that can be used to interface to the DMA control signals on the bus. With this circuit, the DMA function can be used to transfer data from an 8-bit interface port to the system's memory. The interface is enabled by an I/O port bit such that the channel can be reused by other devices when not in operation on this interface.

To transfer a byte of data (assuming that the DMA devices have been initialized), the interface simply applies the data to the input port and raises the REQUEST signal. When this signal makes a positive transition, it latches the input data in the bus register and requests a DMA cycle. When the associated DACK signals go active, the data is transferred to the system's memory and the request is reset. This action is repeated each time the REQUEST signal makes a positive transition and the DMA's terminal count has not been reached.

Figure 6-26 is a diagram of a circuit that can be used, under DMA control, to transfer data from the system's memory to an output port register, to request data from memory, and to simply raise the REQUEST signal. Data is loaded into the port register when the associated DACK signal becomes active (assuming that the DMA channel has been enabled by the I/O port bit and the DMA device has been properly initialized). The DACK signal also resets the request. The operation is repeated each time the REQUEST signal is raised, assuming that the DMA channel has not reached its terminal count.

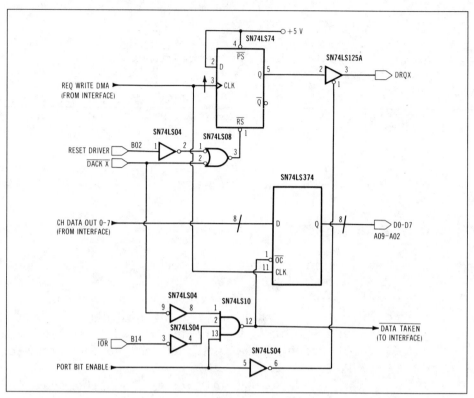

Figure 6-25. Circuit for transferring data from an interface port to PC memory using DMA.

Other Data-Transfer Techniques

If data must be buffered or transferred at a data rate greater than the rate available using the DMA facility, other techniques can be used. A common technique is to dual port high-speed memory so that the microprocessor can read and write to memory on one port and data can be transferred on the other port. (The display adapter regen buffers on the PC use this technique.) Memory is time-division multiplexed with a high-speed clock. On one phase of the clock, memory can be attached to the PC system bus. On the other phase of the clock, an interface may access the memory. This technique allows the processor to access memory at any time, even while data is being read or written to on the other port. However, this technique has two drawbacks. First, new memory must be added to the system. Second, memory must be high speed so that it can support both the microprocessor's accessing requirements and the interface data-rate requirements.

Another technique often used is the ping-pong buffer approach. In

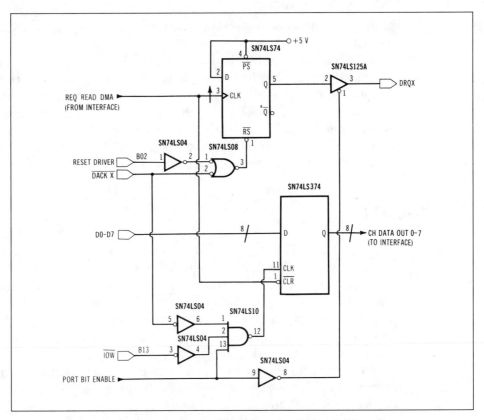

Figure 6-26. Circuit for transferring data from PC memory to an interface port using DMA.

this scheme, two memory buffers are built, each of which is large enough to hold the maximum burst data required by the application. The buffers can be attached to either the PC system bus or the application interface. In operation, one buffer collects or transmits data on the interface while the other is being read or written to by the microprocessor. When the interface buffer is full, the buffers are swapped so that the new buffer can be used to transfer data. This technique is most useful when data comes in short, high-speed bursts.

System Timer Counters

A timing or counting function is often required in an interface design. Three independent timer counters are designed into the PC's base system board. Timer-counter functions are implemented using an Intel 8253-5 timer-counter chip. In general, these timer-counter channels support the basic I/O functions of the PC and are not available for use by an interface design.

Each timer-counter channel has a clock signal and a gate input signal; the gate controls the clock input to the timer counter. Each timer counter has an output signal whose function is set by programming the mode of operation of the channel. In the PC design, the clock input to all channels is the same, a 1.19318-MHz square-wave signal. Thus, each tick of the timer-counter channel is approximately 838.1 nanoseconds in duration. Each timer-counter channel is 16 bits in length.

Channel 0

Channel 0 is used as a general system timer. Its gate is tied high, or on, all the time and the clock input signal is a 1.19318-MHz square-wave signal. The output of the channel 0 timer is tied to interrupt level 0, the highest maskable interrupt level. This channel is set by the PC BIOS to generate an interrupt request on level 0 every 54.936 milliseconds, or 18.206 times a second. These interrupt requests are counted by a BIOS routine that generates a time-of-day clock count that can be read or written to. This routine uses the interrupt count to also generate the motor-off delay after a seek operation on the diskette drives. At each interrupt request, the routine updates the time-of-day clock, checks to see if the motor on the diskette drive needs to be shut off, and attempts to invoke a user-defined routine.

The last function of the BIOS timer channel 0 routine may be of interest to an interfacing application. On each interrupt, or every 54.936 milliseconds, the BIOS routine issues a software interrupt to interrupt level 1C hex. This interrupt vector table value is set with an offset and a code segment value that simply returns control to BIOS. An applications program can alter the interrupt vector value and direct the periodic interrupt to a user routine. As an example of where this may be useful, consider an interface design that must scan for activity on a periodic basis, yet has other tasks it must perform. It would not be practical to devote the entire capability of the PC to looping and waiting for an interface event. A simple solution is to write a sensing routine that is invoked on each timer channel 0 interrupt (or on multiple timer channel 0 interrupts). The address of this routine is then entered into the interrupt vector table for the 1C hex interrupt.

You can use the time-of-day count routine to also time between events because the count can be easily read at any time. It can be set at any time, but care should be taken when doing this because the time-of-day clock function of DOS will be affected.

It is also possible to affect the operation of the diskette drive. To read the count value, first set the AH register to 0; this indicates a read operation. Next, issue a software interrupt to interrupt 1A hex. Upon return from the interrupt, the CX register contains the high value of the count and the DX register contains the low portion of the count. If the counter has not passed 24 hours since it was last read, the AL register is zero. To initialize the time-of-day count, first set the AH register to one, then set the high count value in the CX register and the low portion of the count in the DX register. Next, issue a software interrupt on level 1A hex. Upon return from this interrupt, the time-of-day count will be initialized. Remember that the values in the CX and DX registers are a binary count of time in increments of 54.936 milliseconds, or 0.054936 second.

Channel 1

Timer-counter channel 1 is used in a dedicated manner to support the memory refresh function of the system. The clock input is tied to the 1.19318-MHz square-wave signal and the gate is tied high, or always on. The output of the timer channel is used to generate a direct memory access (DMA) cycle request on DMA channel 0. DMA channel 0 is used to refresh the system's dynamic memory by creating dummy memory-read cycles every 72 processor clock cycles (210 nanoseconds), or every 15.12 microseconds.

The PC BIOS initializes the timer-counter channel in a mode that allows the output to generate an 838-nanosecond output pulse every 18 ticks of the input clock, or approximately every 15 seconds. (Because the input clock is approximately 838 nanoseconds in duration, the timer-counter output is generated approximately every 15 microseconds.) Because the system's dynamic memory refresh function is critical to the proper operation of the system, it is highly recommended that this timer-counter channel not be modified or used in any manner.

Channel 2

Timer-counter channel 2 serves a dual purpose in the PC. First, it is used to output serial data written to the audio cassette port of the system. Second, it is used to drive the audio speaker of the system unit. The clock input is the same 1.19318-MHz signal that is attached to the other channel's clock inputs. The gate signal is tied to an I/O port bit such that it can be controlled by the system's software. The gate to timer-counter channel 2 is controlled by writing to I/O port address 0061 hex, bit 0. A one written to this bit enables the clock input to the timer-counter channel; a zero disables the clock input.

The output of timer-counter channel 2 is used in two places. First, it is used to write serial data to the audio cassette port of the system unit. In this mode, the timer-counter channel is programmed to write either a 250- or a 500-microsecond pulse, depending on the data bit to be written, on the audio cassette's tape. A 0 bit is a 250-microsecond pulse with 250 microseconds of blank space, and a 1 bit is a 500-microsecond pulse with a 500-microsecond blank space. If an interface application design requires access to a programmable timing signal, you can pick up the output of timer-counter channel 2 in the 5-pin DIN connector used to attach an audio cassette. The signal is available at pin 5 of the connector. Note that the signal level is not a TTL level. Depending on the position of the cassette microphone auxiliary select jumper, the signal will be 75 millivolts, or 0.7 volt amplitude. When the auxiliary select is set to the 0.068 volt jumper position, the signal is 0.7 volt.

The second place where the output of timer-counter channel 2 is used is as an input to the system unit's audio speaker. The output is ORed with an I/O port bit such that both can be used to drive the speaker. The I/O port bit addressed is bit 1 of hex address 0061. The speaker and the cassette write functions cannot be run simultaneously. Figure 6-27 shows a block diagram of the timer-counter function of the system unit.

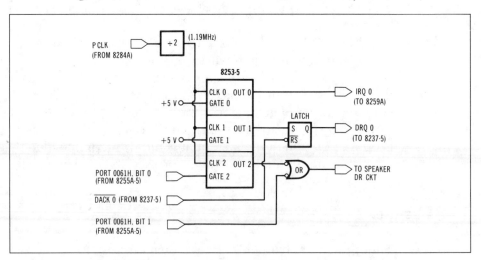

Figure 6-27. A block diagram of the timer counter.

Programming the Timer Counters

The following section defines the PC I/O port addresses and internal timer counter register's bits and bit field. This section should be consulted if you intend to custom program the PC's timer counters.

Timer-Counter I/O Address   The system unit's timer counters in the 8253-5 chip can be addressed by using IN and OUT instructions at addresses 0040 through 0043 hex. The decoding of the timer counter is not unique because some bits in the address field are not included in the decode circuits. Figure 6-28 shows the bits used and not used.

```
ADDRESS BITS   9  8  7  6  5  4  3  2  1  0
8253-5 DECODE  0  0  0  1  0  Z  Z  Z  A  A

Z = NOT IN DECODE
A = ADDRESSES BITS DECODED IN THE 8253-5
BITS 10-15 ARE NEVER USED IN I/O PORT DECODES
```

Figure 6-28. PC 8253-5 I/O port address definition.

The following comments give a brief description of the functions of the 8253-5 timer-counter chip's addresses when they are read and written to:

Write Operations

Hex address 0040	Load count value into counter 0
Hex address 0041	Load count value into counter 1
Hex address 0042	Load count value into counter 2
Hex address 0043	Set channel's mode of operation

Read Operations

Hex address 0040	Read count value in counter 0
Hex address 0041	Read count value in counter 1
Hex address 0042	Read count value in counter 2
Hex address 0043	Invalid operation; cannot read mode registers

Mode Control Registers   Because each channel of the 8253-5 timer counter has a variety of operational modes and no reset goes to this chip, it must be initialized before use. The PC BIOS initializes the modes of operation that it requires.

The mode of operation for each channel is set by writing an 8-bit mode control word to each channel using I/O port address 0043 hex. The definitions of the bits in the mode control word are defined in Figure 6-29 and are summarized as follows:

Bit D0	Selects the counting mode of the counter with binary or binary-coded decimal.

Bits D1–D3   Select the mode of operation of the channel.

Bits D4 and D5   Select the number of bytes and the sequence to be used when reading and loading the timer-counter channels.

Bits D6 and D7   Select the timer-counter channel that the mode control word is directed to.

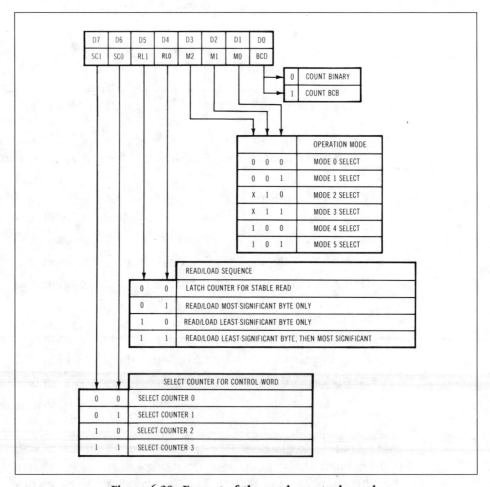

Figure 6-29. Format of the mode control word.

Reading and Writing the Counters   When reading and writing to the counters in the 8253-5 timer counter, care should be taken to use the order and number of bytes programmed into each channel mode control register. Otherwise, invalid operations and results will occur. Another feature of the 8253-5 counter that may cause confusion is that the channel clock input must have a positive- and negative-edge transition before the channel's value can be read. You cannot load a channel counter and simply read back its value; the clock input must make both a positive and a negative transition first.

Reading a counter "on the fly" can also create a problem. It is possible to read the contents of any timer-counter channel at any time, but if the counter is in the process of decrementing, you may get invalid results. One way to avoid this is to delegate the clock input before reading so that the counter will not decrement as you are reading it. The 8253-5 timer counter has a special mode control command that latches the current value of the counter into a read register so that the counter can be read correctly without stopping it. This command was defined in Figure 6-29. It should be noted that all timer-counter channels are countdown counters.

Timer-Counter Modes of Operation

As defined in the mode control word for each channel, there are six program-selected modes of operation for each channel of the 8253-5 timer counter. The following sections describe each of these modes.

Mode 0: Interrupt on Terminal Count   In mode 0, interrupt on terminal count, the output of the channel is set low after the mode control word is written. After the count value is loaded into the selected channel, the output remains low and the counter begins to count. When the terminal count value has been reached, the output goes high and remains high until the counter is reloaded. If a counter channel is rewritten while it is still decrementing, the writing of the first byte of the count value stops the counter, and the writing of the second byte restarts the counter with the new count.

Mode 1: Programmable One-Shot   In mode 1, programmable one-shot, the output is initially high after the mode and count are loaded. The output is set low on the count following the rising edge of the channel's input signal. The output remains low for the value of the count loaded in the counter. Thus, a one-shot pulse of a programmable duration is triggered by the rising edge of the channel's gate signal. This function can be retriggered and, thus, repeated on each rising edge of the gate signal.

Mode 2: Rate Generator   In mode 2, rate generator, the count value is used to divide the input clock by the counter value. Counting begins as soon as the count value is loaded. After the input clock has counted to the counter value, the output of the channel goes low for one period of the input clock. If a new count value is loaded between output pulses, the present period is not affected but the next period reflects the new period value. If the gate is low, it forces the channel's output high. When the gate input goes high, the counter starts from the initialized value. Thus, it is possible to use the gate signal to synchronize the counter's divided function. When this mode is selected, the channel's output goes high and remains high until the count is loaded, then it goes low after the count has been reached. Thus, the counter can be synchronized also by software.

Mode 3: Square-Wave Rate Generator   Mode 3, square-wave rate generator, is similar to mode 2 (rate generator) except that the output remains high until half the count has been completed (for even numbers) and goes low for the other half of the count. This is accomplished by decrementing the counter by two on the falling edge of each clock input pulse. When the counter reaches the terminal count, the state of the output is changed, the counter is reloaded with the full count, and the whole process is repeated. If the count is odd, the output is high for $(N+1)/2$ counts and low for $(N-1)/2$ counts, where N equals the counter value programmed.

Mode 4: Software-Triggered Strobe   After mode 4 (software-triggered strobe) is set, the output is high. When the count is loaded, the counter begins counting. On the terminal count, the output goes low for one input clock period, then goes high again. If the count register is reloaded between output pulses, the present period is not affected, but the next period reflects the new value. Reloading the counter register restarts the counting, beginning with the new number.

Mode 5: Hardware-Triggered Strobe   In mode 5, hardware-triggered strobe, the counter starts counting after the rising edge of the gate input. The output goes low for one clock period when the terminal count is reached. The control of the channel's gate signal is important and is different for some modes of operation. The gate signal operations for each mode are summarized in Table 6-5.

Many modes of operation are not practical to use with the system unit's 8253-5 timer counter because its functions are more or less dedicated to supporting the base function of the PC. Using this device in an interface design is simple because it attaches easily to the system bus. It is treated in detail here because this knowledge may be useful in incorporating timing and counting functions when using the 8253-5 timer-counter device.

Adding Extended Timing and Counting Functions

Many interfacing applications require extensive timing and counting functions. Although the baseboard of the PC has a built-in timer counter,

Table 6-5.   Gate Input Control Summary of the 8253-5 Counter

| Mode | Low or Going Low | Signal Status | |
		Rising	High
0	Disables counting	—	Enables counting
1	—	1. Initiates counting	—
		2. Resets output after next clock	
2	1. Disables counting	1. Reloads counter	Enables counting
	2. Sets output immediately high	2. Initiates counting	
3	1. Disables counting	Initiates counting	Enables counting
	2. Sets output immediately high		
4	Disables counting	—	Enables counting
5	—	Initiates counting	—

its functions are typically tied up in supporting the base functions of the system. Further, none of the interesting control or input signals of the timer counter are available on the system bus.

As previously discussed, the timing and counting functions of the baseboard are implemented using an Intel 8253-5 timer counter. This device has three 16-bit timer counters with five independent modes of operation. Each timer counter has a clock input signal that is used to decrement the counters, a gate input signal that is used to start and stop the counters, and an output signal that can be programmed to perform several functions depending on the mode of operation.

The modes of operation and the input/output signals of the system board's 8253-5 counter are fixed and not available. Because the 8253-5 timer counter is a bus-attached device, you can add another timer counter as part of the interface design and dedicate it to a specific application. In the next section, we demonstrate how an 8253-5 timer counter, when combined with a little extra circuitry, can be used to create a very versatile and capable timing and counting function.

Timer-Counter Design

Because the system bus is available in the card slots, attaching an 8253-5 device is not difficult. Figure 6-30 shows the system-bus interface circuitry needed to decode a set of I/O port addresses and buffer the system bus. In this design, several port addresses are decoded: a group or chip select for the four port addresses of the 8253-5 timer counter and three port addresses for addressing three output ports. These three output ports provide 24 programmable signal lines that are used to control the support circuitry necessary to extend the functions of the 8253-5 counter.

The decode circuitry is designed such that the location of the de-

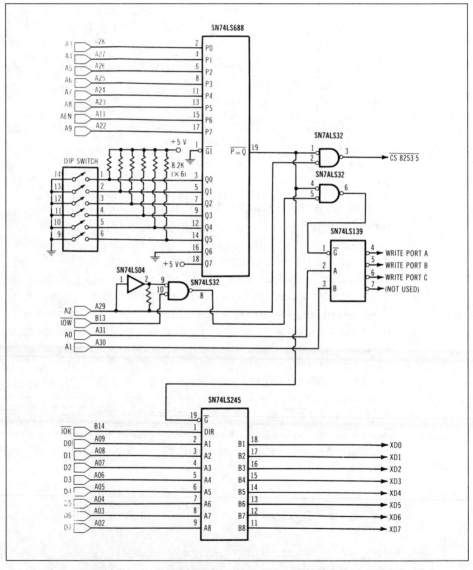

Figure 6-30. Address decode and bus buffers for the I/O ports and the 8253-5 timer counter.

coded addresses can be set in the I/O-port address space by simply setting a value in the DIP switches. The complement of the value set in the DIP switches is compared with the address on the bus; when a match is detected, the card's bus buffer is enabled. This technique allows addresses to be moved such that an I/O-port address overlap can be easily avoided.

Figure 6-31 is a circuit diagram of the three output I/O port registers that provide the control function for the timer-counter extension circuitry. Each 8-bit output register controls the extended function circuits of an 8253-5 timer-counter channel.

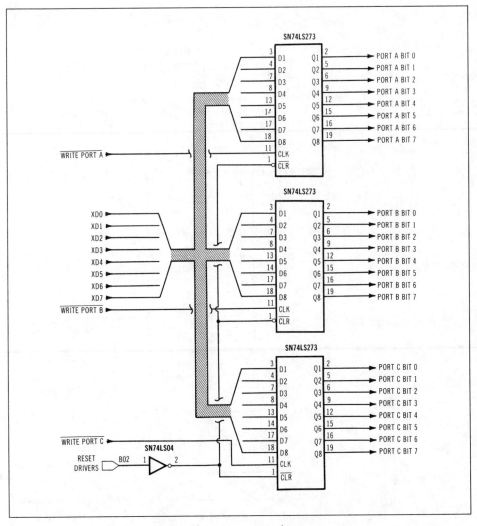

Figure 6-31. Control I/O ports.

Figures 6-32 through 6-35 are circuit diagrams of an 8253-5 timer counter with extended gating and control circuits added. The extra circuitry greatly extends the timing and counting function. The capabilities added include the following.

1. Channels can be chained under program control, providing timing and counting functions up to 48 bits in length.
2. The gate on a timer-counter channel can be controlled by the output of another channel or by an external condition.
3. The clock input on a channel can be selected from an external source, an internal source, or another channel's output.

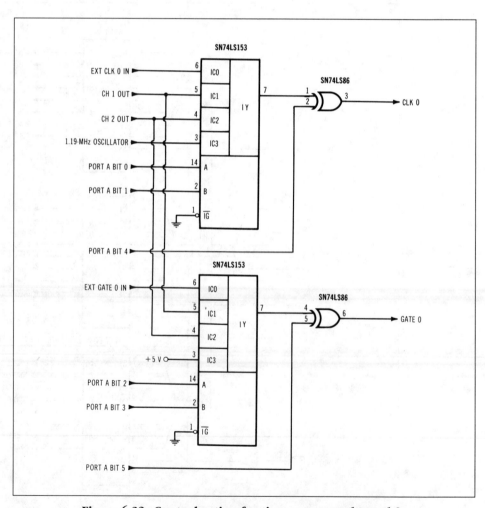

Figure 6-32. Control gating for timer-counter channel 0.

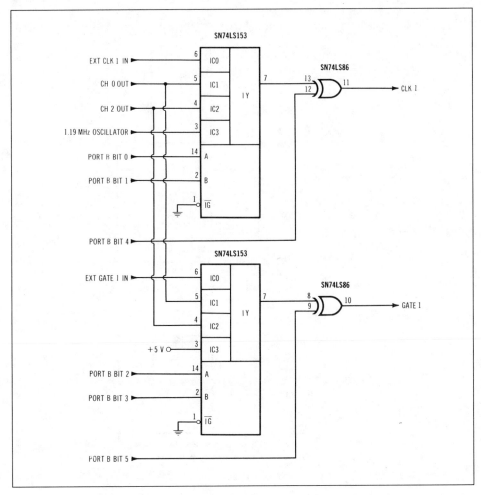

Figure 6-33. Control gating for timer-counter channel 1.

4. The active level of the gate or clock input to a channel can be selected as high or low active under program control.

5. The output of a timer counter can be program selected as either active high or low.

6. The output of each timer-counter can generate a system-bus interrupt request.

When the different control combinations possible through the use of the port bits are added to the modes of operation for each timer counter, the operational modes of this circuit are nearly limitless. This same circuit can be used in a PC AT system design exactly as shown. In a PS/2 design, the

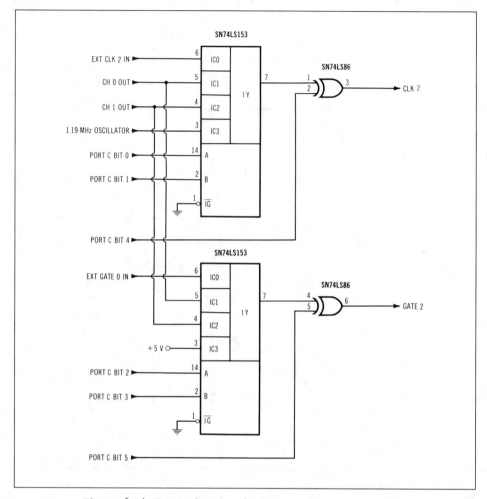

Figure 6-34. Control gating for timer-counter channel 2.

bus interface needs to be modified to support the MCA bus. See Chapters 11 and 12.

Circuit Description   As can be seen from the circuit diagram, each clock output signal is attached to the input of an eXclusive-OR gate. The inputs of these gates are the output of a 4-to-1 selector and a programmable port bit. By programming the active level of the port bit, you can change the active level of the signal from the selector before it is fed to the clock input of the timer-counter channel. An active low level from the port bit passes the output of the selector with no inversion. An active high level from the port bit inverts the signal. The selector inputs are attached to four different sources: the outputs of the other two timer-counter channels, a

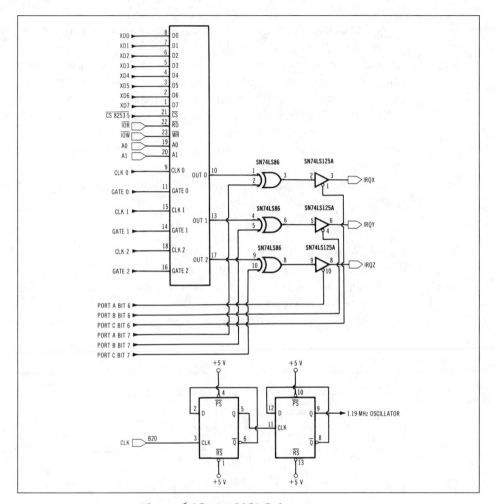

Figure 6-35. An 8253-5 timer counter.

1.19-MHz clock, and an external source. Two bits from the I/O-output port registers select the source from the selector that will be used to drive the clock input. The selector circuit is an SN74LS153, a dual 4-to-1 selector. In the design, only half the circuit is used.

The gate input to each channel has a similar circuit. Again, the active level of the gate input is controlled by programming the state of an I/O-port output register bit. The selector circuit is controlled by two port bits such that any four different gate signals can be used. The four inputs to the gate selector circuit are: the outputs of the two other timer-counter channels, an external gate source, and a tied high-level condition. Under program control, you can force a gate active by selecting the tied high condition.

The active level of the output of each timer-counter channel can be controlled through the setting of a port bit. Again, the port bit controls an eXclusive-OR circuit that either passes the output or inverts the output. An active low signal on the port bit will not invert the channel's output. An active high output will invert the channel's output. The output of the eXclusive-OR circuit can be used to drive an interface or create an interrupt on the system bus. The output of each channel is attached through a tristate buffer to an interrupt-request signal input on the system bus. Under program control, you can activate a port bit that enables the buffer and attaches the channel output to the interrupt request on the system bus.

Bit Definitions of Control I/O Ports   Inspection of the circuit diagrams reveals that eight control signals are required for each channel to control the function of selectors, invertor circuits, and interrupt-enable control. Figures 6-36 through 6-38 define the functions of the three output registers and the signal definitions of the 8 bits in each register.

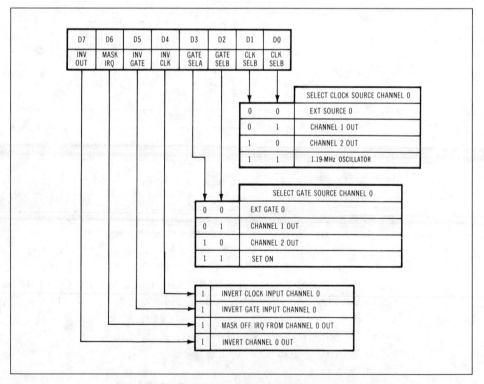

Figure 6-36. Port A control-bit definitions.

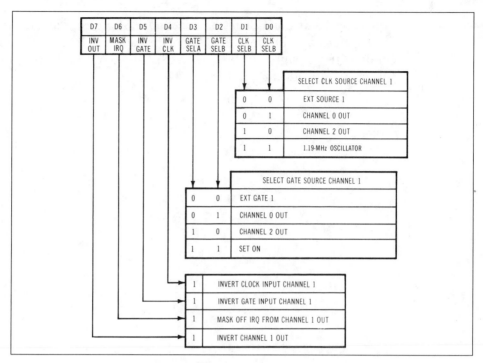

Figure 6-37. Port B control-bit definitions.

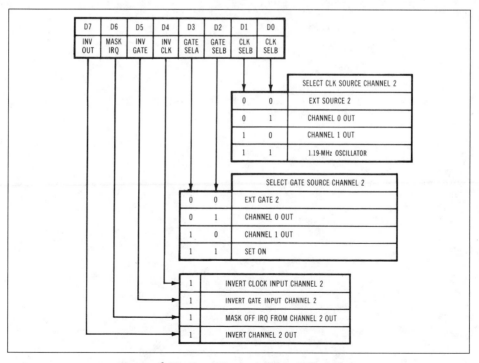

Figure 6-38. Port C control-bit definitions.

Expanding Timing and Counting Functions   If an interface design requires more timer-counter functions than are supported by a single 8253-5 timer counter, the design can be easily expanded by replicating the circuitry and providing additional decoding.

Chapter 7

PC and XT I/O, Memory, and Decoding

THIS CHAPTER PROVIDES INFORMATION on the use of the I/O and memory address spaces of the PC and XT. Maps of the present usage of the I/O and memory spaces are presented. Also covered are decoding techniques that can be used in your interface designs, and the various aspects of bus buffering, transceiver control, and system memory refresh.

Port Addressing

The I/O adapter and most support devices in the PC are controlled and sensed using the digital input and output ports. These ports are addressed using the I/O port address space of the 8088 microprocessor. Data is sent to these ports using the OUT instruction of the 8088 MPU. Data is sensed or read from these ports using the 8088 IN instruction. The 8088 processor architecture supports an I/O port address space of 65,536 unique port addresses. The PC design does not use the full address space; only the lower 10 bits of the address field (bus bits 0 through 9) are used to decode device or port addresses. It is important to note that the 8088 OUT and IN instructions can still be used to specify ports addresses with high-order bits active, but the presently designed devices look at, decode, and respond only to bits 0 through 9.

Bit 9 of the I/O port address field has special meaning in the PC design. When the bit is inactive, data cannot be received on the system bus from the five card slots on the system board. When inactive, this bit enables data only from the devices and the I/O port addresses on the system board. When bit 9 is active, it enables data from the five card slots.

Thus, for input ports, the 1024 port addresses supported in the PC are equally divided into 512 port addresses on the system board and 512 port addresses on the card slot bus.

This restriction does not apply to output ports. Any of the 1024 port addresses can be used as output port addresses in the card slots. Output port addresses used on the system board, however, should not be replicated in the card slot system bus because writing to the port address would write to both ports.

Figure 7-1 illustrates the PC's usage of the I/O address field. Figure 7-2 illustrates how the 8088 address space is allocated in the PC design.

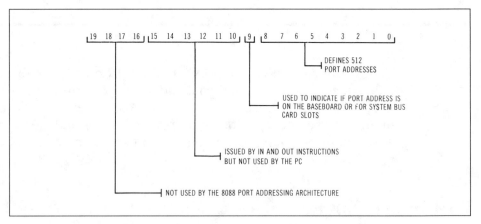

Figure 7-1. I/O port addresses of the 8088 MPU.

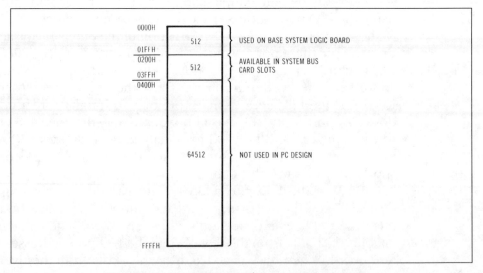

Figure 7-2. Usage of the I/O port address space.

I/O Port Address Map

The I/O port address map can be divided into two parts. The first part is the address space 0000 through 01FF hex or the portion of this address space which resides on the base system board. These port addresses are used to address the 8088 MPU support devices and integrated I/O on the base system board. Figure 7-3 defines the address port's functions on the base system board. For detailed information on the functions of these ports, consult the *IBM Technical Reference Manual.*

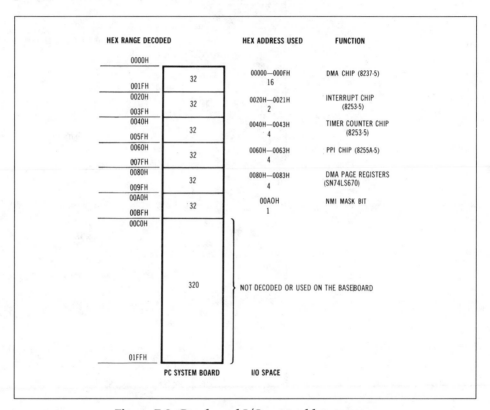

Figure 7-3. Baseboard I/O port address usage.

Addresses 00C0 through 01FF hex are not used as either input or output ports on the baseboard. As previously stated, these addresses cannot be used as input ports, but it is possible to decode these addresses as output ports on the system bus for use in an interface design.

Figure 7-4 defines the present usage of the second part of the PC I/O port address space, addresses 0200 through 02FF hex. This address space is used for port addresses decoded on the system bus and available in the five card slots on the system board. As IBM and other manufacturers provide new feature cards for the PC, more of these address decodes will be used. Because this is occurring at a rapid rate, an accurate map of the usage of these decodes is impossible to maintain. If you do not use some of these devices or feature cards in your system configuration (and you do not plan to do so), you may use those address decodes in your interface designs.

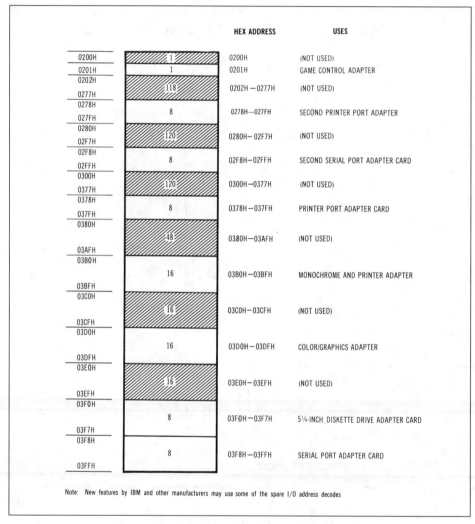

	HEX ADDRESS	USES
0200H	0200H	(NOT USED)
0201H	0201H	GAME CONTROL ADAPTER
0202H – 0277H	0202H – 0277H	(NOT USED)
0278H – 027FH	0278H – 027FH	SECOND PRINTER PORT ADAPTER
0280H – 02F7H	0280H – 02F7H	(NOT USED)
02F8H – 02FFH	02F8H – 02FFH	SECOND SERIAL PORT ADAPTER CARD
0300H – 0377H	0300H – 0377H	(NOT USED)
0378H – 037FH	0378H – 037FH	PRINTER PORT ADAPTER CARD
0380H – 03AFH	0380H – 03AFH	(NOT USED)
03B0H – 03BFH	03B0H – 03BFH	MONOCHROME AND PRINTER ADAPTER
03C0H – 03CFH	03C0H – 03CFH	(NOT USED)
03D0H – 03DFH	03D0H – 03DFH	COLOR/GRAPHICS ADAPTER
03E0H – 03EFH	03E0H – 03EFH	(NOT USED)
03F0H – 03F7H	03F0H – 03F7H	5¼-INCH DISKETTE DRIVE ADAPTER CARD
03F8H – 03FFH	03F8H – 03FFH	SERIAL PORT ADAPTER CARD

Note: New features by IBM and other manufacturers may use some of the spare I/O address decodes

Figure 7-4. Card slot I/O port address usage.

I/O Port Address Decoding Techniques

Several I/O port addressing decode techniques can be used in your designs. The following sections investigate several alternatives.

Fixed Address Decode

The simplest way to decode an I/O port address or group of addresses for an interface design is to find a block of unused addresses in the address space, then construct the proper decode circuitry. Most current IBM feature cards use this technique. Figure 7-5 is an example of a fixed I/O port decode design. In this example, four port addresses are decodes that begin at address 02F0 hex. These decodes can be further ANDed with the IOR and IOW bus signals to generate output and input strobe signals for digital output and input registers. The back edge of the WRITE REGISTER signals can be used to clock data from the data bus into the digital output registers. The READ REGISTER signal can be used to gate data from an input register onto the system bus. The GROUP SELECT signal is generated such that it can be used to enable a bus transceiver when any of the four register decodes are detected. Note that address bit 9 has to be active for the decode, indicating that the port address is in the address space supported in the system-bus card slots. The AEN bus signal is used to degate the decode. This is necessary to prevent an invalid port address decode during DMA cycles.

There are two timing concerns when decoding a port address. The first is at the beginning of an I/O port bus cycle. If the port address decode has a lot of delay, it may occur after the IOR and IOW bus control signals become valid. Because the address bits from the system are skewed, the decode may momentarily decode some other port address. If these invalid decodes are late and are ANDed with the bus control signals, data may be written to the wrong port address. In the PC, the worst-case delay permitted in the decode is 92 nanoseconds.

The second timing concern is at the end of the I/O port bus cycle. Here, if the IOW bus control signal is delayed sufficiently and the decode is very fast, the back edge of the write signal may write data to an address that is decoded from the next bus cycle. In the PC design, the IOW signal delay should be less that 200 nanoseconds. The tightest timing, however, is in the relationship of the back edge of the IOW signal to valid data on the data bus. If the IOW signal is delayed more that 120 nanoseconds, the port address may be written with invalid data. Similarly, if the IOR signal is delayed, it will reduce the read access time available to the I/O port. The timing charts in Chapter 5 should be consulted to ensure sufficient margin in your designs.

Switch-Selectable Decode

The problem with a fixed decode design is that it may overlap that of a feature card you want to add to your system. Figure 7-6 illustrates a decode

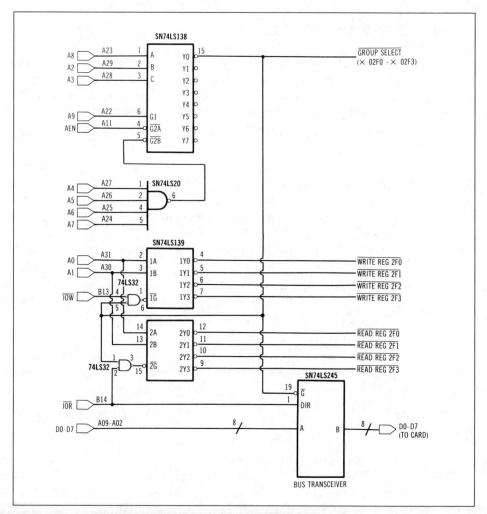

Figure 7-5. Example of a fixed I/O port address decode.

design in which you can move the address of a block of eight port addresses in the address space by simply setting a new value in a bank of DIP switches. In this design, an SN74LS688 octal compare circuit is used. On one side of the compare circuit, address bus bits A3 through A9 and the AEN signal are attached. On the other side, the output of the DIP switches is attached. When the value set in the DIP switches equals the value on the address bus, the compare equal output is activated and can be used as the GROUP SELECT control signal. When a switch is open, or off, it is equivalent to a high level on the associated address bus signal. You can generate a fixed address decode using the same compare circuit by replacing the switches with a hard-wired pattern or address.

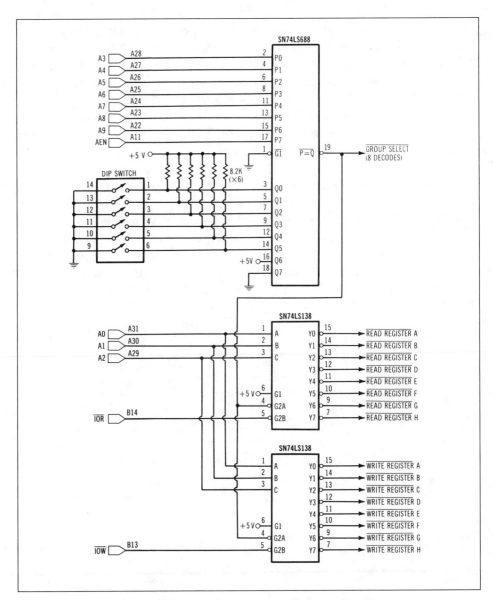

Figure 7-6. Switch-selectable I/O port decode.

PROM Select Decode

Sometimes you need to decode widely different port addresses on a card. This would be the case if you were combining onto a single card the functions of several cards, but maintaining the original port addresses. The fixed decodes would require a large amount of logic to decode. A common solution to this problem is to use PROM (programmable read-only memory) to generate the decode outputs. The address input signal to a PROM decode is a unique output bit pattern that has been written into a device at manufacturing time. The data written into a PROM corresponds to the output signal states required to select a port. Then the port address is applied as an address to the device. Using this technique, it is possible to select any decode as active by simply programming that condition into PROM when it was manufactured.

Figure 7-7 is a circuit design that uses a 512-byte PROM organized as 512 bytes by 8 bits to decode eight different port addresses. Figure 7-8 presents the data that would have to exist at the PROM addresses to decode the port select signals for the different port addresses. All other PROM addresses would be programmed to the zero state. Note that the PROM access time must be faster than the minimum decode time of 92 nanoseconds specified previously. The technique is most often used in high production designs in which the cost of a unique PROM can be justified.

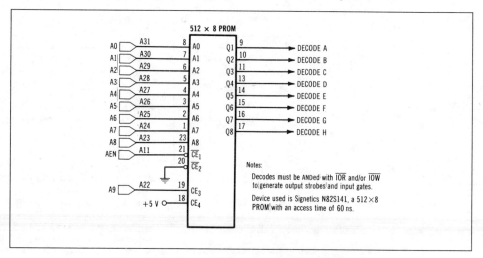

Figure 7-7. PROM I/O port address decoding.

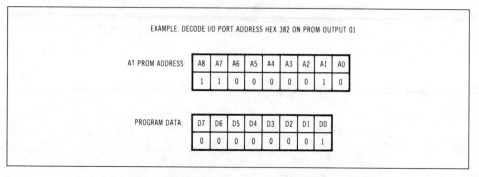

Figure 7-8. PROM decode programming example.

Expanding Port Addressing on the PC

Because the PC design supports only 512 port addresses on the system bus and because a large number of these addresses are used, interfacing designs with requirements for large numbers of I/O ports are difficult to implement. This section describes some techniques you can use to increase the maximum number of port addresses available on the PC.

High-Order Address Bit Usage

As mentioned, the PC design does not use address bits 10 through 15 when decoding port addresses. But your design can use these bits and remain compatible with cards that do not use them. To use the additional bits, we must first satisfy the requirements of the other cards that will be attached to the bus. This means that the cards must not be read or written to when the additional bits are used. To do this, we must find a single unused address in the normal 512-address field. This address becomes the GROUP SELECT decode for the addresses decoded from bits 10 through 15. We use one normal address to enable the decode of bits 10 through 15, thus expanding the decode by 64 addresses.

Using this technique, you can expand each unused address in the normal 512-address space to an additional 64 addresses. For example, if a block of 8 unused addresses is decoded and used as the GROUP SELECT, an additional 512 addresses can be supported, as shown in Figure 7-9. (A net of 504 new addresses is generated because 8 addresses are used to generate the GROUP SELECT decode.) In this design, the block of 8 unused addresses is selected by a DIP switch.

Indirect Port Addressing

Another common method for expanding I/O port addressing is to use indirect port addressing. In this scheme, the contents of a port are used to address other ports. Thus, if 8-bit ports are used, a single port address can specify an additional 256 port addresses. Actually, two port addresses are required to implement indirect addressing. The first port address is a digital output port that, when written to, contains the indirect port address. The second port address is the data port. When data is written to the second port address, the data actually is written to the port address specified in the first digital output register. Similarly, when the second port is read, the data comes from the indirectly addressed port.

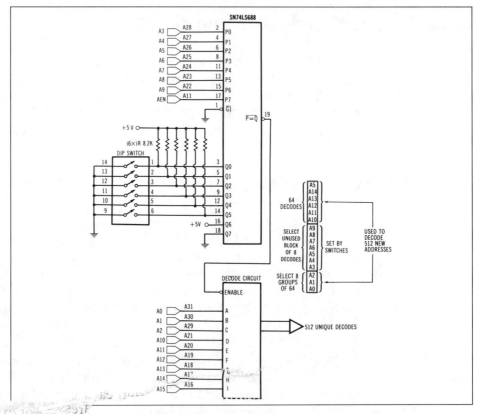

Figure 7-9. Extending port addressing by using high-order bits.

Figure 7-10 is a circuit schematic that indirectly addresses four ports using the indirect addressing technique. It should be noted that to address an indirect port, an additional OUT instruction must be used. Thus, there is a small performance loss using this scheme.

Memory-Mapped I/O Port Addressing

The PC normally uses I/O-mapped addressing, but nothing in the design precludes using memory-mapped I/O port addressing. This scheme simply uses memory addresses as I/O port addresses. It is commonly used to expand I/O port addressing and, in many microprocessor architectures, is the only means of addressing I/O ports.

Because the 8088 MPU has a 1M address space, limitations of port addresses are normally not a concern. A design that uses memory-mapped I/O also has the advantage of not conflicting with other I/O port mapped addresses. Figure 7-11 is an example of a circuit that decodes and imple-

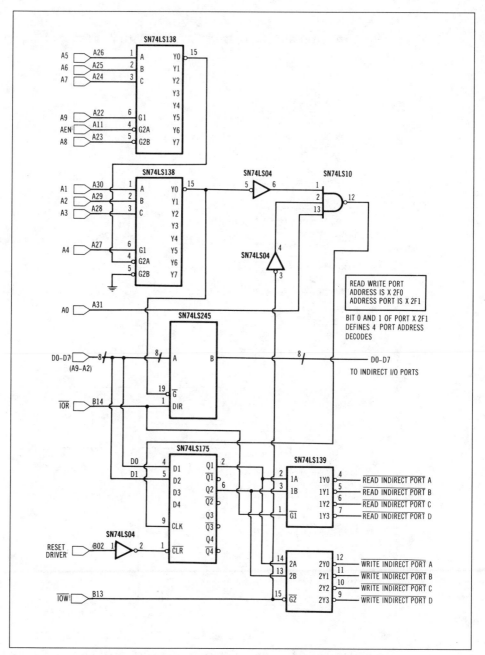

Figure 7-10. Example of indirect port addressing decode.

ments a digital input and output port using memory-mapped I/O port addressing. Aside from removing the I/O port addressing conflicts and expanding the number of available port addresses, memory-mapped I/O has an additional advantage. Because ports are addressed as memory locations, the full power of the 8088 microprocessor instruction set can be used to manipulate the data associated with a port.

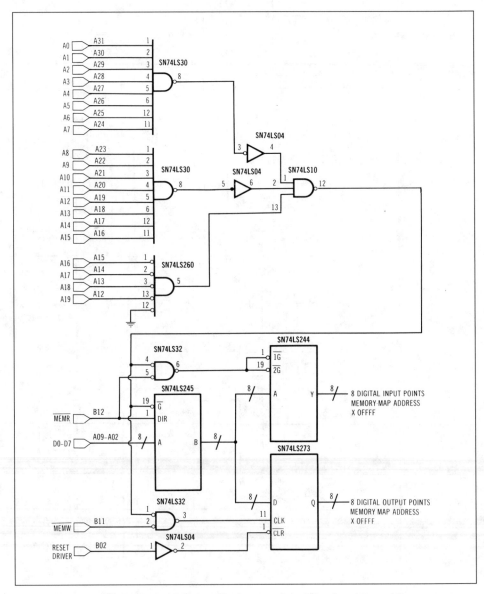

Figure 7-11. Memory-mapped I/O port input and output registers.

There are some disadvantages to memory-mapped I/O addressing. First, all 20 bits of the system-bus address must be used in decoding a port address, thus increasing the amount of circuitry. Second, a define segment register instruction may be needed before each port access to set the proper segment portion of the memory address. This may result in a performance loss when the segment value is different than the value normally used by the program. Last, memory bus cycles are four clocks in length, but I/O port cycles are five clocks in length. Thus, the access time requirement for a memory-mapped device is less than that for an I/O-mapped device.

Memory Usage Map

The 8088 microprocessor supports 1M of memory address space. The PC design uses both the high and low ends of the 8088 MPU address space. In addition, the PC display adapters use a portion of the address space for display buffers. At the high end of the address space, the PC's ROM is decoded. A 64K space is decoded at the high end of the address space and is occupied by 40K of ROM. This ROM space is decoded on the base system board and cannot be decoded or used on the system bus in the card slots. The ROM contains PC BIOS, diagnostics, the bootstrap loader, the cassette operating system, and the BASIC interpreter. An additional 8K of ROM may be added using the spare module socket on the system board. The remaining 16K in the 64K block that is decoded on the system board cannot be used.

RAM is added to the PC starting from the low end of the address space. The first 64K of RAM is decoded on the base system board, and any additional RAM must be added as cards in one of the five card slots on the system board. When DOS is in the system, it occupies approximately the first 12K of system RAM space. When DEBUG is loaded, an additional 10K of space is used. Thus, in a 64K system, this would leave approximately 36K of space for a BASIC workspace. These numbers are approximate values; with each new release of system software, they will vary.

Each of the PC's display adapters decodes a 32K block of storage for use as a display regen buffer. The color graphics card uses only 16K of the 32K that it decodes. The remaining 16K block is not usable in the system. The monochrome display adapter uses 4K of the 32K that it decodes. The remaining 28K is not usable. When one of the display adapters is not in the system, the memory space that it would have used is free and can be used by the system.

The PC design has reserved certain areas of system memory for future enhancements. To ensure compatibility with future devices, avoid using these reserved areas of the memory address space. Figure 7-12 illustrates the memory map, usage, and reserved area of the PC system memory.

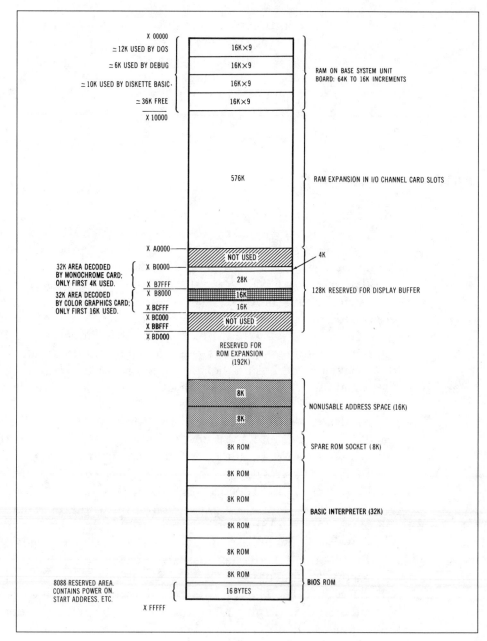

Figure 7-12. The PC memory map.

Memory Address Decoding

Decoding memory addresses is very similar to decoding I/O port addresses, with two major differences. First, 4 extra high-order bits are used in addressing the 1M address space. Second, the AEN bus signal is not used to degate the decodes, as was done with the port addresses. The techniques of fixed and switch-selected decodes still apply, however, and can be used in memory address decoding.

Figure 7-13 is an example of a circuit that can be used to address a block of 8K of static memory on the system bus. The circuit includes a bus buffer, and shows how the bus buffer can be enabled and how its directions can be controlled. This technique can be used to add small amounts of memory in an interface design.

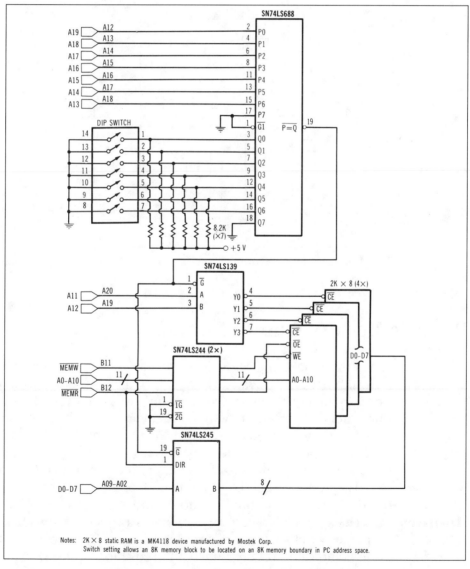

Figure 7-13. Decoding 8K of static memory.

If larger blocks of memory are required, a more efficient method is to use 64K-by-1-bit dynamic memory devices. Figure 7-14 is a circuit diagram that decodes a block of 64K memory addresses and allows the block to be placed on any 64K boundary in the system-address space by simply setting the appropriate value in a set of DIP switches. This scheme allows a memory design that can skip over areas of memory being used by setting in the DIP switches the desired location of each 64K block.

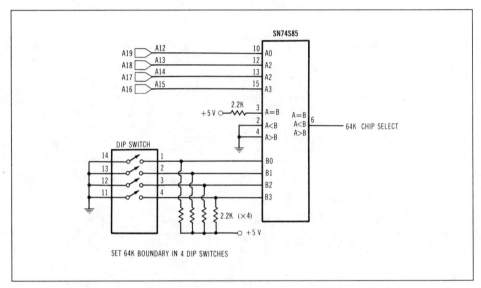

Figure 7-14. A switch-selectable decode for a 64K block of memory.

Dynamic Memory Refresh Function

When dynamic memory devices are added to the system, they require a refresh function. Typically, the memory devices require that each of the first 128 memory locations be read at least once every 2 milliseconds. If this is not done, memory will not maintain its data. To perform this function, two problems must be solved. First, a refresh address must be generated and applied to the memory devices. Second, the refresh cycle must be arbitrated with the normal system processor and DMA cycles.

The PC is designed to provide both of these functions so that a memory device using dynamic memory can be easily attached to the system bus. The system automatically generates a special refresh bus cycle every 72 processor clocks, or approximately every 15 microseconds. This bus cycle is indicated on the bus by the activation of the DACK0 bus signal.

During this bus cycle, the address bus contains a valid refresh address and performs a memory read using this address, thus fulfilling the memory refresh requirements. The memory should be designed such that each time a DACK0 signal is activated, the memory is attached to the bus and a refresh cycle is taken.

Chapter 8

PC Interfacing
Techniques

THE MOST COMMON METHOD of interfacing a microprocessor system such as the PC is through the use of programmable digital input and output registers. The microprocessor can write data into the digital output register, treating the register as an I/O port or memory location. The output of the register could be wired to an interface device, such as a relay. Then, by writing data to the output register, you could activate and deactivate a relay. The relay, in turn, could control the power to a motor, for example.

Digital input registers are similar but are used to sample the status of signals attached to their inputs. For example, you could tie a switch to the input of a digital input register, then read its state to determine if the switch was open or closed. A digital input register can be thought of as a memory location or an I/O port address that has wires attached to individual bit locations. When read, the data results reflect the state of the signals on the wires. In general, digital input and output registers allow the microprocessor to sense information about the outside world and emit control signals that cause actions to occur outside the computer.

Figure 8-1 illustrates the typical components of an interface design and the microprocessor functions available to implement that interface design. As illustrated in the block diagram, the three basic functions used in an interface to a microprocessor are (1) interrupts to signal and synchronize external events, (2) DMA to transfer data at high speeds to or from system memory, and (3) digital input and output registers to sense and control interfacing circuitry or the attached interface.

Often, functions cannot be done easily by the system program using digital input/output registers directly because software programs are not fast enough or require too much software to perform efficiently. In the block diagram, this function is referred to as the interface's *unique inter-*

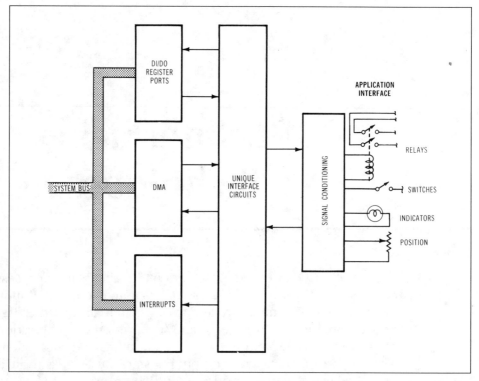

Figure 8-1. Block diagram of an interface design.

face circuits. A goal in any design is to reduce or eliminate the need for unique and custom interface adapter circuitry. This chapter discusses several digital input and output register techniques that can help reduce custom designs in an interfacing project.

The last element of an interface design is the attachment of the design to the real world. Unfortunately, the real world is not digital, and the signals to and from such interfaces require a conversion to other forms, such as relay drivers, switch sensors, indicator drivers, and non-digital voltage levels. This is referred to as the *signal-conditioning section* in the block diagram. The functions of interrupts, DMA, and signal conditioning are covered in specific chapters on these subjects and will not be discussed here.

DI/DO Registers

In this chapter, we discuss several general-purpose digital input (DI) and digital output (DO) register types. This discussion provides a variety of DI/DO register approaches that can be used to implement a specific interface attachment function. The goal is to provide a set of DI/DO registers that have sufficient functions to allow direct interfacing with a minimum of extra circuitry.

The DI/DO register designs in this chapter are a general-purpose set and can be used in a large number of interfacing applications. Parts and pieces of these designs can be incorporated in one specific interface design, thus achieving an optimal solution for a specific project.

Register Address Decoding

A DI/DO register is addressed in two basic ways: as a memory-mapped device or as an I/O-mapped device. There are many advantages to the I/O-mapped method. Segment register manipulation is not required, a separate address space that does not conflict with the memory address space is used, fewer address bits are needed to decode a specific address, and DMA operation between I/O ports and memory is accomplished in one bus cycle. The basic limitation of this method is that only the IN and OUT instructions of the 8088 microprocessor can be used to read and write to the DI/DO registers.

One advantage of the memory-mapped method is that the 8088 microprocessor has a very large address space (that is, lots of available addresses). Also, any 8088 MPU instruction that references memory can be used to access the registers. Thus, the full power of the instruction set can be used to manipulate data in the registers.

The designs discussed here use the I/O method, but they could be easily modified to use the memory-mapped method of addressing. Figure 8-2 is a circuit diagram that decodes eight DO register addresses. Note that only eight addresses are actually decoded. The $\overline{\text{IOR}}$ and $\overline{\text{IOW}}$ bus signals are used to further condition the decodes to provide the 16 possible DI/DO register read and write control signals.

Decode and Bus Buffer Circuit

The PC system bus supports nine address bits for decoding I/O port addresses. Bits A0 through A8 can be decoded to select one of 512 port addresses. Bit A9 is used as a tenth bit in the decode, but its purpose is to indicate to the system bus the source or the destination for the IN or OUT instruction data. The AEN bus signal is used to degate the decode of an I/O port address during DMA bus cycle operation.

With relatively few I/O port addresses supported on the system bus, there is a high probability that a fixed decode would overlap with that of

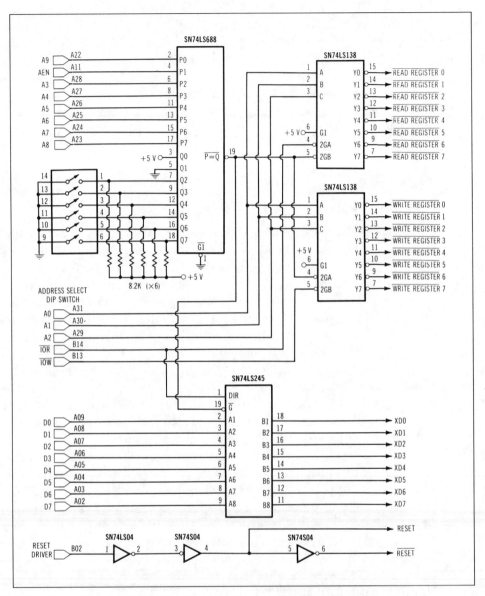

Figure 8-2. I/O port address decode and bus repower.

another card on the system bus. To avoid this problem, the eight decode addresses can be placed on any eight address boundaries in the 512 address space. This is accomplished by the comparator circuit, which compares the address value on the bus (from the seven address bits, A3 through A9) with the value set in the DIP switches, then generates a card-selected signal. The card-selected signal is used to enable the SN74LS245 bus transceiver buffer. The signal enables also the further decode of the

DI/DO addresses from A0, A1, A2, IOR, and IOW by using the two SN74LS138 3-to-8 decode circuits. The IOR signal is used also to set the direction of the enabled SN74LS245 bus transceiver.

DO Register Design

Figure 8-3 is a circuit diagram showing the simplest form of an 8-bit DO register design. In this figure, an octal D-type latch device (an SN74LS273 latch) captures the data sent by the OUT instruction. The input to each bit of the latch is the repowered data bus from Figure 8-2. Data from the bus is written on the back edge of the $\overline{\text{WRT REG0}}$ control signal. The signal is activated when an OUT instruction is executed and the I/O port address is decoded.

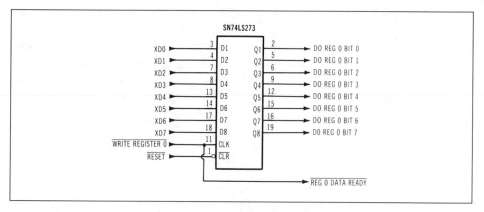

Figure 8-3. Latched DO register.

To write data to a DO register, first load the port address into the DX register. Next, load the data into the AL register and execute an OUT variable port instruction. The data in the AL register will appear in the DO register. The following assembly language example writes the hex pattern AA to port address 0300 hex.

```
MOV DX,0300H   Load DX reg with port address
MOV AL,AAH     Load accumulator with data
OUT DX,AL      Write data in AL to port in DX
```

The same result can be obtained using BASIC. The BASIC command to write to an I/O port is called an OUT command. The following coding example performs the same function as the preceding assembly language program:

```
OUT &H300,&HAA
```

Using these commands with the DO register, you can manipulate (under program control) the output signals of the DO register and thus control external devices. A function that is sometimes useful is to provide the WRT REG signal as an interface signal. The attaching device's circuitry can sense this signal and use it to indicate that new data has been loaded into the DO register. The DO register should be brought to a known state when the system is powered on, particularly if the DO register bits control things such as motors or valves. When the system is powered on, these control functions should not be activated accidentally. This can be accomplished using the RESET bus signal, which holds a reset condition in the register during power on and clears it to an initial state of all bits off.

With the clever selection of components, you can construct a DO register that can be used also for shifting and counting functions. Consider the DO register design in Figure 8-4. In this figure, the DO register operates as a normal output register but has the added capability of transmitting and receiving serial data by utilizing the extra functions of its components. This design uses two 4-bit bidirectional universal shift registers (SN74LS194A devices), which can be used as serial output or input devices and can shift either left or right. In addition to normal output signals provided on the interface, the following controls are available to the interface.

Shift Left Serial IN data

Shift Right Serial IN data

Select Shift Right Mode

Select Shift Left Mode

Shift Data Clock

DO Register Written

The register operates as a DO register until the Shift Left or Shift Right Mode is selected. In these modes, the interface may control the register and can shift data into or out of the register using the extra interface signals. As will be demonstrated later, the output of the DO register can be attached to the input of a DI register and the shift function can be used to transmit serial data loaded by the OUT instruction. It can also receive and read serial data using the IN instruction. Further, DO registers of this type can be chained to create shift registers that are greater than 8 bits in length.

Simple timing and counting functions can be added as extra functions to the DO registers by using counter devices as the latching elements in the DO register design. Figure 8-5 illustrates a DO register design that adds counting capability to the DO register. The DO register

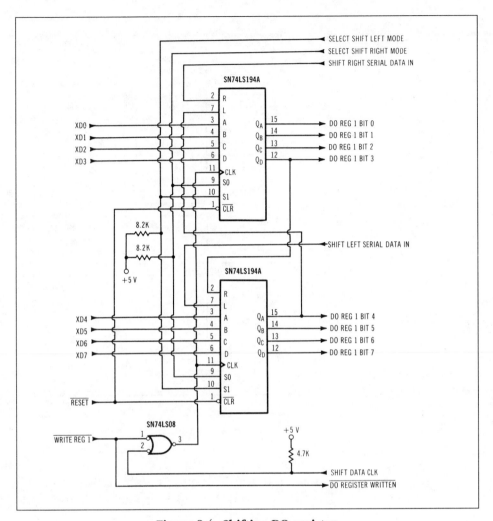

Figure 8-4. Shifting DO register.

function is implemented using SN74LS193 devices, synchronous up/down counters. In addition to the normal outputs of the DO register, the following signals are present to the interface:

Count Up CLK Input

Count Down CLK Input

Counter Carry Output

Counter Borrow Output

DO Register Written

With this design, the counter may be preset with a value, using the OUT instruction, and then decremented or incremented from the inter-

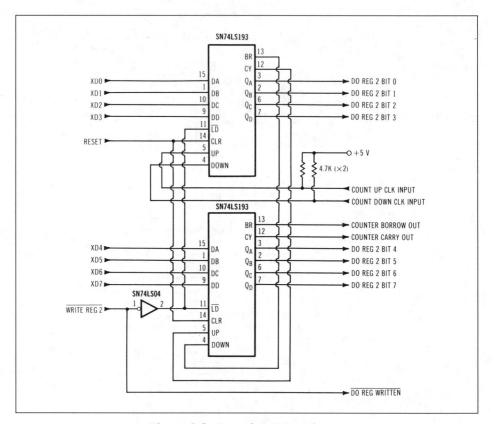

Figure 8-5. Counting DO register.

face. The Carry and Borrow outputs can be used to indicate a count reached or a done function. The output of this type of DO register can also be attached to the input of a DI register in such a manner that count values may be read after being incremented or decremented by the interface. Registers of this type may be chained to give counting functions greater than 8 bits in length.

DI Register Design

Usually, information from an interface is sensed using a DI register. The simplest form of this type of register is illustrated in Figure 8-6. In this design, data from the interface is simply gated onto the system data bus when the address is decoded and an IOR signal occurs. These conditions are generated by the execution of the 8088 microprocessor IN instruction. The IN instruction takes the data at the input of the addressed DI port register and places the data in the AL register of the 8088 MPU, where the data may be operated on by the system's software program. The following

8088 MPU assembly language program reads a DI register, decoded at address 0301 hex:

```
MOV DX,0301H   Load port address in DX register
IN AL,DX       Read port value into AL register
```

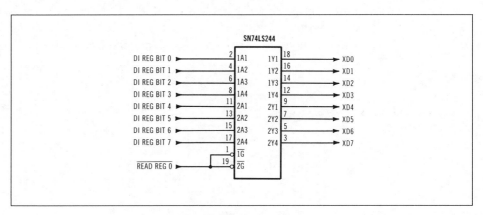

Figure 8-6. DI register.

A DI register may also be read using the INP BASIC command. The following BASIC command reads the value of a port, then places it in the variable named PORTDATA:

```
PORTDATA = INP(&H0301)
```

It is important to note that data at the input of the DI register type illustrated in Figure 8-6 is sampled only at the time of the execution of the IN command. Further, the data is actually sampled at the trailing edge of the IOW signal generated by the IN instruction. Thus, if an interface event is of short duration, it is possible to miss an interface signal when using this type of register. A DI register design that overcomes this problem is discussed next.

Level-Latching DI Register

A common problem in interface design occurs when the signals that need sensing are very short in duration, such as the signals generated when a switch is opened or closed or a photodetector is triggered. A program loop executing continuous IN instructions may not see a short duration signal because it samples the register value only on the back edge of the IOW signal. In addition, the 8088 MPU may have other functions to perform and cannot dedicate its time to a sampling loop. This problem is even more critical in BASIC because its execution time is relatively slow and the sample time is very long.

The level-latching DI register in Figure 8-7 provides a solution to this problem. In this design, a set/reset latch is placed in front of a normal DI register and the output of the latch is used as an input to the DI register. When an interface signal goes low, even for a few nanoseconds, the latch is set and the event is captured. When an IN instruction is executed later, the latch and the DI register reflect the occurrence of the short duration event.

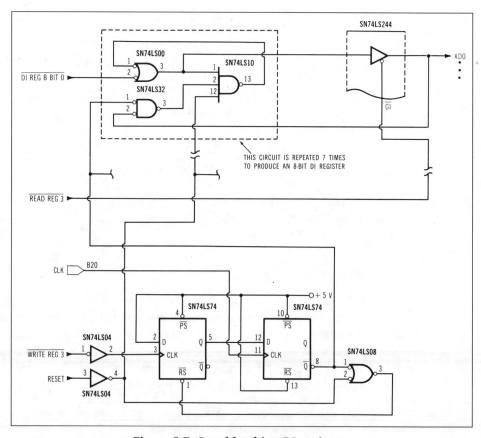

Figure 8-7. Level-latching DI register.

The next task is to reset the latch such that later events can be captured and sensed. This is accomplished with a pulsed-output register function. A special timing circuit generates a timing signal that is ANDed with the data from the data bus, $\overline{\text{IOW}}$, and pulsed-output register decode to generate a reset latch. At first, it would appear that ANDing the register write signal with the data bus would produce a reset pulse. If the $\overline{\text{IOW}}$ signal comes before the data bus is valid, however, it would result in invalid reset pulses.

The timing generator circuit in Figure 8-7 generates a reset timing pulse that is delayed until the data bus is valid. With this design, you can reset the level-sensing latches of this DI register by simply issuing an OUT instruction with the zero bit set in the position that requires a reset on the DI latch. The circuit is designed also such that a set condition on the input of the DI register overrides a reset command on the latch. This may be a useful function because a reset can be issued and the latch read after the reset. If the latch is still set, the input has not been deactivated. Thus, you can follow the state of the input signal by continually issuing resets and reading the latch.

The following 8088 assembly language code can be used to both read a level-sensitive latching DI register and reset all the bits that may be latched. The DI register is read by issuing an IN instruction to port address 0302 hex. The register latches are reset by issuing an OUT command to the same hex address.

```
MOV DX,0302H   Load DX reg with port address
IN AL,DX       Load AL reg with DI data
MOV BL,AL      Save DI data in BL register
MOV AL,0       Set AL register to all zeros
OUT 0302H,AL   Write zeros to port and clear latches
```

Transition-Detection DI Register

Another common problem when dealing with a DI register is detecting signal transitions on an interface. After the transition is sensed, you need to reset the DI register bit so that it can detect the next transition. This should be possible even though the signal is still active.

Figure 8-8 illustrates the design of a DI register that can be used to detect the rising-edge signal transition of interface signals. The design is similar to that of the level-sensing DI register. An edge-triggered D-type latch replaces the set/reset latch used as the input to the DI register. The D input is tied high, and the input is the transition-setting clock signal. Thus, any time the input signal goes from a low state to a high state, the latch is set and can be read through the DI register using an IN instruction. The transition-detection latches are reset using the same pulsed-output DO register design as was used with the level-detecting DI register. The major difference is that the reset always clears the latch, regardless of the state of the input signal to the latch. As with the level-sensing DI register design, if a zero is written to a bit position in the pulsed-output register, the latch is cleared.

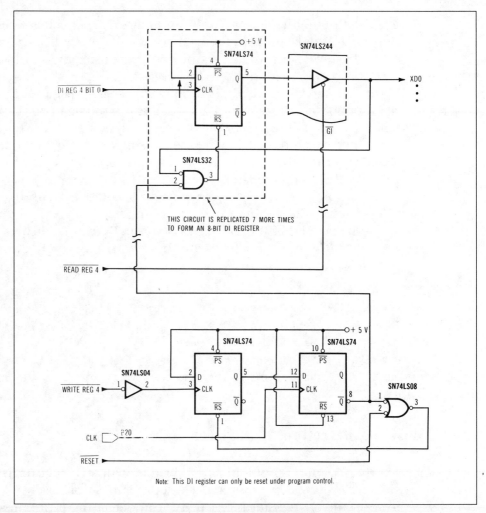

Figure 8-8. Transition-detection DI register.

The following 8088 processor assembly language code can be used to sense the status of a transition-detection DI register and reset only bit 2 of the DI register. We assume that the DI and DO registers are at port address 0304 hex.

```
MOV DX,0304H    Load port address in DX reg
IN  AL,DX       Read port data into AL reg
MOV BL,AL       Move data from AL reg to BL reg
MOV AL,FBH      Set data in AL reg with only bit 2 off
OUT DX,AL       Write data to port, resetting bit 2
```

Interrupts from the DI Register

The level- and transition-latching DI register designs just presented can be used also as source interrupts. Before the output of these types of latches is fed into the DI sensing circuitry, it can be wired to interrupt requests on the system bus. Thus, the latches can serve a dual function: detecting levels and transitions using the DI function and creating interrupts that can be cleared under program control.

Bidirectional DI/DO Registers

You can design a port register that can be changed under program control to act as either a DI register or a DO register. Further, you can program each bit so that it can be either a DI bit or a DO bit. This capability is of interest when the design will support a variety of interfacing functions, each requiring different numbers of DI and DO bits. The register is customized by software to configure the required number of DI or DO bits.

Figure 8-9 illustrates a port design that has individually programmable DI or DO bits. The output portion of the port design is similar to a standard latched-output DO. Each output bit of the DO register is used to drive an open-collector device, which is an SN74LS05 in this design. The output of each open-collector device is pulled high through a 4.7K resister to +5 volts, which provides a load for the SN74LS05. The outputs of the SN74LS05s are not tied to the input of a standard DI register.

To use a bit of this register as an output bit, simply write the desired level of the bit to the DO register using an OUT instruction. To use a bit as an input bit, first write a zero bit to the bit position in the DO register. This will turn off the open-collector driver and remove it from the circuit. Now an input signal can drive the signal line either high or low, and its state can be read in the DI portion of the circuit using an IN instruction. Note that after a power-on reset, the port is configured as an input port. In addition, when configured as an output port, the output signals are the complement of the data written to the port.

Pulsed-Output Port Design

We have used a pulsed-output port function to reset the latches in level-transition DI register designs. This function is often useful by itself in an interface. A pulsed-output type of register can be used to strobe data into a

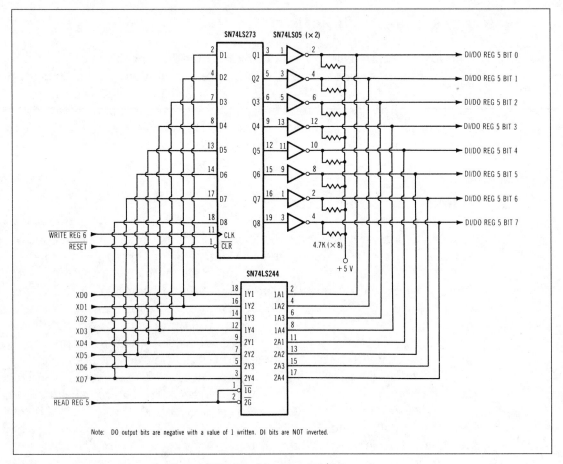

Note: DO output bits are negative with a value of 1 written. DI bits are NOT inverted.

Figure 8-9. Combination DI/DO register.

register under program control, reset interface status latches, and generate interrupt requests to another attached system. Figure 8-10 is a circuit diagram of an 8-bit pulsed-output register. This circuit produces a 420-nanosecond output pulse at a port bit when a one bit is written to the port bit position using an OUT instruction.

DO Register Output Drive

In the DO register designs in this chapter, we used LS-type devices. These devices have a limited signal drive capability; typically, they can sink only 8 mA. To obtain additional drive capability, you can substitute S-type devices, which support a 20-mA drive-current or sink-current capability.

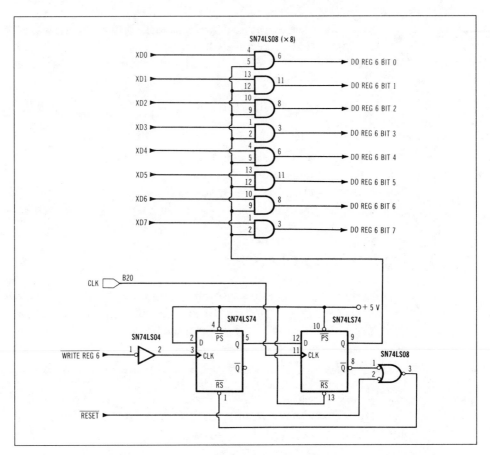

Figure 8-10. Pulsed DO register.

Setting and Resetting Bits in a DO Register

Setting and resetting bits in a DO register may appear to be a simple task; just load the AL register with the desired pattern and execute an OUT instruction. But in this technique, each routine that uses the DO port must know the proper setting of all bits in the port, even though it uses only one bit or a few bits in the register.

The following code can be used to manipulate a bit or bits in a DO register without disturbing the other bits. For this technique to work, you must maintain an image of the current state of the DO register by reading the DO register contents using a DI register. In this example, we turn on bit 3 without changing the state of the other bits in the DO register. We assume that the DO register can be read and written at port address 0305 hex.

```
MOV DX,0305H   Load DX reg with port address
IN AL,DX       Read DO reg into AL register
OR AL,08H      OR bit 3 on in AL register; other bits not affected
OUT 0305H,AL   Write AL reg to port; only bit 3 is affected
```

Similarly, the following code can be used to reset only bit 3 in a DO register:

```
MOV DX,0305H   Load DX reg with port address
IN AL,DX       Read DO port into AL register
AND AL,F7H     AND bit 3 off in AL reg
OUT 0305H,AL   Write data in AL reg to DO port with only bit 3 set off
```

Testing Bits in a DI Register

Following are some 8088 assembly language coding techniques for testing the state of a DI register bit or an interface signal state. In the following example, we test bit 6 and assume that the DI port is at address 0307 hex.

```
MOV DX,0307H   Load DX reg with port address
IN AL,DX       Read DI port into AL reg
AND AL,40H     AND all bits off in AL reg except bit 6
JZ BITOFF      Jump to bit off routine
JMP BITON      Jump to bit on routine
```

If the signal is tested often or has a tight timing requirement, both code and time can be saved if the signal is assigned to bit 7 in a DI register. In this bit position, no logical operations need to be performed on the data because it can be tested using the jump on sign instruction. The following example illustrates the savings:

```
MOV DX,0307    Load DX reg with port address
IN AL,DX       Read DI port into AL reg
JS BIT70N      Jump to bit 7 on routine
JMP BIT70FF    Jump to bit 7 off routine
```

Other DI/DO Devices

Several devices provide DI/DO functions in single chips and can be easily attached to the system bus of the PC. Following is a list of devices that may be of use in an interface design. The operations and characteristics of these devices are specified in their data sheets and are not covered here.

Intel 8255A-5 (supports 24 DI/DO bits)

Zilog Z80-P10 (supports 24 DI/DO bits)

Motorola 6820 (supports 16 DI/DO bits)

Cards and Ports for Interfacing

For smaller interfacing projects, you may be able to use interfaces that exist on the PC system unit baseboard or on some of the feature cards that IBM provides for the PC. For example, consider the cassette port on the system unit. If your system is diskette based, the cassette port on your system is probably not being used. This interface provides a serial input point and a serial output point for the system. In addition, the cassette port has a set of relay points that can be controlled from the system's software. Two other feature cards are of interest also. The parallel printer port card can be used as a general-purpose digital input/output register group, and the game I/O port can be used as both a digital and an analog input interface.

Interfacing with the Cassette Port

The interface to the cassette-adapter function is through a 5-pin DIN-type connector at the rear of the system unit. Figure 8-11 defines the signals present on each of the pins in the connector.

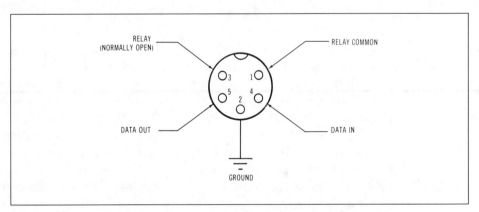

Figure 8-11. The cassette-connector signals.

The channel 2 output of the system's 8253-5 timer counter drives the circuit shown in Figure 8-12. The output of this circuit is then sent to the

DIN connector pin. As indicated in Figure 8-12, the output level of the signal can be selected by a jumper on the base system board. By proper programming control of the timer counter channel 2 output, data can be sent out on this port. With a simple modification, this circuit can generate a TTL signal at pin 5 of the DIN connector. The circuit will produce a TTL-level output signal if you replace the 4.7K resistor with a jumper wire, remove the 1200-ohm resistor, and set the jumper to select the 0.68-volt output. Note that the output level is inverted from the output of timer counter channel 2.

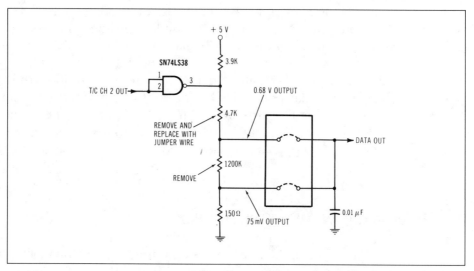

Figure 8-12. The cassette drive circuit with modifications for TTL output.

The data from the cassette input is read as an 8255A-5 I/O digital input port bit. The port address is 0062 hex, and the signal is on bit 4 of this port. Figure 8-13 illustrates the receiving circuit. Note that the input is capacitively coupled to the input of the noninverting operational amplifier. Thus, only ac signals are passed to the digital input port bit. This circuit can be modified to accept a TTL-level input signal. The simplest approach is to remove the 0.047 µF capacitor and 18K resistor that are in series with the output from the operational amplifier and place a jumper wire from the input side of the 0.047 µF capacitor to the cathode of the diode. A high level at the input of the connector will produce a 1 at the input to the port bit.

A digital output port bit of the 8255A-5 device also controls the motor relay on the cassette interface port. Writing a zero to bit 3 of I/O port address 0061 hex will activate and close the contact of the relay. However, the relay points can handle only 1 ampere of current and voltages that are

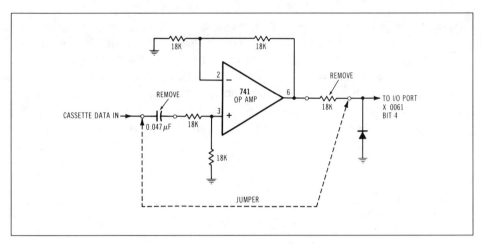

Figure 8-13. Cassette input circuit modified to accept TTL levels.

no higher than 50 volts. Do not use the relay to switch large dc currents because arcing will cause the system to fail.

Interfacing with the Parallel Printer Port Card

The parallel printer adapter card can be used as a general-purpose set of digital input and output points for interfacing other devices. This card provides an 8-bit digital output register that can also be read, a 4-bit output register that can be read and changed to an input register, a 5-bit input register, and an output register bit that can be enabled to generate an interrupt on level 7. The card's address can be modified so that it will not conflict with another printer port card in the system. All input/output port bits are available for interfacing on a 25-pin D-type connector at the back of the card.

Address Modification   The parallel printer port card normally decodes I/O port addresses 0378, 0379, and 037A hex. But the card can be easily modified such that the port addresses are moved to addresses 0278, 0279, and 027A hex. Inspection of the card and the circuit diagram, provided in the *IBM Technical Reference Manual*, reveals that the address modification can be implemented by deleting a single signal trace. A location for two jumper pins, called J1, is identified on the card. When the signal trace is deleted between these two pin positions, the new addresses are decoded.

An 8-Bit Output Port   An 8-bit digital output register is at address 0378 hex, or 0278 hex on a modified card. The output of this register is connected to the connector pin, as defined in Figure 8-14. Thus, an OUT instruction to either port address can write data directly to the connector pins. A one-bit written to the port will result in a high TTL level at the connector pin. The output of the digital output register, and the state of the connector pins that it is connected to, can be read through a digital input register at the same port addresses. The purpose of the input register is to verify that the digital output register was loaded properly. A simple modification on the card can convert this output port to an input port. To disable the output function of this port and use it as an input port, remove the ground connection on pin 1 of the U4 component (an SN74LS373) and tie this pin to +5 volts.

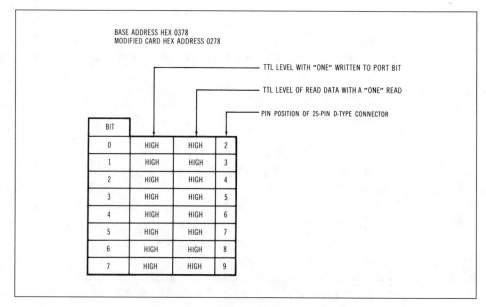

BASE ADDRESS HEX 0378
MODIFIED CARD HEX ADDRESS 0278

TTL LEVEL WITH "ONE" WRITTEN TO PORT BIT

TTL LEVEL OF READ DATA WITH A "ONE" READ

PIN POSITION OF 25-PIN D-TYPE CONNECTOR

BIT			
0	HIGH	HIGH	2
1	HIGH	HIGH	3
2	HIGH	HIGH	4
3	HIGH	HIGH	5
4	HIGH	HIGH	6
5	HIGH	HIGH	7
6	HIGH	HIGH	8
7	HIGH	HIGH	9

Figure 8-14. A printer-port 8-bit output port.

A 4-Bit Input/Output Port   A 5-bit digital output register is at address 037A hex, or 027A hex on a modified card. Four of the output bits are wired to the 25-pin D-type connector. The fifth bit is used to enable and disable interrupt requests on level 7. The output of the digital output register, and the connector pins that is attached to, can be read by issuing an IN command to the same port address.

Figure 8-15 defines the active levels of the register bits and the connector pins that they are attached to. Because the four output bits attached to the connector pins are driven with open-collector drivers, you can use these points as input bits. If the output register is set to a value that produces a high TTL logic level at the connector pins, the outputs may be driven low by incoming signals on these pins. Thus, an external driving circuit can control the level of these pins and, by using the input portion of this register, their states can be sensed. By programming the output bits to a high level, they can be used as input port bits.

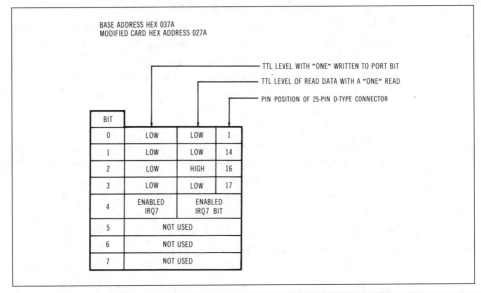

Figure 8-15. A printer-port 4-bit input/output port.

A 5-Bit Input Port   A 5-bit digital input register is at address 037B hex, or 027B hex on a modified card. Figure 18-6 defines the active signal levels and the connector-pin assignments for this register. Bit 7 of this register can be used to create an interrupt on level 7 if it is enabled by the port bit in the 5-bit input/output register port.

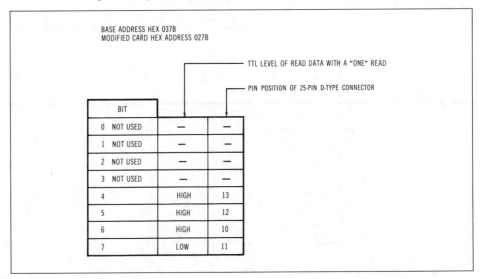

Figure 8-16. A printer-port 4-bit input port.

Interfacing with the Game Control Card

The game control card is designed to connect joysticks and game paddles to the PC, but its functions could be used to interface other devices to the PC. This card is an input-only device. It provides four digital input points and four resistance-sensing input points. These points are typically used to sense the trigger buttons and joystick potentiometer positions.

The game control card is decoded at address 0201 hex. An OUT instruction, with any data, will fire four one-shot circuit devices. The outputs of the one-shot devices can be read using an IN instruction at address 0201 hex. The input register at address 0201 hex also contains the four trigger inputs from the connector. The outputs of the one-shot circuits are determined by an RC time-constant circuit attached to each one-shot device. The resistive portion of the time-constant value is added by the user's interface. Thus, by measuring the length of the one-shot output and knowing the capacitive value of the circuit, you can determine the value of the resistance attached to the input.

The resistive element must be attached to +5 volts for the circuit to operate properly. Thus, any external condition that can be represented as a resistive value can be sensed and read using this circuit. For a joystick, the resistance represents the position of the joystick. Figure 8-17 defines the address and bit map of the card and shows the level and connector pin positions that correspond to each port bit.

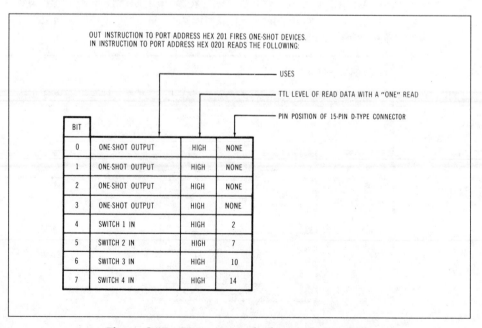

Figure 8-17. Game control adapter input port.

The relationship of the one-shot output pulse length and the external resistance is defined by the following equation:

$$Time = 24.2 + 0.011(Resistance)$$

The time is in microseconds. This equation will give only an approximate value in a range of resistive values from 0 to 100,000 ohms. If the cable length to the resistive value is long, extra capacitance and resistance will be added to the circuit, changing the time constant. The sample rate obtained using this circuit is dependent on the maximum resistive value being measured. The larger the resistance, the longer the time. It should also be pointed out that the one-shot circuits cannot be fired individually; all are fired at once. Figure 8-18 illustrates how an external resistive value can be measured.

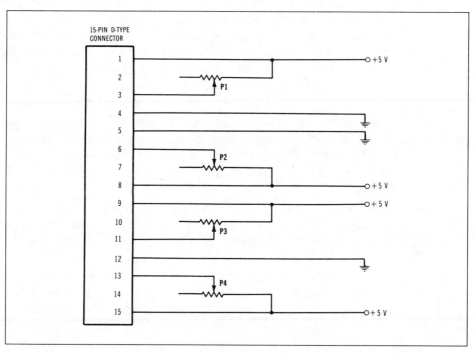

Figure 8-18. Resistor connections to the game port card connector.

Interface Signal Conditioning

In general, the typical interfaces for controlling and sensing information from the PC are digital, for example, digital input and output registers, interrupt-request inputs, timing and counting functions, and DMA data-transfer ports. All these interfaces, in addition to being digital, present a TTL logic-level interface.

If the devices that you are interfacing with are electronic-type equipment with digital interfaces, attachment may be straightforward. Sometimes, however, the interface that needs to be sensed and controlled is not digital, or the signals may be digital but not at TTL logic levels. Other times, digital signals must interface at great distances, creating special problems. We will investigate some common interfacing problems and present specific signal-conditioning circuits.

RS-232C Interface

RS-232C refers to a very old and popular standard typically used to attach data processing equipment to data communication equipment (for example, terminals to modems). The RS-232C standard covers the mechanical, electrical, and functional characteristics of the interface. Many interesting devices, such as terminals, plotters, logic analyzers, tape drives, and printers, use an RS-232C interface as an attachment method. If your interfacing application will be attaching a device to an RS-232C interface, you need to convert the TTL logic level signal to the non-TTL interface required by the RS-232C standard. A good example of the use of this interface can be obtained by inspecting the IBM PC serial-interface feature card. The circuit schematic and functional description are in the *IBM System Reference Manual.*

The RS-232C signal lines provide one-way data transmission on single-ended lines for distances up to 50 feet, at a maximum data rate of 20 kilobits per second. For a signal to be considered a positive-one level, it must exceed 5 volts but not be over 15 volts. A negative-level or zero-level signal must exceed −5 volts but not exceed −15 volts. Figure 8-19 is an example of a circuit that can be used to convert TTL logic level signals to RS-232C levels and convert RS-232C levels to TTL logic levels.

RS-423 Interface

The RS-423 interface is an improved version of the RS-232C interface. Many newer devices, particularly ones with high data-transmission rate requirements, support this interface. The RS-423 standard provides one-way single-ended data transmission at up to 100 kilobits per second at distances up to 40 feet.

The receiver is a balanced-line receiver and, thus, permits a ground potential difference between the driver and receiver. A logical one state

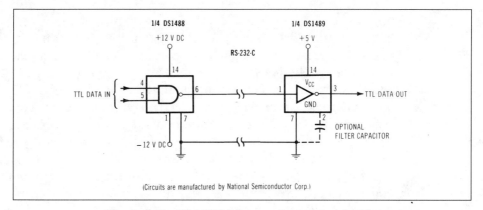

Figure 8-19. RS-232C driver and receiver circuit.

must exceed 4 volts but not exceed 6 volts. A logical zero must exceed −4 volts but not exceed −6 volts.

Figure 8-20 is an example of a circuit that can be used to convert TTL signals to an RS-423 interface and convert an RS-423 interface to TTL signals.

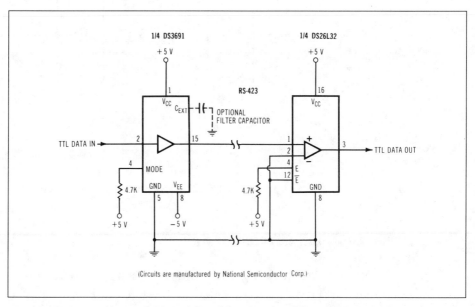

Figure 8-20. RS-423 driver and receiver circuit.

RS-422 Interface

The RS-422 standard is a further improvement of the RS-423 standard, permitting even higher data rates and a much greater distance between transmitter and receiver. The RS-422 standard provides one-way balanced-line transmission at data rates up to 10 megabits per second and at distances up to 1000 feet. Lower data rates permit data transmission at distances of up to 4000 feet. The interface permits driver outputs of ±2 volts to ±6 volts, and the receiver will detect input signals as low as 200 millivolts.

Figure 8-21 is an example of a circuit that can be used to convert TTL signals to an RS-422 interface and convert an RS-422 interface to TTL signals. Several manufacturers provide a tristate control on the driver circuit that permits data to be transmitted bidirectionally on a single pair of interface lines. This facility also enables a multidrop capability, in which several devices can receive and transmit data on a single pair of interface lines in half-duplex mode.

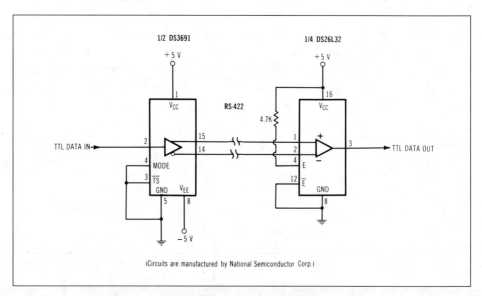

(Circuits are manufactured by National Semiconductor Corp.)

Figure 8-21. RS-422 driver and receiver circuit.

Current-Loop Data Transmission

Another frequently used transmission scheme that permits data to be transmitted over great distances is the current loop. With a current loop, the voltage levels are converted to currents in a closed-loop circuit. Because current-mode circuits are low-impedance circuits, they are less sensitive to noise and are often used to transmit signals in noisy environments. It is also possible to provide ground isolation between two different systems by using a current-loop scheme.

Figure 8-22 is an example of an isolated current-loop transmitter and receiver circuit. This circuit can be used to transmit data at rates up to 50 kilobytes per second and at distances up to 3000 feet. The distance is limited by the resistance of the loop wire. In this design, the loop resistance should not exceed 30 ohms. The use of the optical isolator is not limited to this circuit; this scheme can be used any time you need power isolation between systems or circuits that do not share the same ground or power system.

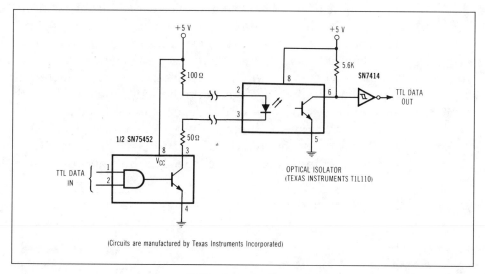

(Circuits are manufactured by Texas Instruments Incorporated)

Figure 8-22. Current-loop circuit.

Switch Sensing

Often, an interface design requires that switches be interfaced and sensed. These could be switches to indicate a movement, such as a limit switch, or operator-controlled panel switches that indicate an action should be performed by the system. A switch can be easily made to emit TTL signals for direct attachment to a normal TTL-circuit input. Figure 8-23 is an example of a switch that provides, when open, a 5-volt level to the circuit and presents, when closed, a ground level to the TTL input.

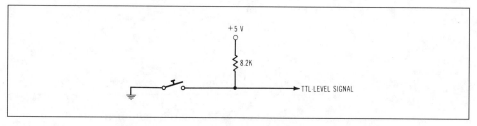

Figure 8-23. Switch to a TTL signal level circuit.

The most common problem with switch interfacing is switch bounce. When a mechanical switch is opened or closed, the contacts bounce and emit a burst of noise that the sensing circuits may interpret as a rapid opening and closing of the switch. There are several solutions to this problem. A common solution is to sample the state of the switch several times to determine if it has reached its final state. This approach works if the system has time to dedicate to a software sampling algorithm. A simple hardware solution can be obtained if the switch presents both a normally open contact and a normally closed contact.

Figure 8-24a shows a circuit for a switch that will not exhibit switch bounce. When the switch is activated, the first detected bounce sets a latch, thus eliminating bounce on the activation. Similarly, the latch is reset on the first bounce of the deactivation. This circuit works only with switches that have both normally open and normally closed contacts and that break the normally closed contact before the normally open contact is made. The timing chart in Figure 8-24b illustrates the principle.

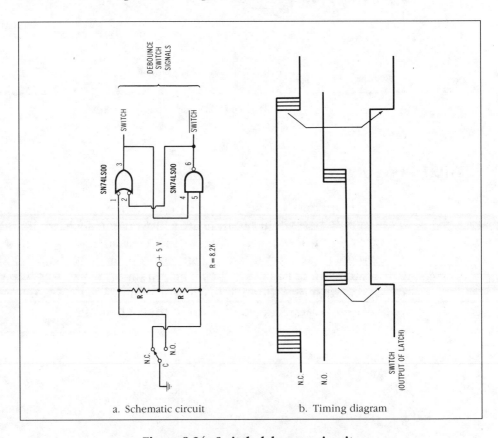

a. Schematic circuit   b. Timing diagram

Figure 8-24. Switch debounce circuit.

Indicator Driving

It is often necessary to present a visual indication of an event on an interface. For example, you may need to notify an operator that intervention is required or simply determine the status of a process. Following are a few examples of how TTL signals can be conditioned to drive some popular indicator types.

For low-level light output, light emitting diodes (LEDs) are an easily implemented solution. Several manufacturers provide LEDs that can be driven directly from standard TTL or S-type (Schottky) devices. Do not attach LEDs to LS-type devices or NMOS LSI devices because these devices normally do not have sufficient drive to operate an LED.

After an LED is tied to a TTL output, the output should not be used to drive the circuits because the LED will clamp the output at an invalid logic level and cause improper circuit operation. Thus, all signals that need to be sensed with an indicator should be buffered with a driving circuit. Figure 8-25 is an example of an LED and a circuit that can be driven from any TTL source.

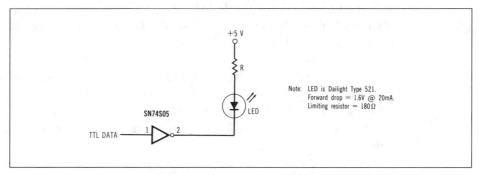

Figure 8-25. LED driver circuit.

When brighter indicators are required, an incandescent lamp can be used. Lamps of this type require much higher current and a special driver circuit. Figure 8-26 illustrates a lamp and circuit that can be driven from TTL signals.

When the displayed information is numeric data or hexadecimal characters, special display devices are needed. Several manufacturers provide DIP-type display devices that can be driven directly from a TTL source and can decode and display numeric or hex data directly from encoded TTL signals.

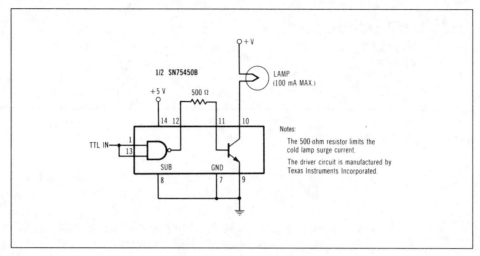

Figure 8-26. High-current lamp driver circuit.

Relay Driving

When an interface design needs to operate relays or solenoids, which in turn control higher power levels, special circuits are normally required because the devices typically cannot be driven directly from TTL signals. The current required to operate relays or a solenoid may be much more than can be provided by normal TTL circuits. In addition, the driving circuit usually requires special protection from the inductive kickback of the relay or solenoid coils. The SN75475 dual peripheral-driver device manufactured by Texas Instruments can operate a wide variety of relays and solenoids. The device can provide 300 milliamperes drive from voltages as high as 100 volts. In addition, it can be driven from a standard TTL circuit and provides an output clamp diode for transient suppression from inductive loads. Figure 8-27 illustrates how this circuit can be used to drive a relay.

Stepper Motors

Many times, an interface application requires that the PC control motion or move an object. A stepper motor is often used to power or move a shaft in precise increments, directions, and speed. It is capable of very accurate, repeated movements. Depending on the cost and design of the stepper motor, it can have as few as 12 steps and as many as 200 steps per

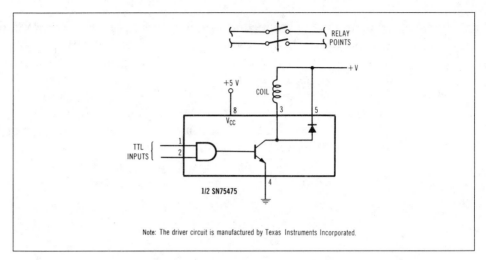

Figure 8-27. Relay driver circuit.

revolution. Stepper motors are manufactured in a wide range of sizes and torque capabilities. Several types of stepper motors are available; each has advantages and disadvantages.

Following is a brief list of manufacturers of stepper motors. In most cases, the manufacturers will provide data sheets describing the drivers and control sequences required for proper operation of the motors.

Portescap U.S., Micromotor Division, 31 Fairfield Place, West Caldwell, New Jersey 07006

Oriental Motor U.S.A. Corporation, 2701 Toledo Street, Torrance, California 90503

Airpax North American Philips Controls Corporation, Chesire Division, Chesire Industrial Park, Chesire, Connecticut 06410

Litton Clifton Precision, Marple at Broadway, Clifton Heights, Pennsylvania 19018

Superior Electric, 1200 Middle Street, Bristol, Connecticut 06010

Permanent-Magnet Stepping Motor

The permanent-magnet stepping motor operates by having a set of permanent magnets attached to the rotor of the motor. A set of windings can be energized on the stator portion of the motor. The north and south poles of the rotor's permanent magnets rotate to a position where the north and south poles of the stator and rotor line up because unlike poles attract. Rotation is achieved by energizing adjacent sets of stator windings and reversing the currents in other windings. The rotor will then move to the new position where the unlike poles can line up. By properly energizing and reversing the currents in the stator windings, a continuous rotation of the shaft can be obtained.

The major disadvantage of this type of stepper motor is the requirement of reversing the currents in the stator windings. This typically requires a power supply with both a positive and a negative output, or relatively complex drive circuits. The major advantages are low cost and the shaft being held in its last position by the permanent magnet when the power is removed.

Bifilar Stepping Motor

The bifilar stepping motor is similar to the permanent magnet motor. The major difference is in the design of the stator pole windings; each stator pole position has two windings. With this design, a stator pole may be either a north pole or a south pole, depending on which winding is energized. The major advantage of this type of motor is its capability of operating from a single-output dc power supply. This motor also has a permanent magnet rotor and, thus, will stay in the last position stepped to when power is removed.

Variable-Reluctance Stepping Motor

A variable-reluctance stepping motor does not use a permanent magnet in the rotor. The rotor is moved by the magnetic attraction of the rotor to the energized poles of the stator. Because there is no permanent magnet, this type of stepper motor will not hold the shaft in the last stepped position. Thus, to maintain a fixed position, the driving circuits must maintain power to the appropriate poles of the motor.

Pulse Stepper Motor

In a pulse stepper motor, the stepping phase control and the winding coiled drivers are part of the motor. To step the motor one position, a single TTL pulse can be sent to the motor for each step. Increasing and decreasing the pulse rate to the motor will accelerate and decelerate the motor.

Analog-to-Digital Conversion

Much of the information concerning the state of an interface is represented as a voltage that is proportional to an external condition. This condition is converted by a transducer into a current or voltage output, which cannot be sensed with digital signals. To transform the voltage or current level into a digital value, a device called an analog-to-digital converter (ADC) is used. Rapid advancements have been made in the design of these devices, and they are now highly integrated. Many ADC devices now incorporate a precision voltage reference, an analog multiplexer, and a microprocessor bus port. The following characteristics of ADC devices should be considered when selecting one for an interfacing application.

What is the input range of the ADC? This specification is a concern for two reasons. First, it determines if you can attach the input directly to your source. In general, this will not be the case because the source may produce a voltage level that is too large or small to be directly sensed. If the input level is too small, you have to amplify the signal using a positive-gain operational amplifier. If the input signal is too large, a simple precision resistor-divider network can be added. Second, to determine the minimum value that can be measured, you can divide the range by the resolution. For example, if the input you want to measure is 0 to 5 volts, and the device has 8 bits of resolution, the minimal measurable value is 5 divided by 256, or 0.0195 volt.

Can the ADC measure differential, positive, and negative voltages? This may be important, particularly if the transducer output is not referenced to a known ground or it outputs either negative voltages or positive and negative voltages.

Does the ADC contain a precision voltage reference for calibration? Most conversion techniques require a precision voltage reference. If it is not part of the device, it will have to be added as a separate component, thus adding to the cost and using card space.

What is the offset error introduced by the ADC? If the voltage level you are trying to measure is small, the offset error will be of concern. The offset error must be much smaller than the smallest voltage to be measured. Many devices provide mechanisms for correcting the offset error.

What kind of load does the ADC present to the source that it will be sensing? You must ensure that the device does not overload the source and alter the true value being measured. If this is the case, you can add a unity-gain operational amplifier with high-input impedance to buffer the input to the device. Note that this can introduce an additional offset error in the system.

How many bits of resolution can the ADC provide over the input range? As mentioned, the number of bits of resolution determines the minimum value that can be measured by the system. For example, an 8-bit device measures 256 levels, and a 12-bit device measures 4096 levels over the voltage range of the input.

How is the digital data presented to the system? This may be important for two reasons. First, if the device provides a microprocessor bus port, it will be easy to attach to the PC. Second, if it is difficult to obtain the data from the device, this will have an adverse effect on the minimum sample rate that can be achieved by the system. If the conversion rate is very fast, but a complicated set of steps are required to retrieve the data, the total performance of the system is affected. The sample rate is the sum of both steps. Thus, to maintain a high sample rate for the system, the data access method must be simple and fast.

How long does it take the ADC to convert an analog signal to a digital value? This specification is important because it determines the rate at which the device can sample and convert the analog data to a digital value. If a rapidly changing input will be sensed, the conversion rate must be fast. Typically, the faster the conversion speed, the more expensive the device. Some devices have a conversion speed that is dependent on the required resolution or the input signal magnitude.

Digital-to-Analog Conversion

Many times, an interface design requires that the PC generate and control a voltage or current source. This function is typically performed by a digital-to-analog converter (DAC) device. These devices typically accept a binary value from a system such as the PC and generate an output voltage proportional to the digital input value. DAC devices have specifications similar to those of ADC devices. In general, the output of a DAC does not provide the voltage range or power required to drive a device. Thus, DAC devices are usually interfaced with some type of amplifier that provides the voltage gain and output power needed in the design. DAC devices are now available with a microprocessor port for control and precision voltage-reference sources.

Manufacturers of DAC and ADC Devices

Most large semiconductor manufacturers provide a wide range of ADC and DAC devices. These manufacturers provide detailed data sheets and, in many cases, application notes on how the devices can be attached to microprocessors and used. Following is a brief list of manufacturers and some of the more popular devices provided by each.

National Semiconductor Corporation, P.O. Box 60676, Sunnyvale, California 94088—National Semiconductor provides a large range of devices and transducers. In addition, information on these devices and application notes are available by ordering the National Semiconductor *Data Acquisition Handbook*. Its present cost is $7.00.

Texas Instruments Incorporated, Literature Response Center, P.O. Box 202129, Dallas, Texas 75220—Texas Instruments has recently introduced a family of low-cost 8-bit analog-to-digital converters: the TL530, TL531, TL532, and TL533. They are designed for attachment to a microprocessor. All incorporate an analog multiplexer and some incorporate digital input and output ports.

Motorola Semiconductor Products, Inc., P.O. Box 52073, Phoenix, Arizona 85072-2073—Motorola offers a large variety of ADC and DAC devices that can be attached to a microprocessor. Three devices that are of particular interest follow. The MC14435 low-power analog-to-digital convertor is a CMOS part with a multiplex BCD output. It supports 3 1/2 digits of resolution. The MC14431 12-bit analog-to-digital convertor subsystem is a CMOS device. The MC14051B 8-channel analog multiplexer is a CMOS low-power device.

Analog Devices, P.O. Box 9106, Norwood, Massachusetts 02062-9106—This company provides a family of DAC and ADC devices. Two devices that may be of interest follow. The AD571 is a high-speed 10-bit analog-to-digital convertor that contains a precision voltage reference and has a tristate microprocessor-compatible output bus. The device can be configured to support a 10-volt input range. The AD558 is a digital-to-analog convertor that supports 8 bits of resolution at a maximum output voltage of 2.56 volts. The device supports a microprocessor input bus capability for setting output levels.

Chapter 9

PC and XT Bus Extension and Monitoring

BOTH THE PC AND THE XT are designed with five or eight system-bus card slots. Even in a minimum diskette-based system, two are used: one for the display adapter and one for the diskette adapter. The remaining three slots can be used up quickly by adding three commonly used features: a serial port, a printer port, and extra memory. Because PC system-bus card slots are so scarce, a good design project would be to devise a method of extending the system-bus outside the system unit so that additional card slots could be provided. If your interface design will not fit on a PC card, bus extension allows you to use another enclosure that is not limited in space or power.

This chapter investigates two designs that can be used to extend the PC's system bus. The first design is the simplest but has some limitations. This design can be safely used to extend the system bus approximately 3 feet and drive four card slots. If a modest increase in the number of system-bus card slots is required, this method is recommended. The second design is more complex but has the advantages of driving an 8-foot interface between the system unit and the extended card slots and supporting up to ten additional card slots. Also included in this chapter are techniques that could be useful in bus conversions, such as PC bus to S-100 bus. This same approach can be used to extend PC AT and PS/2 micro channel buses.

A Simple Bus Extender Design

We will cover the simple design first, then alter it to the higher function design. The first design involves two parts: a card that fits in one of the system unit's card slots and drives and receives the bus from the extended card slots, and a card that receives and drives the output of the system unit card and contains the new card slots. Figure 9-1 illustrates the components and the concept of the design.

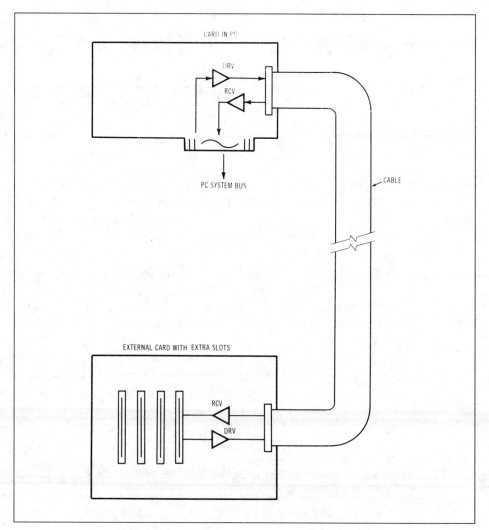

Figure 9-1. A bus extender circuit concept.

Most of the signals on the PC bus can be handled quite simply. The basic concept is to repower and drive output signals from the bus onto the cable. The drive circuit's primary function is to shunt the capacitance of the cable so that it is not reflected on the system bus, which would add delay and signal distortion to the system unit's bus. At the other end of the cable, on a new card slot, the signal is received and repowered to drive the extra slots.

Similarly, the receiver circuit shunts the capacitance of the cable from the new card slots, providing a quiet bus for attaching feature cards in the new slots. Input signals from the extra card slots are similarly treated; that is, they are repowered and driven onto the cable, then received, repowered, and driven onto the system bus. Several circuits could be used to perform the bus repower function; suitable devices are the SN74S240 and SN74LS240 octal buffers and line drivers manufactured by Texas Instruments. These two circuits are identical, except in their signal delay and power consumption.

The SN74S240 has a typical signal delay of 4.5 nanoseconds and a maximum delay of 7 nanoseconds. The SN74LS240 has a typical delay of 12 nanoseconds and a maximum delay of 18 nanoseconds. Both circuits are used in the design: the SN74S240 on signals that cannot tolerate much delay, and the SN74LS240 on signals that are less timing dependent.

Because signals are repowered twice in this design, there is a 10 to 15 nanosecond delay in the bus cycle in the extended bus card slots. This delay is 10 to 15 nanoseconds. This means that memory and I/O-port-address data-access times are shortened by this amount. Because this delay is small, in most cases it will have no effect. Typically, a wide timing margin is designed into feature cards. Figure 9-2 is a block diagram of the signals being repowered.

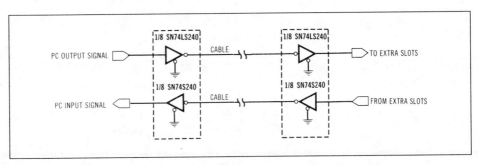

Figure 9-2. Typical driver and receiver circuit for bus extension.

The scheme shown in Figure 9-2 works well for everything except the system data bus. The eight signal lines of the system bus are bidirectional. At first glance, it would appear that a simple solution is to insert a bus transceiver circuit, such as the SN74LS245 octal bus transceiver (manufactured by Texas Instruments). A problem arises when the signals are required to control the transceiver. Both an enable signal and a direction signal are required. The bus transceiver is normally enabled by an address decode, and its direction is controlled by either the IOR or MEMR bus-control signals. Because we don't know what memory or I/O addresses will be used in the extra bus slots, we cannot generate for the transceiver an enable control signal that will work under all conditions. This is a simple design, so the solution is to simply not repower the data-bus lines. The system data-bus signals have sufficient drive to drive the extended card slots as long as there are just a few slots.

The major problem is the extra bus capacitance added by the cable and extra card slots. The extra capacitance delays the data-bus signals and distorts the signal by creating signal undershot. To minimize these problems, a termination circuit, shown in Figure 9-3, can be added to the data bus. This circuit consists of a 220-ohm resistor in series with a 43-picofarad capacitor. One end is tied to the bus line, and the other end is tied to +5 volts. Because the capacitor acts as an open circuit to the steady-state condition of the bus line, the 220-ohm resistor is not tied to the line, except during signal transitions. When the line begins a transition from high to low, the capacitor attaches the load resistor to the circuit, which lowers the circuit's impedance. Thus, the charge stored in the capacitance of the system is dissipated in the lower-impedance circuit and reduces the effect of the undershot.

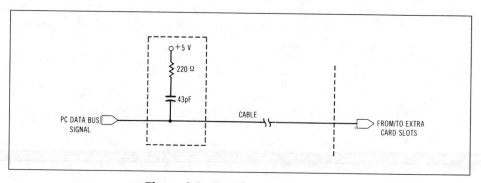

Figure 9-3. Data-bus terminator.

Figures 9-4 and 9-5 are circuit schematics of a simple bus extender design that can drive a 3-foot cable and four card slots. In the design, we assume that the power for the new card slots comes from the system unit. If the new feature cards take a reasonable amount of power, you should not have any difficulty driving them from the system unit's power supply. All system unit power levels are available in the system unit's data-bus card slots and can be easily cabled to the new card slots. Be sure to use heavy gauge wire or multiple wires or both when cabling the power and ground signals to extra card slots. In addition, the power levels should be decoupled as shown in the circuit diagram.

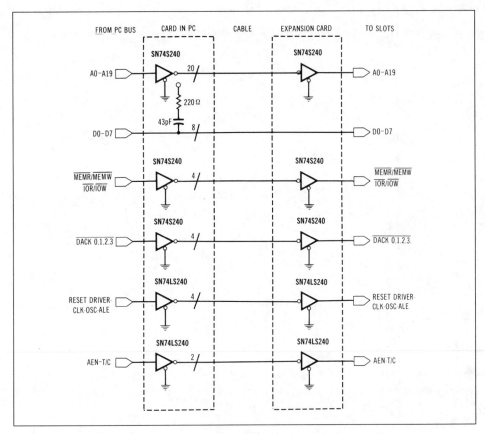

Figure 9-4. Output signals in the bus extension design.

When wiring the signals through the connector and cable, it is recommended that a separate ground lead be provided for each signal. If possible, the ground lead should be placed next to each signal. A better solution is to use twisted-pair cable for the signals and run one signal on one of the signal pairs and run ground on the other signal pair.

An Enhanced Bus Extender Design

If you are not happy with the limitations of the first design, the following modifications will be of interest. The next design enables the use of a longer cable (up to 8 feet) and can drive up to ten extra card slots.

The major problem is the capacitance and signal distortion created by the cable. For all unidirectional signals in the bus, the previous design is sufficient when one small change is made. To reduce the effect of signal

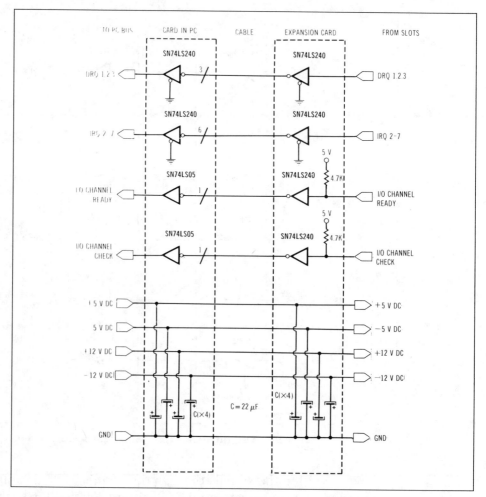

Figure 9-5. Input signals and power in the bus extension design.

undershot, a 270-ohm series resistor can be placed in the driving end of each signal. Figure 9-6 illustrates how these signals are driven and received with the damping resistor. Because the maximum input and low-level current of the drivers is 200 microamperes and the series resistance is 270 ohms, the low-level signals are lifted off from ground by 54 millivolts. The ground shift is not sufficient to cause a problem at the receiver because the receiver has a low-level margin of 800 millivolts before it switches.

The data bus needs to be repowered in this design because the cable and the number of extra card slots add too much capacitance to ensure reliable operation. Figure 9-7 illustrates the design used to repower the system data bus. Only one line is shown because all 8 signals require the same circuit. The basic principle of this circuit is to sense that data from

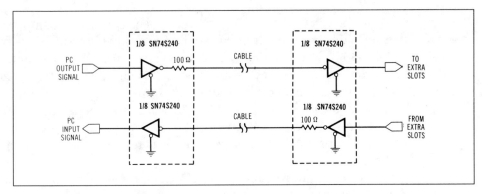

Figure 9-6. Driver and receiver circuit modified for greater distance.

the expansion-interface card slots is being transmitted and to allow the data to drive the bus only if the data is sensed on the other side of the circuit and it is a read operation. Similarly, data is transmitted only if it is a write operation.

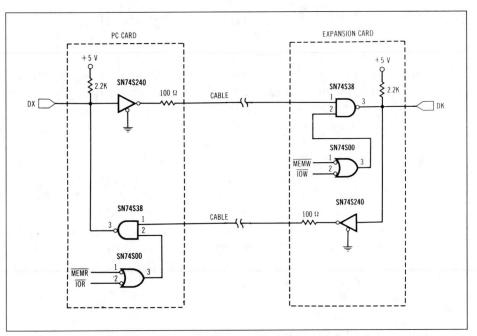

Figure 9-7. Circuit for repowering the data bus.

The circuit doubles the number of data lines from 8 to 16; thus, the cable is larger. The data-bus lines are also delayed in both directions. The maximum circuit delay is 7 nanoseconds for the SN74S240 and 10 nanoseconds for the SN74S38 open-collector buffer driver. This gives a total of 17 nanoseconds, but at least another 10 nanoseconds should be added due to the capacitance of the cable. This circuit uses a damping resistor in series with the signal lines. The value is reduced to 100 ohms because the SN74S38 has only a 400-millivolt margin before it will switch.

The only potential problem with this circuit is the tighter access-time requirements caused by the loss of approximately 27 nanoseconds from circuit and cable delay. Most feature cards have more than sufficient timing margin in their design, so this should not be a problem. If it does become a problem, a simple solution is to swap the card with one in the system unit.

Another interesting characteristic of the enhanced bus extension design's data-bus repowering circuit is that it generates a split data bus, with a data bus in and a separate data bus out. This could be a useful function if you are interested in converting the PC data bus into an S-100 bus because the S-100 bus requires a separate data bus in and out.

Hardware and Software for Testing Designs

After a design is completed and built, it must be tested and debugged. Rarely does a design operate correctly the first time it is tried, particularly if the design is complex. The opportunity for errors—from simple wiring errors, improperly assigned component pins, and circuit loading and timing problems to a faulty design concept—is great. In this section, we discuss hardware-support circuit designs and software that will aid you in inspecting and verifying the proper operation of your designs.

First, a smart card extender design is presented. This design detects all types of bus cycles directed at port address or memory address locations. It displays data to be written to or read from any specified port address or memory location and generates an oscilloscope synch signal based on bus conditions and specified external conditions. Second, the functions and capabilities of the IBM DEBUG monitor supplied with IBM DOS are summarized.

Smart Card Extender Design

This section describes how a simple card extender can be enhanced to provide information on the operation of the system bus. This information can then be used to assist in debugging a new PC bus adapter design.

Functional Description   Card extenders are used to extend the bus in a system unit card slot above the rest of the cards in the unit. The card being debugged is then inserted into the top of the extender card so that it is now above the rest of the cards and is easy to access for inspection and signal probing.

Typically, no circuitry is on an extender card; bus signals are simply bused to the connector at the top of the card, where the card being tested is inserted. By adding a small amount of circuitry on an extender card, you can create a powerful debugging aid. This is simple to do because all system-bus signals are already available on the extender card.

The circuitry can be used to detect the type of bus cycle being issued by the 8088 or DMA controller. Further, it can be used to determine if the bus cycle is directed to any specific port or memory location, and it can trap and display the data on the bus associated with the specific bus cycle. This can be done ''on the fly'' without affecting normal performance or operation of the software or hardware being debugged.

This function can be used to determine if the software is accessing the correct ports or memory locations. When a specified set of conditions on the bus and the interface is detected, the circuitry issues a sync pulse that can be used to trigger an oscilloscope. Thus, sync signals can be generated on both hardware and software conditions to aid in debugging. The sync signal also sets a latch and an indicator, signaling the event has occurred. This type of circuitry is extremely useful when a circuit design operates correctly only at full speed and cannot be easily traced or single-stepped under program control. The circuit is designed so that the compare conditions can be set either with DIP switches or through programmable digital output port bits.

Figure 9-8 is a block diagram of the circuitry used to implement the smart extender card function. The heart of the design is a 32-bit compare circuit, which compares the state of the 32 input signals against the state of either a set of 32 DIP switches or the output of 32 bits of the digital output registers. If the states of the two sides of the comparator are the same, an output pulse equal to the minimum duration of the compare time is issued.

The following signals are fed to the signal input side of the compare circuit:

A0 through A19	Bus address bits
$\overline{\text{IOW}}$	Bus-I/O-Write signal
$\overline{\text{IOR}}$	Bus-I/O-Read signal
$\overline{\text{MEMW}}$	Bus-Memory-Write signal
$\overline{\text{MEMR}}$	Bus-Memory-Read signal
EXT 1	External signal 1
EXT 2	External signal 2

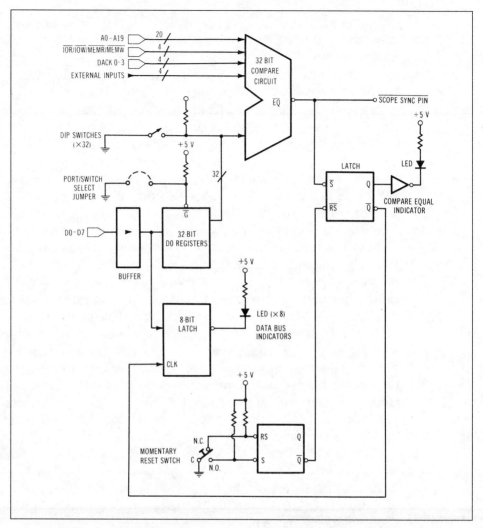

Figure 9-8. Block diagram of the smart card extender circuits.

EXT 3	External signal 3
EXT 4	External signal 4
$\overline{\text{DACK0}}$	Bus Signal DMA Acknowledge Channel 0
$\overline{\text{DACK1}}$	Bus Signal DMA Acknowledge Channel 1
$\overline{\text{DACK2}}$	Bus Signal DMA Acknowledge Channel 2
$\overline{\text{DACK3}}$	Bus Signal DMA Acknowledge Channel 3

A switch or digital output (DO) register bit corresponding to each of these signals is fed into the other side of the compare circuit. By properly setting the switches or the digital output register bits, a compare occurs only when these signals equal the value in the switches or the DO bits. Thus, by setting the switches or the DO registers, you can specify that a sync signal be generated only on a specific set of bus conditions and the state of four external conditions.

To select between the use of the switches or the programmable DO register, a simple jumper is either removed or added. The output of the compare circuit is fed to a sync pin on the card and is also used to set a latch. The latch then drives an LED indicator. The latch and indicator can be reset by activating a momentary push-button switch. This function provides a visual indication (without the need of an oscilloscope) that a specific set of conditions did occur.

Following is an example of how this circuit may be used. Suppose that we want to examine, with an oscilloscope, the design's operation when a DMA cycle (on channel 3) reads data from a specific memory location. In addition, the test is further conditioned by an external signal attached to external input number 1. To do this, a sync signal is required. First, we need to set the address of the memory location of interest in the DIP switches or the DO port register bits. Next, the switch corresponding to DACK3 would be set to its active state. Because it is a DMA cycle with a memory read and write to I/O, the MEMR and IOW DIP switches (or DO bits) are set active. To include the external signal in the sync condition, its proper level is set in the DIP switch or DO bit that corresponds to external input number 1. The remaining external inputs are pulled high by the pull-up resistors. The DIP switches or DO bits are set inactive. The circuit now generates a sync pulse each time the set conditions are detected. Further, the latch and indicator are set the first time the condition appears. To determine if the condition is looping or repetitive, press the reset button. If the indicator comes on again or does not go out, the condition is being repeated.

Another feature of this circuit is the capability to capture data on the system data bus on the back edge of the sync pulse and display the bus data in the LED indicators. The back edge of the sync signal is used because the MEMR, MEMW, IOR, and IOW signals can be a condition of the compare, and data is always valid on the back edges of these bus signals.

Circuit Description   Figure 9-9 is the circuit schematic of the address decode and port write signals for the eight digital output registers used to specify the compare condition from software. The four decoded port addresses are 03E0, 03E1, 03E2, and 03E3 hex. The data bus is also buffered here with the SN74LS244 octal driver.

Figures 9-10 and 9-11 show the circuit schematic diagrams for the digital output port registers. The output registers are formed using SN74LS374 octal D-type latches with tristate outputs. Note that the multiplex function between the switches and output port bits is accomplished

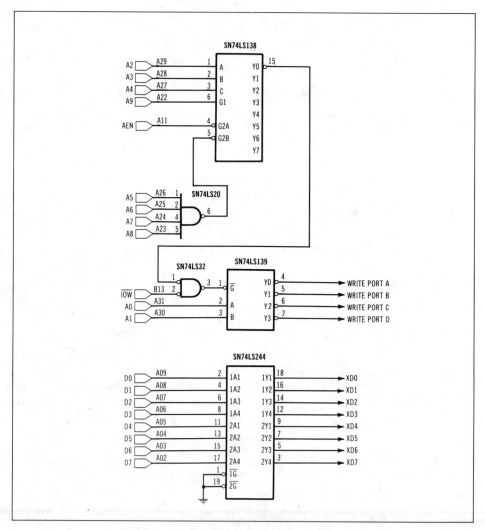

**Figure 9-9. Smart card extender bus repower and
port decode circuits.**

using the tristate function of the octal latches. When the switches will be
used, the output of the octal latches is disabled by removing a jumper. In
this state, the switches drive the input to the compare circuits and the DO
outputs are removed from the circuit. When a switch is on, or closed, it
corresponds to an active low-level compare condition.

When the compare conditions will be specified from the digital output port bits, the jumper is added, enabling the output of the octal latches.
Before the DO register bits can properly drive the compare circuits, all
switches must be opened. With all switches open, or off, the compare condition may now be specified under program control by writing the proper

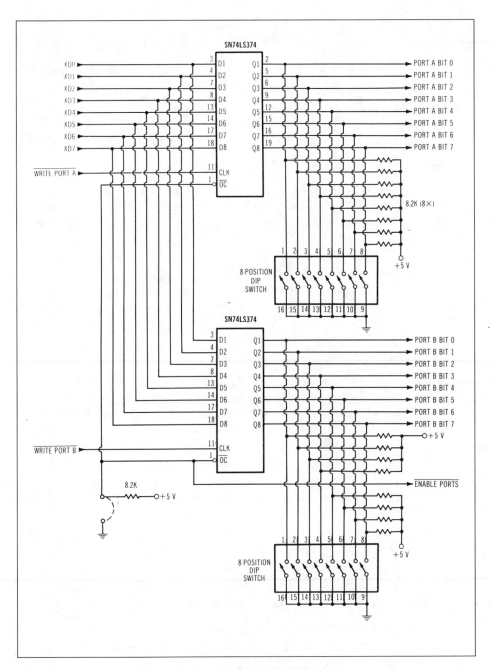

**Figure 9-10. Port bits and switch compare
selector schematic diagram.**

bit patterns to the DO register ports using the 8088 microprocessor OUT
instruction. A one written to a port bit corresponds to a high-level compare condition on the associated input signal.

Figure 9-12 (Parts A and B) is the circuit schematic for the compare circuit. This function is implemented using the SN74LS688 octal compare device. This device compares the value of the two bytes and generates a compare equal signal if the two bytes are equal. Four such devices form the required 32-bit compare function. The outputs of each of the four SN74LS688 octal compare devices are ANDed together. Thus, all four devices must have a compare equal condition before a sync signal is generated.

Figure 9-13 is the circuit schematic for the compare equal latch and indicator and the data-bus latches and indicators. When a compare equal signal is generated, it is fed to three portions of the circuitry. First, it goes to the sync pin, where it can be used as a sync or a trigger for an oscilloscope.

Second, the signal is used to set a latch that, in turn, drives an LED indicator. The latch and indicator may be reset from a momentary-on push-button switch on the card. The indicator provides a visual indication of a compare condition, without using an oscilloscope. Even if the compare condition is very short or occurs only once, it will be detected and indicated in the LED. The reset button allows the latched compare condition to be reset so that the next condition selected can be detected. The reset button can also be used to determine if an event occurs repeatedly. To determine this condition, simply select the condition that you want to detect. When it lights the indicator, press the reset button. If the indicator does not go out or comes back on, the event is looping and occurring repeatedly.

The last place that the compare equal signal is used is in the data-bus capture and indicator circuits. In this circuit, the back edge of the compare equal or sync signal is used to latch the status of the system data bus. When the bus is captured in the latches, its value is indicated in the eight LEDs attached to the latch outputs. The back edge of the sync or compare signal is used because it can be conditioned with $\overline{IOR}$, $\overline{IOW}$, $\overline{MEMR}$, or $\overline{MEMW}$. To obtain valid data-bus status on a bus cycle, you must include one of the preceding bus command signals to ensure that the sample takes place when the data bus contains valid data.

I/O Port Address and Bit Definitions   Following is a summary of the digital output addresses and the definition of the signals that each bit controls in the compare circuit.

DO port address 03E0 hex
Bit 0   Bus address bit 0

Bit 1   Bus address bit 1

Bit 2   Bus address bit 2

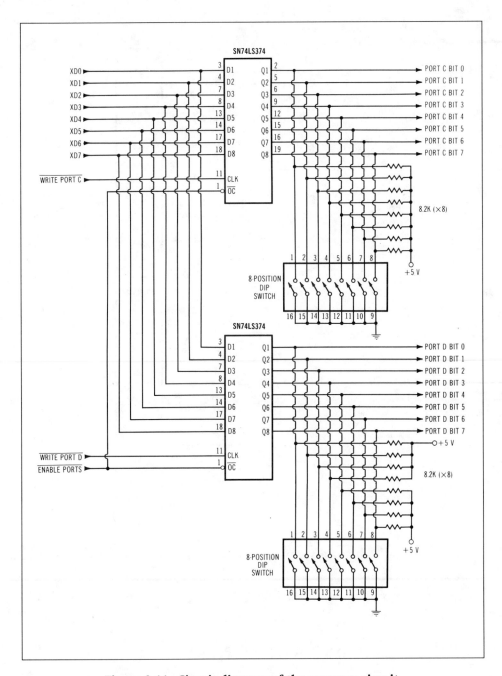

Figure 9-11. Circuit diagram of the compare circuit.

Bit 3   Bus address bit 3
Bit 4   Bus address bit 4
Bit 5   Bus address bit 5

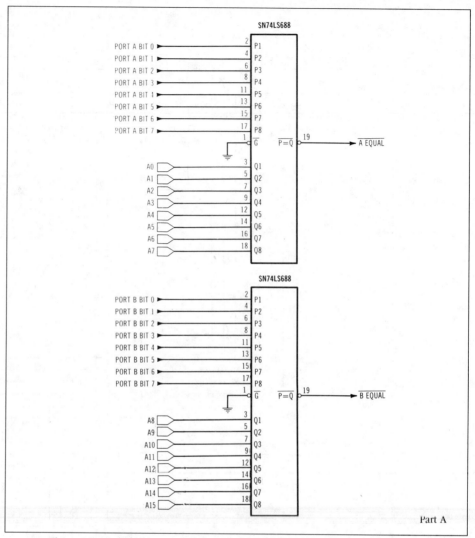

Figure 9-12. Diagram of the compare latch and indicators circuit.

| Bit 6 | Bus address bit 6 |
| Bit 7 | Bus address bit 7 |

DO port B address 03E1 hex

Bit 0	Bus address bit 8
Bit 1	Bus address bit 9
Bit 2	Bus address bit 10
Bit 3	Bus address bit 11
Bit 4	Bus address bit 12

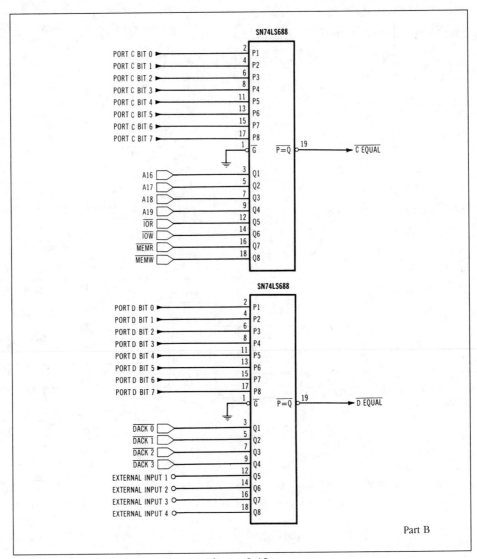

Figure 9-12.

Bit 5	Bus address bit 13
Bit 6	Bus address bit 14
Bit 7	Bus address bit 15

DO port C address 03E2 hex

Bit 0	Bus address bit 16
Bit 1	Bus address bit 17
Bit 2	Bus address bit 18

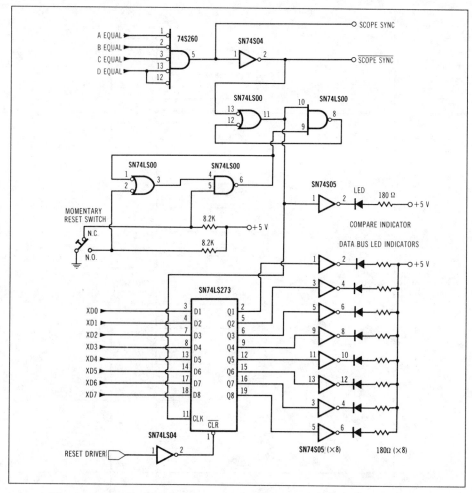

Figure 9-13. Diagram of the compare latch and indicators circuit.

Bit 3	Bus address bit 19
Bit 4	Bus signal $\overline{\text{IOR}}$ (negative active)
Bit 5	Bus signal $\overline{\text{IOW}}$ (negative active)
Bit 6	Bus signal $\overline{\text{MEMR}}$ (negative active)
Bit 7	Bus signal $\overline{\text{MEMW}}$ (negative active)

DO port D address 03E3 hex

Bit 0	Bus signal $\overline{\text{DACK0}}$ (negative active)
Bit 1	Bus signal $\overline{\text{DACK1}}$ (negative active)
Bit 2	Bus signal $\overline{\text{DACK2}}$ (negative active)
Bit 3	Bus signal $\overline{\text{DACK3}}$ (negative active)

Bit 4   External input 1

Bit 5   External input 2

Bit 6   External input 3

Bit 7   External input 4

DOS Debug Program

The DEBUG program is provided as part of the IBM DOS package. This program is extremely useful in debugging both hardware and software. It provides a system debug monitor with many useful functions. Following is a summary of the commands available in DEBUG:

- Compare two blocks of system memory
- Display the contents of system memory
- Display and modify the contents of system memory
- Fill memory with a data byte or data from a string of bytes
- Go and execute the program at a specified address
- Specify break points in a program and display the system's status
- Load data from a diskette into memory
- Move the contents of memory from one location to another
- Send data to an I/O port
- Display the contents of the 8088 registers and flags
- Search system memory for data specified in a string
- Trace the execution of a program and display the 8088 MPU status
- Disassemble an assembly language program
- Write a block of system memory to a diskette

You will find a full description of DEBUG and its capabilities in section 6 of the *IBM Disk Operating System Manual.*

Chapter 10

PC AT System and Bus Architecture

THE PC AT was a significant extension to the expansion slot bus architecture of the PC and PC XT. One of the most important features of the new AT bus was its backward compatibility with the PC and XT bus. Thus, adapter boards designed for the PC and XT bus architecture can still be used in AT expansion bus slots.

The AT expansion bus is often called ISA (Industry Standard Architecture). Following are the key new attributes of the PC AT (or ISA) bus:

- Addition of a second 2-by-18 signal bus extension slot adjacent to the existing 2-by-31 PC and XT bus slot
- Support for both 8- and 16-bit wide data buses
- Support for both 20- and 24-bit memory addressing
- Addition of three 16-bit DMA channels
- Addition of six more interrupt level requests
- Higher speed bus cycles
- Support for zero wait-state I/O bus cycles
- Support for alternate bus masters
- Support for larger adapter boards

PC AT and ISA Bus Slot Configuration

The original IBM PC AT supported a total of eight bus expansion slots, the same as the PC XT. Two slots were 8-bit bus slots with 62-pin card-edge connectors identical to the PC XT; six slots were 16 bits made up of one 62-pin card-edge connector XT slot and one 36-pin AT extension card-edge connector. Most AT and ISA bus compatible systems retain this slot arrangement. Figure 10-1 illustrates the AT slot configuration. Figure 10-2 illustrates the signal names and card-edge pin definitions for the AT bus expansion slots. Figure 10-3 illustrates the signal names and card-edge pin definitions for the PC AT 8-bit and XT compatible bus 62-pin connector.

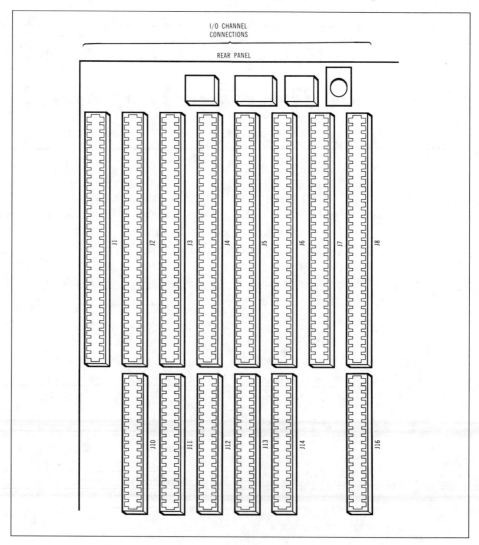

Figure 10-1. PC AT and ISA bus slot configuration.

Signal Additions and Changes in XT Slots

The 62-pin edge-connector XT compatible slots have four changes. First, the unused signal on B8 is now called 0WS (zero wait state). This signal is

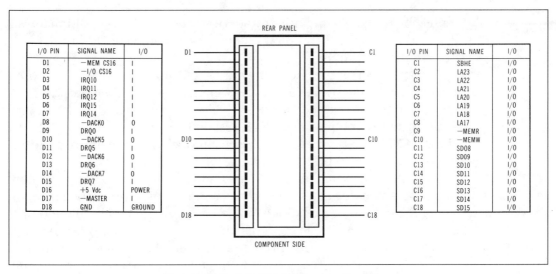

Figure 10-2. PC AT 16-bit extension slot.

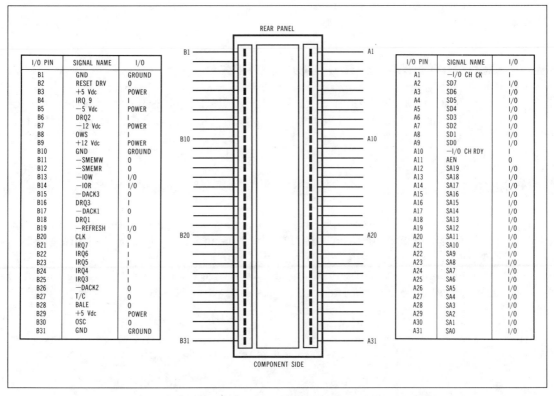

Figure 10-3. 62-signal 8-bit bus slot definition for the PC AT.

an active low input signal and should be driven with an open collector or tristate device capable of sinking 20 milliamps. This signal is used to force the present 16-bit bus memory cycle to proceed with no additional wait states. If the bus cycle is an 8-bit memory cycle, only two additional wait states are inserted in the cycle.

Second, interrupt request signal 2 (IRQ2) on pin B4 became IRQ9. Interrupt level 2 is now used to accept interrupts from the second 8259A interrupt controller added in the PC AT design. Third, the MEMR and MEMW signals on pins B12 and B11, respectively, are changed to SMEMR and SMEMW. These signals are only activated when the memory cycle address is below the 20-bit address range of 1M.

Last, the CLK signal on pin B20 is no longer 4.77 MHz. This pin now reflects the processor clock rate on the system's microprocessor, the substrate of the processor clock, or a totally independent clock. In the newer high clock rate 286 and 386 systems, the clock rate can be one-half, one-third, or one-fourth the rate of the processor clock. In some designs, it is an independent clock set at a fixed frequency of 10 MHz. With some new 286 and 386 custom support chips, you can program the bus clock rate from a selection of values.

AT Extension Slot Signal Definitions

Most of the new features of the PC AT (or ISA) bus were added in the 36-pin card-edge slots. The following sections describe the signals in the bus extension slots.

SBHE

The SBHE (system bus high enable) signal is an output signal from the system board. It indicates that the bus-attached device and present bus cycle expect to transfer data on the high byte of the data bus on lines SD8 through SD15. This signal and the low-order address bit A0 can be used to decode the type of bus cycle, as shown in Table 10-1.

Table 10-1. Data Bus Size Operation Decodes

SBHE Value	A0 Value	Function
1	0	16-bit transfer
1	1	Upper byte transfer
0	0	Lower byte transfer
0	1	Invalid

MEMR

The $\overline{\text{MEMR}}$ (memory read) signal is identical to the $\overline{\text{MEMR}}$ signal in the XT bus slot except it is activated on all memory-read cycles, including those above the 1M range. If $\overline{\text{SMEMR}}$ is inactive and $\overline{\text{MEMR}}$ is active, the memory-read cycle is for memory above the 20-bit address range (greater than 1M). This signal is active low, indicating to a memory device to place its data on the system data bus prior to the signal going inactive.

MEMW

The $\overline{\text{MEMW}}$ (memory write) signal is identical to the $\overline{\text{MEMW}}$ signal on the XT bus slot except it is activated on all memory-write cycles, including those for memory above the 1M range. If $\overline{\text{SMEMW}}$ is inactive and $\overline{\text{MEMW}}$ is active, the memory-write cycle is for memory above the 20-bit address range (greater than 1M). This signal is active low, indicating that the system microprocessor has placed on the bus data to be written into a memory device. Data can always be written on the rising edge of this signal.

DRQ5–7

Signals DRQ5–DRQ7 (DMA request 5–7) are similar to the DRQ0–DRQ4 signals on the XT expansion slots and are used by expansion slot devices to request a direct memory access (DMA) cycle. See DRQ0–DRQ4 definitions in the section on XT bus definitions in Chapter 5. The only difference with these signals is that the DMA cycles on channels 5 through 7 are 16-bit bus transfers. These signals are active high, just like DRQ0–4 on the XT bus slots.

DACK5–7

Signals $\overline{\text{DACK5}}$–$\overline{\text{DACK7}}$ (DMA acknowledge 5–7) are similar to the $\overline{\text{DACK0}}$–$\overline{\text{DACK3}}$ signals on the XT bus expansion slots and are used to signal to an expansion slot adapter that its request for a DMA cycle has been granted. These signals acknowledge 16-bit DMA requests on levels 5 through 7 on the bus extension slots. See the $\overline{\text{DACK0}}$–$\overline{\text{DACK3}}$ descriptions in the sections on the XT bus signals in Chapter 5.

MEM CS16

The $\overline{\text{MEM CS16}}$ (memory chip select 16) active low input signal is used to indicate that the expansion slot adapter board can support one wait-state 16-bit bus transfer on the present bus cycle. This signal must be driven with an open collector or tristate device capable of sinking 20 milliamps of current.

I/O CS16

The $\overline{\text{I/O CS16}}$ (input/output chip select 16) active low input signal is used to indicate that the expansion slot adapter board can support one wait-state 16-bit I/O bus cycle on the present I/O bus cycle. This signal must be driven with an open collector or tristate device capable of sinking 20 milliamps of current.

MASTER

The $\overline{\text{MASTER}}$ signal is an active low input signal used with the DRQ5–DRQ7 signals to allow a bus master to take over the system bus. When a $\overline{\text{DACK}}$ signal is returned from a DRQ activation on channels 5–7, the $\overline{\text{MASTER}}$ signal can be activated, which cancels the DMA channel operation and tristates the system address bus, data bus, and control signals. This allows an expansion slot adapter (for example, another processor or a DMA device) to take control of system bus-attached devices and memory. The new bus master, however, must obey all timing requirements of the bus-attached devices and return control to the PC AT processor and DMA channels within 15 microseconds to avoid loss of memory due to a lack of memory refresh cycles.

IRQ10, 11, 12, 14, 15

IRQ10–12, 14, and 15 (interrupt requests 10, 11, 12, 14, 15) are active high input signals that are nearly identical to the IRQ2–IRQ7 signals on the XT bus slots. They are used to generate interrupt requests from expansion slot adapters to the interrupt controller on the system board. In the AT design, a second interrupt controller is added to the system. These interrupt request signals go to the second interrupt controller chip. These signals generate interrupt requests on their rising edge. For additional information, see the definition of IRQ2–IRQ7 in the section on XT bus signal definitions in Chapter 5.

LA17–23

LA17–LA23 (unlatched addresses 17–23) are output signals used to provide memory address information about the present bus cycle. These address signals, unlike SA0–SA20, are not valid during the entire bus cycle. They become valid during the actual time of the BALE bus signal and can be latched on the falling edge of the BALE signal. These signals are provided in this manner to reduce address delay when they are used to decode a block of bus-attached memory.

SD8–15

SD8–SD15 (system data bus bits 8–15) are eight bidirectional signals that support the transfer of data on the high byte of 16-bit transfers on the expansion bus slots. They are similar to the low-byte data bus bits on the XT bus expansion slots. SD8 through SD15 transfer the upper byte of data bus data on all 16-bit bus operations. All 8-bit-wide devices and memory must attach to SD0–7 on the XT bus slots. If the system software requests a 16-bit transfer to the 8-bit device, the AT system board forces two bus cycles on the low-order SD0–7 bits. Adapters must indicate their capability to support 16-bit transfers by activating the MEM CS16 signal for memory devices and the I/O CS16 signal for I/O devices.

+5VDC

One card-edge pin on the expansion slot connectors provides access to the +5 volts direct current (+5VDC) power source on the system board.

GND

One card-edge pin on the expansion slot connectors provides access to the direct current ground (GND) on the system board.

Adapter Board Size

The PC AT expansion slots can accept a taller adapter board than the board supported in the PC and XT. The board can be a maximum of 4.8 inches high, versus the PC and XT board height of 4.2 inches. The PC, XT, and AT have an identical maximum board length of 13.13 inches. The connector and strain relief bracket at the rear of the PC AT board is identical to the PC XT. Although the AT boards are higher, the connector access area was not expanded so that mechanical compatibility could be maintained with the older PC and XT adapter boards. The spacing between adapter boards is .75 inches, the same as in the PC XT.

Aside from the additional height of the PC AT adapter boards, the major difference is the additional set of card-edge tabs on the board. Figure 10-4 illustrates the mechanical dimensions of the PC AT bus adapter boards. AT motherboards can be supplied as upgrades to PC XT systems. To maintain compatibility with XT bus systems, many AT adapter board designs still use the smaller height, even though they support the 16-bit bus extension slot.

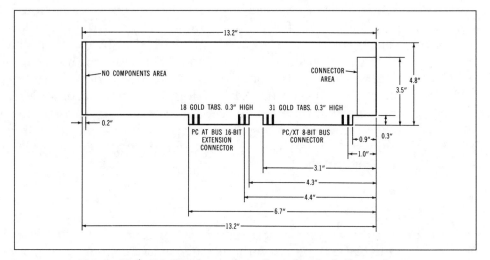

Figure 10-4. PC AT adapter board mechanical dimensions.

Expansion Slot Bus Cycles

Bus cycles targeted for I/O or memory devices on the expansion slots of the PC AT vary greatly in length, depending on the clock rate of the micro-processor and the wait states inserted automatically by the processor board. In general, memory accesses targeted to expansion bus slots contain one wait state, and I/O accesses targeted to expansion bus slots contain a minimum of six wait states.

Wait states can be eliminated using the 0WS signal on the expansion bus XT connectors. Note that bus cycles appear on the expansion slots even though the data transfers are for the local bus on the system board. Steering circuits on the system board disable the data transfers on the expansion slots, but address and control timing signals are still valid. On some designs, this gives the appearance of fast zero wait-state cycles on the expansion slots, but these cycles are valid only on the system board.

Because the 286 and 386 systems use two clocks to execute a bus cycle, the timing of the signals relative to the bus CLK signal is different on the PC AT bus than on the XT bus, which uses four clocks per bus cycle. The original IBM 6-MHz PC AT supported expansion bus transfers with the number of clocks and wait states defined in Table 10-2.

Table 10-2. PC AT Clock Cycles and Wait States

Bus Transfer Type	Number of Clocks	Number of Wait States
8 bit to 8 bit	6 clocks	4
16 bit to 8 bit	12 clocks	10
16 bit to 16 bit	3 clocks	1

Most AT designs for expansion slots follow the bus cycle clock times and wait states in Table 10-2. Some higher clock rate designs, however, insert additional wait states in the expansion bus I/O and DMA cycles. This is done to ensure compatibility with slower adapter boards designed using the lower bus clock rates. Wait states can always be reduced by new adapters using 16-bit transfers and by activating the 0WS bus interface signal.

Figures 10-5 and 10-6 illustrate the basic timing of a typical one wait-state expansion bus cycle for a memory-read operation and a memory-write operation, respectively. Figures 10-7 and 10-8 illustrate the basic timing of a typical four wait-state expansion slot bus cycle for an I/O-read operation and I/O-write operation, respectively. Figure 10-9 illustrates a memory read to an I/O-write DMA operation on the PC AT bus expansion slots.

Bus master devices that take control of the system must follow these basic timings if they will be accessing other system I/O or memory on the system. In general, bus cycle lengths in PC AT bus expansion slots vary widely due to different clock speeds. Care must be taken in a design for a high clock rate system to ensure compatibility with its expansion bus cycles.

PC AT DMA cycles operate differently than those in the PC XT in two respects. First, DMA chips normally operate at half the processor's clock speed. The DMA chips do all transfers in five clock cycles or ten processor clock cycles. Again, additional wait states sometimes are inserted in high clock rate systems to maintain bus cycle speed compatibility with older adapter board designs. Second, the PC AT added a second DMA controller that supports 3 channels of 16-bit DMA transfer. Both 8- and 16-bit transfers take the same number of clock cycles. Figure 10-10 illustrates an I/O read memory-write DMA on the PC AT bus expansion slots.

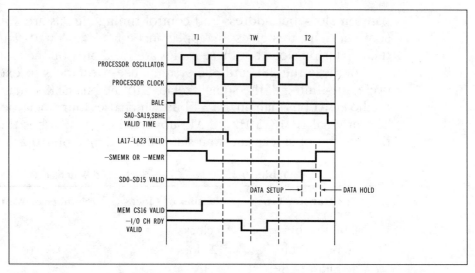

**Figure 10-5. PC AT expansion slot memory-read bus cycle with one
wait state.**

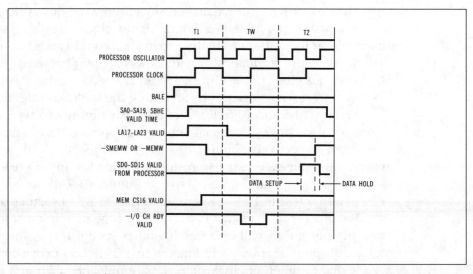

**Figure 10-6. PC AT expansion slot memory-write bus cycle with one
wait state.**

Bus Timing

Due to the significant differences in the speed and technology of
microprocessors and supporting circuits, it is nearly impossible to generate a single set of expansion slot bus timings that are valid across all implementations of the PC AT bus. However, the PC AT bus is a clock syn-

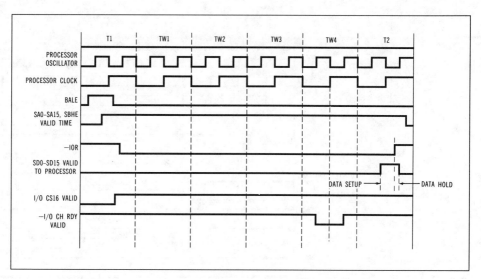

Figure 10-7. PC AT expansion slot I/O-read bus cycle with four wait states.

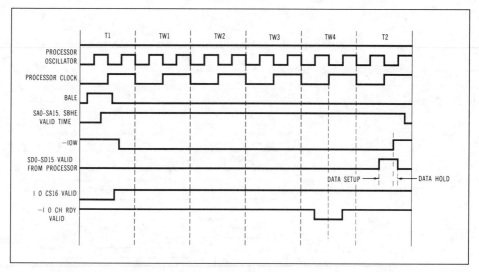

Figure 10-8. PC AT expansion slot I/O-write bus cycle with four wait states.

chronous bus, which means that all bus control, data, and address timings are relative to the processor clock edge. The basic timing diagrams for the various types of bus cycles can be used to obtain ballpark design parameter requirements.

In general, all signals are delayed from a specific clock edge. This delay is in three parts. First, the delay is the result of internal microprocessor delays. These delays vary with the clock speed and technology of the specific microprocessor; if you need detailed information, consult the

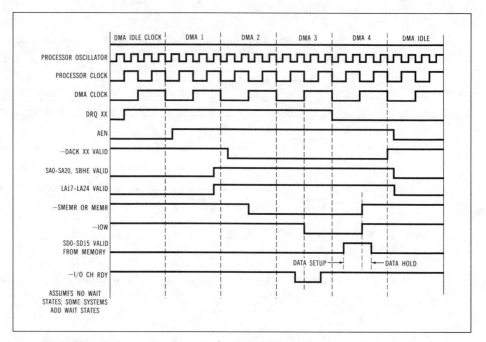

Figure 10-9. Memory-read I/O-write DMA bus cycle on the PC AT expansion slots.

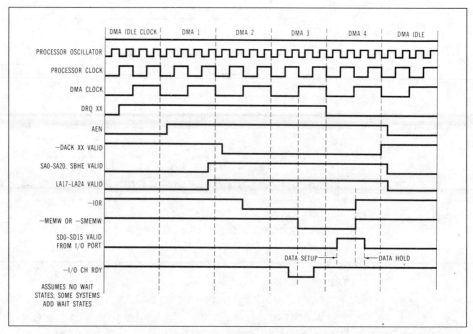

Figure 10-10. I/O-read memory-write DMA bus cycle on the PC AT bus expansion slots.

specifications of the microprocessor chip. Second, delay is induced in signals as the result of decoding and buffering. Again, this delay is highly dependent on the implementation of these circuits. Some custom LSI system support chips are very fast and have little delay; other designs use TTL devices and have significant delay. Third, bus signals are delayed as a result of capacitive loading on the bus. A bus with few installed adapter boards will be faster than one with many boards.

To assist in generating timing information, the following worst-case delays can be assumed for each of the three types of delays for 286 and 386 processor systems:

- Internal microprocessor delay from activating clock edge: 15 ns
- External decode and buffer delays: 15 ns
- Typical bus capacitance delay: 10 ns

Adding these delays from the activating clock edges in the basic timing diagrams will provide a rough indication of the actual signal timings and will be sufficient for all but the most demanding designs.

Read data must be valid on the bus prior to the rising edge of the $\overline{\text{IOR}}$ or $\overline{\text{MEMR}}$ signal. To insure valid read data from expansion-slot memory or I/O-read operations, it is recommended that data be valid on the bus a minimum of 25 nanoseconds prior to the rising edge of either the $\overline{\text{IOR}}$ or $\overline{\text{MEMR}}$ signal.

Bus Loading and Drive

Bus loading and driving requirements on the PC AT bus also are difficult to exactly specify due to the many different implementations. By following some simple adapter board guidelines for number of loads and driving capability, however, problems can be easily avoided. First, never present more than two physical loads to any bus signal. A good rule is to not exceed two 74LSxx device loads on any bus output signal. Second, when driving a bus signal, drive it with at least a 74LSxx equivalent driver capable of sinking 4 milliamps. Do not drive bus signals with the output of NMOS devices because they typically do not have the current sinking capability and perform poorly on highly capacitive signals.

Five input signals on the PC AT bus require an open collector or tri-state driver. The driver should be able to sink 20 milliamps of current. The five signals are

$\overline{\text{I/O CH CK}}$

$\overline{\text{I/O CH RDY}}$

$\overline{\text{MASTER}}$

$\overline{\text{MEM CS16}}$

$\overline{\text{I/O CS16}}$

All signal inputs from each slot are wired together such that any slot can activate the signal.

Bus Wait States

Wait-state generation on the AT is very similar to that on the PC and XT, with only one major difference. The $\overline{\text{I/O CH RDY}}$ signal used to force wait-state insertion in expansion bus slots is sampled on both edges in the PC AT but on only the rising edge in the PC and XT. This is because the circuits controlling the ready signal to the 286 are sampling in asynchronous mode at twice the processor clock speed.

Requests for wait states in a bus cycle from the expansion slots' $\overline{\text{I/O}}$ $\overline{\text{CH RDY}}$ signal must be synchronized by both the clock controller circuit (82284 chip) and the 82288 bus controller chips or their counterparts in custom and 386 system designs. This takes a minimum of one clock cycle or two clock edges. Figure 10-11 illustrates the expansion bus slot timing for the insertion of wait states in the standard memory bus cycle, which already contains one wait state inserted by the system board. Figure 10-12 illustrates the expansion bus timing for the insertion of wait states in the standard I/O bus cycle, which already contains four wait states inserted by the system board.

DMA cycles can have wait states inserted also. The DMA device that samples the $\overline{\text{I/O CH RDY}}$ signal, however, typically runs at half the processor clock rate and samples the RDY signal on the falling edge of the clock. In general, DMA channel wait-state timing in the PC AT is nearly identical to that of the PC XT. Consult the PC XT section on DMA wait-state generation in Chapter 6 for additional details. Figure 10-13 illustrates wait-state timing in DMA cycles.

The 0WS (0 wait states) signal on the bus can be used to eliminate wait states in bus cycles that have been inserted automatically by the system board. This signal is similar in function to the $\overline{\text{I/O CH RDY}}$ signal, except it skips one stage of READY signal synchronization. Figure 10-14 illustrates the timing needed to remove system board wait states by activating the 0WS signal.

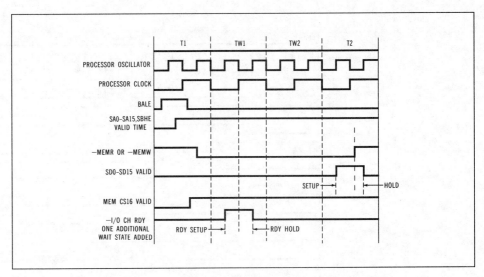

Figure 10-11. Wait-state timing in memory cycles.

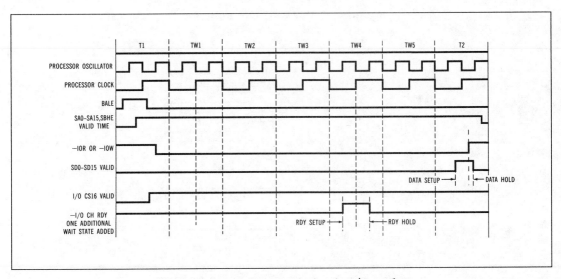

Figure 10-12. Wait-state timing in I/O cycles.

Wait-State Generation Hardware

Due to the nature of the PC AT bus design, the same designs used to insert wait states in the PC and XT will operate on the AT bus. For design examples, consult the section in Chapter 6 on XT wait-state generation. Re-

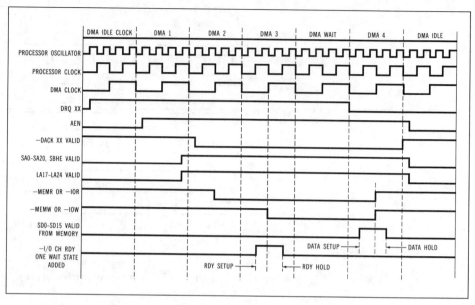

Figure 10-13. Wait-state timing in DMA cycles.

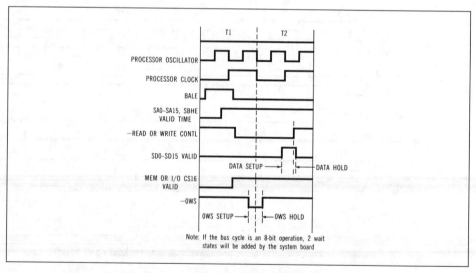

Figure 10-14. Timing for 0WS signal activation.

member, however, that wait states are probably already inserted in expansion slot bus cycles and that the total time will be less at higher clock rates because each wait state is a single, shorter clock period. Further complicating the issue is the fact that, in some newer systems, wait states inserted by the system board are programmable, and the clock driving the DMA channels may be programmable or may not be half the system processor clock.

Programmable Bus and System Parameters

Many new custom chip sets that support the higher clock rate 286, 386SX, and 386 microprocessors can be customized under program control. A good example of this capability is in the Chips and Technology chip set used with 386 processors to build AT bus compatible systems. This chip set runs the 386 at clock speeds of up to 25 MHz using zero wait-state interleave memory designs. The chip set is designed to use three independent clocks: the processor oscillator, a system clock, and a slower AT clock. With this scheme, the processor can run at its optimum speed, the support device DMA can run at its optimum system clock speed, and the AT bus can be configured to run at its selected speed.

The AT setup program is typically used to prompt the user to select the configuration parameters through a set of menus. This information is stored in CMOS battery-backup nonvolatile memory and is used to configure the system for operation automatically on power up. Following is a summary of the configuration parameters available in the Chips and Technology chip set for 386 PC AT designs. The processor clock, the AT bus clock, and the DMA clock sources are selective.

Processor clock sources: processor oscillator and system clock times 2

Bus clock sources: processor clock divided by 2, processor clock divided by 3, and AT clock (normally 10 MHz)

DMA channels clock sources: system clock and system clock divided by 2

The chip set also permits the enabling and disabling of the shadow ROM capability in RAM address space. Shadowing can be enabled at

F0000H segment: 64K (BIOS)

C0000H segment: 16K (display ROM)

C4000H segment: 16K (extended display ROM)

The chip set permits extensive configuration of system memory. ROM may be disabled in 64K segment blocks in the range C0000 to FFFFF hex. RAM may also be enabled in this same ROM area in blocks of 64K segments; this RAM can be specified as either read/write or read-only in 64K segment sizes.

Control registers permit the specification of dynamic RAM type, dynamic RAM timing, parity check, interleave options, minimum memory size, enabling memory above 16 megabytes, specification of boot ROM location, and wait states in memory.

In addition to programmable PC AT bus clock sources, the number of wait states is programmable for 8-, 16-, and 32-bit bus cycles in increments of two bus clocks from two to eight. DMA cycle wait states are programmable in increments of system clocks from one to four. The location of the leading edge of the memory and I/O READ and WRITE signals on the AT bus can be specified independently for 8-, 16-, and 32-bit bus operations.

With these types of chip sets, processor speed can be independent of AT bus speed and timings, and can be tailored to bus and adapter board requirements. High-speed processors can be directly coupled to high-performance memory, rather than limited by the slower operating AT bus, which runs at independent clock speeds. This type of capability also highlights the difficulty in providing a comprehensive AT bus specification because so many bus timing parameters are system programmable and even user programmable.

EISA and ISA Bus Standard

BCPR Services has attempted to convert the PC AT bus to the ISA (Industry Standard Architecture) bus standard. The ISA specification is included in the EISA (Extended Industry Standard Architecture) specification, and is available from BCPR Services Incorporated, 1400 L Street N.W., Washington, DC, 20005-3502.

The EISA specification is available in two packages. The complete package costs $450.00. This includes: the right to make five copies, access to the EISA Forum Electronic Bulletin Board at the highest security level, any updates for a one-year period, and the right to purchase additional copies from BCPR Services for $100.00 per copy.

A partial package costs $125.00. This specification package does *not* include the following: the right to make copies, access to the bulletin board, and assurances of updates. Additional copies of the partial package cost the same as the initial partial package, $125.00 per copy.

There is no guarantee that PC AT bus systems comply with the ISA specification. However, the specification contains an excellent description of the bus and would be a worthwhile reference document for a PC or PC adapter designer.

Power Supply Specifications

Most PC AT systems have DC power supplies in excess of 185 watts capacity. The AT bus provides access to +5, −5, +12, and −12 volts DC. These power levels are provided in the expansion bus slots on the same card-edge connectors as the PC and XT 62-pin connectors. In addition, +5 volts and ground are provided on card-edge connector pins in the AT bus expansion 36-pin connector. The original PC AT system from IBM provided the power level and currents specified in Table 10-3. Manufacturers of AT bus compatible systems provide similar power supply capabilities. A good rule is that approximately half the current available on each DC level is available for expansion slot adapter use. Adapter designs should attempt to keep the total adapter board power dissipation below 7 watts. Although the power supply may be able to support your currents, you may have difficulty cooling the adapter board at high power levels.

Table 10-3.   PC AT Power Supply Specifications

Power Level	Tolerance	Maximum Load Current
+5 volts dc	+5% to −4%	19.8 amps
−5 volts dc	+10% to −8%	300 milliamps
+12 volts dc	+5% to −4%	7.3 amps
−12 volts dc	+10% to −9%	300 milliamps

PC AT Interrupts, DMA, Timer Counters, I/O, and Memory

IN THE AREAS OF INTERRUPTS, DMA, timer counters, and memory and I/O map definitions, the designers of the PC AT tried to maintain compatibility with the PC and XT while extending the capabilities of these functions. For detailed descriptions of these functions, see Chapters 6 and 7. This chapter highlights only the differences and extended functions of the AT design over the PC and XT implementations.

Direct Memory Addressing

The PC AT uses the same chip type (the 8237 or equivalent device) as the PC and XT systems to implement the DMA feature. However, several enhancements and changes were incorporated in the AT design. A second four-channel DMA controller was added to the AT system design. This controller operates in cascade mode and supports three 16-bit transfer channels. The fourth channel is used to accept the cascade input from the first controller. Figure 11-1 illustrates the configuration of DMA channels on the PC AT. Table 11-1 defines the use of DMA channels in the AT system.

Second, channel 0 on the first controller was made available for general use by removing the memory refresh function from this channel. This was implemented by independent hardware on the PC AT. Third, the DMA page register was extended in size to support the 24-bit 16-megabyte address space of the 286 microprocessor. Figure 11-2 illustrates the generation of DMA memory addressing using the extended DMA page register.

The use of the channels was also modified. As indicated, channel 0 was freed from the memory refresh function and made available. DMA

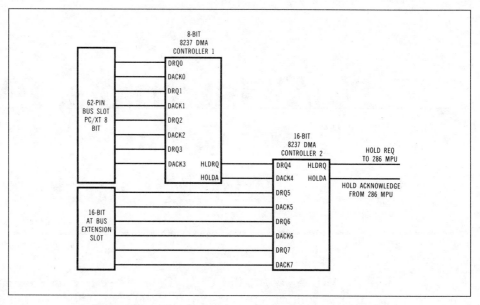

Figure 11-1. Configuration of PC AT DMA channels.

Table 11-1.   PC AT DMA Usage

Controller 1 (I/O Addresses 00H to 1FH) for 8-Bit DMA Channels

Channel 0	Spare
Channel 1	SDLC communications adapter
Channel 2	Diskette controller
Channel 3	Spare

Controller 2 (I/O Addresses C0H to DFH) for 16-Bit DMA Channels

Channel 4	Controller 1 cascade input
Channel 5	Spare
Channel 6	Spare
Channel 7	Spare

SOURCE	DMA PAGE REGISTERS	8237A-5
ADDRESS	A23 ← → A16	A15 ← → A0

ADDRESS GENERATION FOR DMA CHANNELS 3 THROUGH 0

SOURCE	DMA PAGE REGISTERS	8237A-5
ADDRESS	A23 ← → A17	A16 ← → A1

ADDRESS GENERATION FOR DMA CHANNELS 7 THROUGH 5

Figure 11-2. PC AT DMA address generation with page registers.

channel 3 was no longer used to support hard disk data transfers. Table 11-2 defines the I/O port addresses used by the AT DMA controller and page register.

Table 11-2. PC AT DMA and Page Register I/O Addresses

Device	I/O Address
DMA controller 1	00H to 1FH
DMA controller 2	C0H to DFH
DMA CH 0 page register	87H
DMA CH 1 page register	83H
DMA CH 2 page register	81H
DMA CH 3 page register	82H
DMA CH 5 page register	8BH
DMA CH 6 page register	89H
DMA CH 7 page register	9AH
Refresh page register	8FH

There is one other significant difference in the operation of DMA channels in PC AT bus compatible systems. DMA channels normally do not operate at the same clock rate as the system microprocessor; they often operate at one-half, one-third, or one-fourth the processor clock rate. In addition, the 286 and 386 microprocessors require more clock cycles to transfer the bus to and from the DMA channels. DMA channels in the PC and XT designs often operate at higher data rates and require fewer clocks than 8-bit mode AT designs.

Interrupts

Interrupts were expanded on the AT in a manner similar to the expansion of the DMA channels. A second 8259A controller (or equivalent device) added seven hardware interrupts to the PC AT design. Five of these additional interrupts are available on the PC bus 16-bit expansion slot connector. The unused interrupt level 2 on the first controller now serves as an input for the requests from the second controller. The level-2 interrupt was replaced with interrupt 9 on the second controller. To maintain compatibility with old adapters that use level 2, software redirects level-9 interrupts to level-2 service routines. The first interrupt controller's interrupts are still initialized to vector to INT 9 through F, or low memory vector locations 20H to 3FH. The second interrupt controller is initialized to INT 70 through 77, or low memory vector locations in the memory block 1C0H to 1DFH.

The first interrupt controller is accessed as in the PC and XT at I/O addresses 20H through 3FH. The second interrupt controller is accessed at I/O addresses A0H through BFH. Information on the operation and programming of the 8259A interrupt controller can be found in the section on PC and XT interrupts in Chapter 6. Table 11-3 illustrates the PC AT dual interrupt controller configuration and the use of the interrupts in a PC AT design.

Table 11-3. PC AT Interrupt Controller Configuration and Interrupt Level Request Usage

Level		Function
Microprocessor NMI		Parity or I/O channel check
Interrupt Controllers		
8259A-1	*8259A-2*	
IRQ0		Timer 0 output
IRQ0		Timer 0 output
IRQ1		Keyboard interrupt input
IRQ2		Interrupt input from 8259A-2
	IRQ8	CMOS real-time clock interrupt
	IRQ9	Replaces bus IRQ2
	IRQ10	Not used, extension slot IRQ
	IRQ11	Not used, extension slot IRQ
	IRQ12	Not used, extension slot IRQ
	IRQ13	Numeric coprocessor IRQ
	IRQ14	Fixed disk adapter IRQ
	IRQ15	Not used, extension slot IRQ
IRQ3		Serial port 2 if installed
IRQ4		Serial port 1
IRQ5		Parallel port 2 if installed
IRQ6		Diskette controller
IRQ7		Parallel port 1

Note: IRQ8 through IRQ 15 are cascaded through IRQ2.

Timer Counter

The PC AT timer counter is nearly identical to the PC and XT timer counter. Each of the three channels of the timer counter is configured in hardware the same as in the PC and XT designs. Channel 0 is still driven by a 1.190-MHz input signal with its output tied to interrupt controller 1's level-0 interrupt request. Channel 1 input is driven by the same 1.190-MHz clock, and the output is used to generate a memory refresh request. However, channel 1's input no longer generates a DMA channel 0 request. Channel 2 is still used to generate speaker tones, which is driven by the 1.190-MHz clock and its gate input controlled by bit 1 of PPI port 61H. For detailed information on the configuration, operation, and programming modes of the timer counter chip, see Chapter 6.

The PC and XT use the 8253 Intel timer counter chips; the PC AT uses the newer 8254 device. This device is a superset of the functions and performance of the 8254. The major differences are the capability of the 8254 to operate at a higher input clock rate and the addition of a new read back mode. By defining a new control word command, the read back mode latches the status and count of any of the three counters. See Figure 11-3. The 8254 timer counter device is still accessed using the same I/O addresses (40H to 5FH) as defined in the PC and XT systems.

Real-Time Clock and CMOS Memory

The PC AT enhanced the timing capability of the system by providing a CMOS battery-backup real-time clock chip—the Motorola MC146818—and support circuits. Detailed information on this device can be found in *Motorola Microprocessor, Microcontroller, and Peripheral Data Manual, Volume 2.* This device provides 64 bytes of nonvolatile CMOS RAM. The first 14 bytes control and sense the real-time clock features of the device. The remaining 50 bytes are user-defined RAM; in the PC AT design, these 50 bytes of RAM contain system configuration data. Since the original design of the PC AT, the content of the configuration data has changed with the different adapters, hard disks, and memory configurations supported. Modifying information in RAM can easily cause systems to fail. It is recommended that this device be accessed only as provided with the system CMOS setup programs.

The real-time clock and CMOS RAM is accessed indirectly at I/O address locations 70H and 71H. Before a read or write to any of the 64 bytes

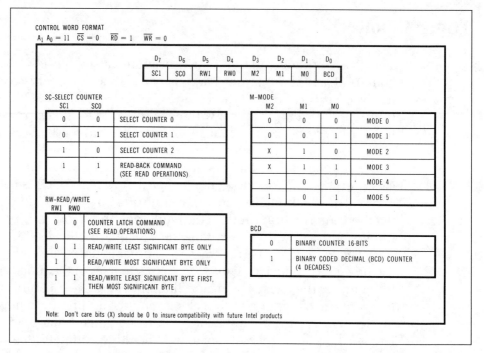

CONTROL WORD FORMAT
$A_1 A_0 = 11$ $\overline{CS} = 0$ $\overline{RD} = 1$ $\overline{WR} = 0$

D_7	D_6	D_5	D_4	D_3	D_2	D_1	D_0
SC1	SC0	RW1	RW0	M2	M1	M0	BCD

SC-SELECT COUNTER

SC1	SC0	
0	0	SELECT COUNTER 0
0	1	SELECT COUNTER 1
1	0	SELECT COUNTER 2
1	1	READ-BACK COMMAND (SEE READ OPERATIONS)

M-MODE

M2	M1	M0	
0	0	0	MODE 0
0	0	1	MODE 1
X	1	0	MODE 2
X	1	1	MODE 3
1	0	0	MODE 4
1	0	1	MODE 5

RW-READ/WRITE

RW1	RW0	
0	0	COUNTER LATCH COMMAND (SEE READ OPERATIONS)
0	1	READ/WRITE LEAST SIGNIFICANT BYTE ONLY
1	0	READ/WRITE MOST SIGNIFICANT BYTE ONLY
1	1	READ/WRITE LEAST SIGNIFICANT BYTE FIRST, THEN MOST SIGNIFICANT BYTE

BCD

0	BINARY COUNTER 16-BITS
1	BINARY CODED DECIMAL (BCD) COUNTER (4 DECADES)

Note: Don't care bits (X) should be 0 to insure compatibility with future Intel products

Figure 11-3. New control word command for the 8254 timer counter.

in the device, the address must be set with an OUT instruction to I/O port address 70H. An IN or OUT instruction to I/O port 71H reads or writes, respectively, the register previously specified in the OUT to I/O port 70H. Table 11-4 defines the functions of each of the 64 bytes in the original PC AT design.

Memory Map

In real mode, the PC AT memory map is similar to the PC and XT memory map because memory is limited to 1 megabyte. The PC AT can operate also in protected mode, which supports memory above the 1-megabyte boundary. The amount of memory addressed above the real mode limit depends on the system design and the microprocessor. The 286 and 386SX support a maximum of 16 megabytes of physical memory. This is the same maximum supported by the PC AT expansion bus slots. The 386 and 486 microprocessors support a full 32-bit address and can thus support up to 4 gigabytes of physical memory. PC AT expansion bus slots cannot support more than 16 megabytes, unless a special 32-bit slot (or

Table 11-4. Real-Time Clock and CMOS RAM Address Definitions

Addresses	Description
00-0D	Real-time clock information*
0E	Diagnostic status byte*
0F	Shutdown status byte*
10	Diskette drive type byte—drives A and B
11	Reserved
12	Fixed disk type byte—drives C and D
13	Reserved
14	Equipment byte
15	Low base memory byte
16	High base memory byte
17	Low expansion memory byte
18	High expansion memory byte
19–2D	Reserved
2E–2F	2-byte CMOS checksum
30	Low expansion memory byte*
31	High expansion memory byte*
32	Date century byte*
33	Information flags (set during power on)*
34–3F	Reserved

*These bytes are not included in the checksum calculation and are not part of the configuration record.

slots) is provided to support memory expansion beyond this limit. Figure 11-4 defines the memory use of a typical PC AT system.

I/O Map

Significant changes are made to the AT I/O map compared to the original PC and XT maps. First, the boundary between system board address space and expansion slot address space was moved from 200H to 100H, providing an additional 256 I/O addresses on the PC AT expansion bus slots. The PC AT fixed disk adapter uses eight I/O addresses in this block. Most PC adapters chose not to use these I/O addresses because they would lose compatibility with the installed base of PC and XT systems. Second, the

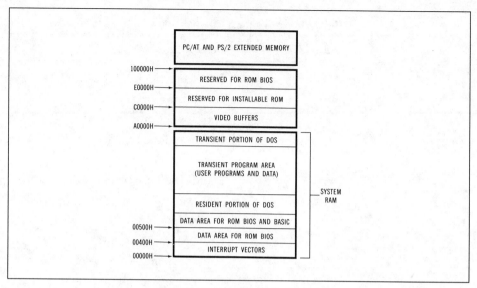

Figure 11-4. PC AT memory map.

addition of more DMA channels and interrupt levels combined with new controls for the numeric coprocessor and the real-time clock added significantly to the use of I/O address space on the system board. Table 11-5 defines I/O address space use on a typical PC AT system.

Table 11-5. PC AT I/O map.

Hex Range	Device
000–01F	DMA controller 1, 8237A-5
020–03F	Interrupt controller 1, 8259A, master
040–05F	Timer, 8254, 2
060–06F	8042 (keyboard)
070–07F	Real-time clock, NMI mask
080-09F	DMA register, 74LS612
0A0–0BF	Interrupt controller 2, 8259A
0C0–0DF	DMA controller 2, 8237A-5
0F0	Clear math coprocessor busy
0F1	Reset math coprocessor
0F8–0FF	Math coprocessor
1F0–1F8	Fixed disk
200–207	Game I/O
278–27F	Parallel printer port 2

Table 11-5.   *(cont.)*

Hex Range	Device
2F8–2FF	Serial port 2
300–31F	Prototype card
360–36F	Reserved
378–37F	Parallel printer port 1
380–38F	SDLC, bisynchronous 2
3A0–3AF	Bisynchronous 1
3B0–3BF	Monochrome display and printer adapter
3C0–3CF	Reserved
3D0–3DF	Color/graphics monitor adapter
3F0–3F7	Diskette controller
3F8–3FF	Serial port 1

Chapter 12

PS/2 Micro Channel Architecture

WITH IBM'S INTRODUCTION of the PS/2 model 50 and above, a new expansion slot architecture was defined supporting 8-, 16- and 32-bit operations. This new expansion slot architecture, called Micro Channel Architecture (MCA), is technically different than the PC AT bus. This was the first time IBM fully defined the bus architecture by providing a full specification, including signal timing and loading information. The bus was also unique in its attempt to isolate the characteristics of the system microprocessor from the expansion bus slots. The AT and PC buses were little more than extensions of 8088 and 286 microprocessor-demultiplexed local buses.

Full specifications of MCA are beyond the scope of this book. (It would require several hundred pages to specify all the features, timing, and loading for each PS/2 model implementation.) If you plan to implement an MCA compatible adapter, it is recommended that you get a copy of the appropriate system reference manual or the MCA specification from IBM. Following are the best documents:

IBM Personal System/2 Model 50/60 Technical Reference, IBM number 68X-2224

IBM Personal System/2 Model 88 Technical Reference, IBM number 68X-2256

IBM Personal System/2 Models 50, 60, 70, 80 MCA Architecture, IBM number G360-2637 (revision 5.3, May 1987)

Several chip manufacturers provide chip sets that interface directly to the MCA and convert the bus to a more familiar Intel chip interface. These suppliers provide detailed specifications and design examples for using their chips in MCA designs. Two such suppliers are ALTERA Corporation and Chip and Technologies Incorporated. ALTERA has two EPLDs (electrically programmable logic devices) that support the MCA interface: EPB2001 and EPB2002. They also provide chip specifications, design examples, and a *Micro Channel Handbook* to support the use of their devices. Their address is ALTERA Corporation, 3525 Monroe Street, Santa Clara, California, 95051.

Chips and Technologies Incorporated provides three chips for interfacing to the MCA. The 82C611 supports multifunction memory and I/O slave adapters. The 82C612 additionally supports DMA slave device adapter implementations. The 82C614 supports MCA bus master and slave DMA devices on the bus. The chips are provided with excellent specifications and design examples. The address is Chips and Technologies, Incorporated, 3050 Zanker Road, San Jose, California, 95134. It is recommended that you contact MCA suppliers and read their documentation before starting any MCA design. This chapter provides information on the key technical capabilities and operation of MCA.

Capabilities and Characteristics

MCA is unique in several respects when compared to PC AT bus implementations. This section highlights the areas that differentiate MCA from the PC AT expansion slot bus architecture.

Family of Buses

MCA is actually a family of buses providing 8-, 16-, and 32-bit versions of MCA with extensions supporting a video interface, an audio channel, and a special matched memory interface for high-speed system memory expansion. Some PS/2 models support both 16-bit and 32-bit slots. Figure 12-1 illustrates the family of bus sizes and extensions supported by MCA. The newer versions of IBM RISC architecture workstations also have incorporated MCA as their expansion slot architecture. IBM has indicated that extensions to MCA supporting higher speeds and wider bus paths may be used in newer systems in the future.

Asynchronous Bus Operation

A notable feature of MCA is the lack of a bus clock. Bus signals are not referenced to any system or bus clock, unlike the PC AT bus. This permits

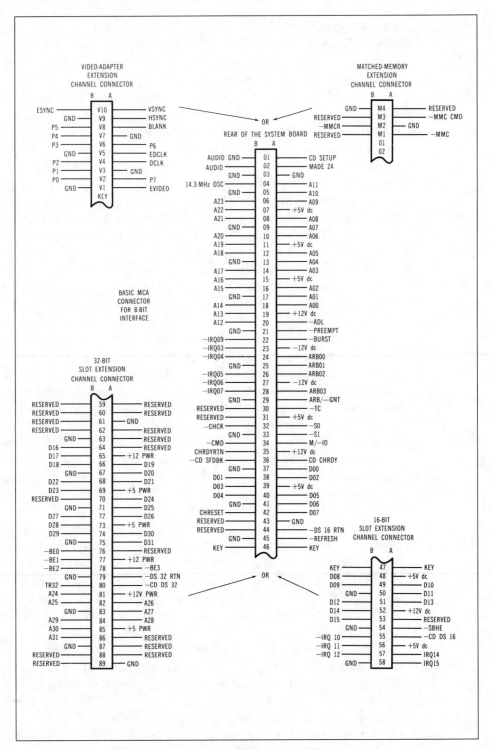

Figure 12-1. MCA bus definition and extensions.

MCA to operate in *asynchronous mode.* This scheme does not lock MCA operation to any specific speed defined by the system microprocessor; it allows a mixture of high- and low-speed devices on the same bus, each operating at optimum speed.

Careful analysis of each implementation of MCA reveals that it is a quasi-asynchronous bus. Bus cycles, although they are not referenced to a system or processor clock, are not smoothly variable in length; they are executed in increments of the processor or system clock. A device that acknowledges a bus cycle within a specified time will execute in the minimum number of system clocks. This is analogous to providing a synchronous response using an MCA signal as a clock edge reference and obeying the setup time on the acknowledged signal. If the MCA response is not within the specified synchronous response time, the cycle is considered asynchronous and is extended a specified clock increment.

When devices cannot respond in the synchronous response time, the cycle incurs a two-clock synchronization effect on both ends of the bus. The device receiving the bus cycle must first synchronize the request with a local clock to generate the desired delayed response. When this acknowledge signal is received, it must be synchronized with the bus master clock. Because no bus clock is provided, the master and slave use two asynchronous clocks to generate their signals. Thus, two clock edges are required on each end to synchronize the bus interchange. To minimize this effect, high-speed clock sources are now required on the adapter boards. If the adapter just misses meeting the synchronous response time, it can pay up to a two-clock delay in bus cycle penalty. Because the PC AT bus provides a system bus clock, the adapter does not have to add a separate clock and avoids the extra bus time needed to synchronize request and acknowledge signals.

Both MCA and PC AT buses extend their length in incremental clock period cycles. The argument over which type of bus is better has been going on for years. Synchronous buses are generally considered easier to implement and best for nonvariable-length bus cycles to devices such as memory. Asynchronous buses are considered best for mixed speed devices and slower, longer buses. Synchronous buses are generally considered to operate open ended, which means no response is required before the bus cycle proceeds. Asynchronous buses normally require a response from the addressed device before the bus cycle proceeds. Using these definitions, the PC AT, which is normally considered a synchronous bus, can operate in an asynchronous mode that supports variable-length cycles interlocked by the CH RDY response signal. The MCA bus, which is considered an asynchronous bus, is synchronized to the processor or system clock and extends its bus length in increments of the processor or system clock. Both buses operate in a similar manner and have attributes of both asynchronous and synchronous operation.

Programmable Option Select

The programmable option select feature of MCA is intended to eliminate the use of jumpers and DIP switches on adapter boards for setting addresses, interrupts, DMA channels, and so on. The concept of the scheme is quite simple. Each MCA slot is addressed using a common block of 8 I/O-port-byte addresses. A slot is enabled to respond to these 8 I/O addresses by setting one of 8 bits in the card select register on the system board. The adapter responds with a unique 2-byte identification code. This ID code is then used to look up an adapter description file, whose contents define the adapter and provide information on how to set up the adapter. Table 12-1 defines the POS functions and I/O register definitions.

Table 12-1. POS Address Register Decodes

Address (Hex)	Function
0094	System board enable/setup register
0095	Reserved
0096	Adapter enable/setup register
0097	Reserved
0100	POS register 0: adapter identification byte (least significant byte)
0101	POS register 1: adapter identification byte (most significant byte)
0102	POS register 2: option select data byte 1. Bit 0 of this byte is designated as Card Enable (CDEN)
0103	POS register 3: option select data byte 2
0104	POS register 4: option select data byte 3
0105	POS register 5: option select data byte 4. Bit 7 of this byte is designated as −CHCK. Bit 6 of this byte is reserved.
0106	POS register 6: subaddress extension (least significant byte)
0107	POS register 7: subaddress extension (most significant byte)

The register at I/O port address 96H is used to enable the setup of POS addresses 100H to 107H on the system board. Bit 7 enables the setup of system board devices such as DMA, the serial port, and the printer port. Bit 5 enables the setup of the integrated VGA display adapters on the system board. I/O port 96 is used to select which expansion slot is to be mapped into the POS address range 100H to 107H. Table 12-2 defines the value set in I/O port address 96H to select a specific MCA expansion slot position for POS access.

Table 12-2. MCA Channel Slot Selection Register Definition

Channel Position Selected for Setup	7	6*	5*	4*	3	2	1	0
None	0	0	0	0	0	X	X	X
1	0	0	0	0	1	0	0	0
2	0	0	0	0	1	0	0	1
3	0	0	0	0	1	0	1	0
4	0	0	0	0	1	0	1	1
5	0	0	0	0	1	1	0	0
6	0	0	0	0	1	1	0	1
7	0	0	0	0	1	1	1	0
8	0	0	0	0	1	1	1	1
Channel Reset	1	0	0	0	X	X	X	X

*These bits are written to as 0 but read as 1.

After an MCA expansion slot is selected, I/O port addresses 100H to 107H can be accessed for information concerning the adapter present in the selected slot. POS registers 0 and 1 are read-only and always contain the adapter ID code. The remaining POS registers, 2 through 7, generally contain free-form POS information. However, IBM has published guidelines on how to use the free-form POS registers. Three register bits are not free-form and are defined in specific registers and bit positions. Register 2, bit 0 is defined as the adapter enable bit; when this bit is set to zero, the adapter is disabled and will respond only to a channel setup access. Register 5, bit 7 is used to indicate that a channel check condition has been generated by this adapter. Register 5, bit 6 indicates that additional status information on the channel check can be found in POS registers 6 and 7.

Some fields are required when certain features are implemented on the adapter boards. Adapter devices that use burst mode with the arbitration feature of MCA must implement a fairness enable bit; when this bit is active, all other priority devices are serviced before this device is serviced again. Devices using the arbitration scheme for bus access must implement a programmable arbitration level field. Devices that have an adapter ROM mapped into system address space must support a programmable segment locator address. All devices that can be in more than one slot at a time in the system must provide for a programmable I/O address and interrupt level. This scheme is not new; the Apple II supports slot specific ROM and RAM locations that can be used to support adapter specific configuration and initialization information and programs.

It is also possible to detect the presence of an adapter board by sensing bit 0 of I/O-port register address 91H. This bit is set by the detection of the card select feedback signal, which the adapter generates when it is accessed. It is reset automatically with a read operation.

Bus Arbitration Feature

MCA uses a centralized bus arbitration scheme that permits other bus masters to take control of the system bus. The centralized bus arbitration control point supports up to sixteen arbitrating devices, including the system microprocessor, eight channels of processor board DMA channels, and expansion slot bus master devices.

Seven bus signals are used to support the alternate bus master feature. These signals communicate with the central arbitration control point and the adapter's local arbitration circuits. These signals are

PREEMPT	Requests bus control
ARB/GRT	Indicates an arbitration cycle
BURST	Indicates a request for multiple cycles
ARB0–ARB3	Indicate to the central point arbiter the requested arbitration level

Table 12-3 defines the relationship of the processor, DMA channels, and free arbitration level in the system.

The bus arbitration feature supports a special mode. When an adapter implements this feature, the central arbiter services each adapter bus request in priority sequence with one bus cycle, then moves to the next priority device. With this scheme, all adapters have access to the bus without being locked out by a higher-level device taking all bus cycles.

MCA Interrupts

Interrupts on the MCA channel are similar to those on the PC AT. They are implemented using the same 8259A controller device or equivalent cir-

Table 12-3. Arbitration Priority Level Assignments

ARB Level	Primary Assignment
−2	Memory refresh
−1	NMI
0	DMA channel 0*
1	DMA channel 1
2	DMA channel 2
3	DMA channel 3
4	DMA channel 4*
5	DMA channel 5
6	DMA channel 6
7	DMA channel 7
8	Reserved
9	Reserved
A	Reserved
B	Reserved
C	Reserved
D	Reserved
E	Reserved
F	System microprocessor

*These DMA channels are programmable to any arbitration level.

cuits. Because two controllers are used, a total of fifteen interrupt requests, plus the NMI interrupt, are provided in the system. Interrupt levels 3, 4, 5, 6, 7, and 9 are present on the 8-bit bus interface, similar to PC AT interrupt levels. Levels 10, 11, 13, 14, and 15 are on the 16-bit MCA extension, the same as on the 16-bit PC AT extension slot.

MCA interrupts are different than PC AT interrupts in two significant features. The MCA channel interrupts are negative-active level-sensitive and driven with open collector devices. This permits easy sharing of interrupt levels between adapters in different slots and sharing of multiple interrupt sources in a single slot adapter. PC AT bus interrupts did not share between slots because they were rising-edge sensitive interrupt requests. IBM has published a proposed software algorithm that, if implemented by adapter software, allows an orderly identification of the interrupting source in a shared-level sensitive interrupt environment. For an adapter with high-performance interrupt service routine requirements, sharing may not be possible or practical.

Physical Characteristics of MCA Adapters

MCA adapter boards are significantly smaller than those of the PC, XT, and AT. Table 12-4 compares the sizes of these expansion channel architectures.

Table 12-4. System Expansion Adapter Size Comparison

Adapter Type	Height	Length	Total Area
PC/XT	3.9 in.	13.2 in.	51.48 sq. in.
PC AT	4.5 in.	13.2 in.	59.40 sq. in.
MCA	3.05 in.	11.5 in.	35.075 sq. in.

Note: Actual usable area is smaller due to restrictions on components placed near edges of the adapter board and in connector areas.

The long thin aspect ratio of the MCA adapter makes signal routing difficult and often forces the use of multiple signal-layer adapter board designs. See Figure 12-2. The design of MCA adapter boards is also aggravated by the high number of card-edge signals and their close spacing requirements of .05 inch apart. The area of external connector access in the MCA adapter board is also smaller than that on the PC, XT, and AT boards. All these factors tend to make adapter designs for the MCA more expensive than equivalent designs on the older PC, XT, or AT bus.

MCA Power and Ground

MCA significantly increased the grounding and power distribution capabilities to the expansion slots. In a 16-bit slot, for example, seventeen grounds are provided and arranged such that each signal has a ground within 0.1 inch. In addition, on a 16-bit MCA slot, seven card-edge tabs provide +5 Vdc and two provide +12 Vdc. Note that a −5 Vdc power source is no longer available on the bus, as it is on the PC XT and AT buses. IBM also specified the typical and maximum allowed currents available for each MCA adapter slot. See Table 12-5.

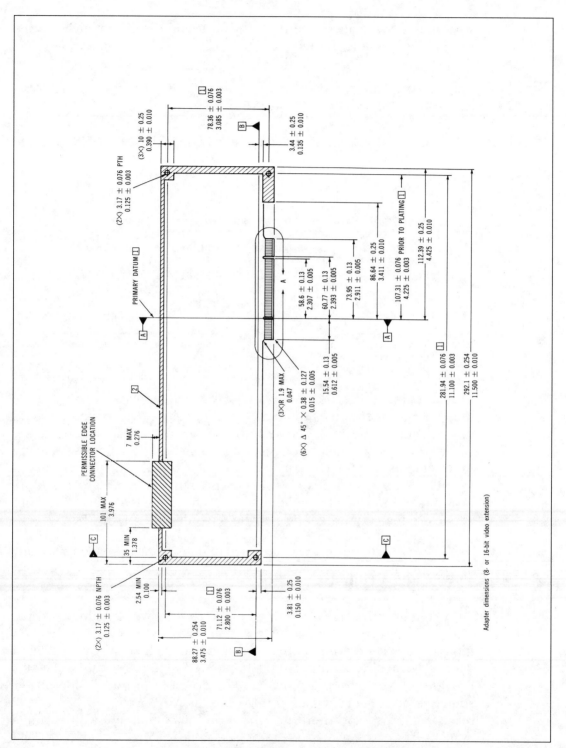

Figure 12-2. MCA adapter board dimensions.

Table 12-5. MCA Adapter Current Capacity per Slot

Supply Voltage	Typical Current per Connector	Maximum Statistical Current per Connector
+5.0 Vdc	1.4 A	1.6 A
+12.0 Vdc	0.100 A	0.175 A
−12.0 Vdc	0.040 A	0.040 A

MCA Signal Definitions

For a familiarity with the basic MCA bus operations, it is necessary to define the functions of the basic MCA signal set used in 16-bit bus mode. This section describes the functions of the 16-bit MCA bus signals.

A0–23

A0 through A23 (address bits 0–23) provide the bus with memory and I/O addresses. They are driven by the present bus master and thus must be tristatable when another bus master takes control. They support a full 24-bit 16M memory range and a 16-bit 64K I/O address space. During I/O operations, A16–A23 are not used. The address signals are not latched and active throughout the bus cycle. If this is required by the adapter design, the rising edge of the ADL bus signal or the falling edge of the CMD bus signal can be used to latch the address bits.

D0–15

Data bus bits D0 through D15 are used to transfer data between slave and master devices on the bus and must be driven with tristate devices. Only 8-bit devices use the low-order data bits D0–D7. During memory-write or I/O-write cycles, the write data must be held valid on the bus the entire time the CMD signal is valid. During memory-read or I/O-read cycles, the data bus must be driven with read data prior to the rising edge of the CMD signal. The setup timing varies with MCA systems.

$\overline{\text{ALD}}$

The $\overline{\text{ALD}}$ (address decode latch) signal is driven by the present bus master and indicates when the bus address and status signal are valid. Its trailing edge can be used to latch the status and address information on a slave device adapter.

M/$\overline{\text{I/O}}$

The M/$\overline{\text{I/O}}$ (memory/input/output) signal is driven by the present bus master and indicates the type of bus cycle: either a memory cycle or an I/O address space cycle. It is typically latched by the trailing edge of the ADL signal or the leading edge of the CMD signal.

$\overline{\text{S0}}$ and $\overline{\text{S1}}$

The $\overline{\text{S0}}$ and $\overline{\text{S1}}$ (status bits 0 and 1) signals are driven by the present bus master and are combined and decoded with the M/$\overline{\text{I/O}}$ signal to determine the exact type of bus operation. Table 12-6 defines the valid decodes of the $\overline{\text{S0}}$, $\overline{\text{S1}}$, and M/$\overline{\text{I/O}}$ signals.

Table 12-6.   Bus Status Decodes

M/$\overline{\text{I/O}}$	$\overline{\text{S0}}$	$\overline{\text{S1}}$	Function
0	0	0	Reserved A
0	0	1	I/O write
0	1	0	I/O read
0	1	1	Reserved B
1	0	0	Reserved C
1	0	0	Memory write
1	1	0	Memory read
1	1	1	Reserved D

CMD

The CMD (Command) signal is driven by the present bus master and defines when the bus master write data is valid on the bus. During bus read operations, the addressed data slave device must place data on the bus before the trailing edge of the CMD signal. This signal is often ANDed with the decodes of the status information to create the more AT-bus equivalent signals MEMR, MEMW, IOW, and IOR needed for control of chip-level devices on the adapter.

SBHE

The $\overline{\text{SBHE}}$ (system bus high enable) signal is driven by the present bus master and indicates that a data transfer will occur on the high byte, bits D8–D15. On 8-bit transfer cycles, this line is not activated. It is valid with the bus address signals.

MADE24

The MADE24 (memory address enable 24) signal is driven by the present bus master and indicates that the maximum system memory address space is 16 megabytes. This signal is valid with the system bus address signals.

CD DS 16

The $\overline{\text{CD DS 16}}$ (card data size 16) signal is returned by an addressed slave device and indicates that it is a 16-bit data bus size adapter. This signal is unique to each slot.

DS 16 RTN

The $\overline{\text{DS 16 RTN}}$ (data size 16 return) signal is similar to the $\overline{\text{CD DS 16}}$ signal, except it is driven with an open collector and wired OR to a similar signal from each slot. When an adapter drives this signal, a bus master can determine that the bus transfer from the addressed slot adapter will be 16 bits in size.

CD SFDBK

The $\overline{\text{CD SFDBK}}$ (card select feedback) signal is driven by a bus slave device when it is addressed as either memory or I/O. It is used to detect the presence of an adapter in the specific slot. There is a unique signal from each DMA slot. The $\overline{\text{CD SFDBK}}$ signal from each slot is latched in I/O port register 91H on the system board. This signal is used by system diagnostics to determine if an adapter is installed in a slot and what memory and address decodes are used.

CD CHRDY

The CD CHRDY (card channel ready) signal is driven by an addressed slave device and indicates that the bus cycle can proceed at the bus master's optimum speed. If the slave drives this signal inactive, the bus master extends the bus cycle time up to 3 microseconds, depending on the time held inactive. This is equivalent to the $\overline{\text{CH RDY}}$ signal on the PC AT bus. This signal is unique to each slot.

CHRDYRTN

The CHRDYRTN (channel ready return) signal is the wired AND of all CD CHRDY signals from the bus slots. It is monitored by the present bus master to indicate a ready or bus extended cycle.

$\overline{\text{PREEMPT}}$

The $\overline{\text{PREEMPT}}$ signal is generated by a DMA slave device or bus master to request access to the system bus through the centralized arbitration function on the system board.

ARB/$\overline{\text{GNT}}$

The ARB/$\overline{\text{GNT}}$ (arbitration/grant) signal is driven from the centralized arbitration point on the system board. Its leading edge indicates an arbitration cycle is in progress. The trailing edge indicates the end of the arbitration cycle and granting a device access to the bus.

ARB0-3

The ARB0–ARB3 (arbitration priority bus bits 0–3) signals are used to indicate the current bus priority level and the current adapter priority level request. These four bits are encoded to support 16 possible priority levels. All bits on is the lowest priority, and all bits off is the highest.

$\overline{\text{BURST}}$

The $\overline{\text{BURST}}$ signal is sent by a bus master or a slave DMA device that has obtained bus control through an arbitration cycle. This signal indicates that the device will transfer a block of data in burst mode.

$\overline{TC}$

The $\overline{TC}$ (terminal count) signal is driven by a channel DMA device. It indicates to the adapter that the total transfers on the specified channel have been reached and DMA operations will cease on this channel.

CD SETUP

The CD SETUP (card setup) signal is unique to each slot and is selected using the POS I/O registers on the system board. It is activated by system setup software to obtain the adapter ID and other setup information at I/O port addresses 100H to 107H on the adapter board. Only one CD SETUP should be active at a time.

$\overline{CHCK}$

The $\overline{CHCK}$ (channel check) signal is generated by the slot adapter boards to indicate to the system board that an error condition exists on one of the adapter boards. This signal is wire ORed with all bus CHCK signals. Identification of which slot adapter has the problem is determined by interrogating the POS register for each slot.

$\overline{IRQ3\text{-}7}$, $\overline{9\text{-}12}$, $\overline{14}$, $\overline{15}$

Eleven IRQ (interrupt level request) signals ($\overline{IRQ3\text{-}7}$, $\overline{9\text{-}12}$, $\overline{14}$, and $\overline{15}$) are used by the bus slot adapter to generate an interrupt request to the system board's interrupt controllers. These signals are nearly equivalent to those on the PC AT bus. They are negative-active level-sensitive and must be driven with an open collector driver to allow slot sharing of the interrupt levels.

AUDIO

The AUDIO signal is used to carry audio signals between adapters and the system board's audio subsystem. It supports a maximum 2.5 volt peak-to-peak signal reference around audio ground.

AUDIO GND

The AUDIO GND (audio ground) signal provides a separate audio ground return path for the audio signal.

$\overline{\text{REFRESH}}$

The $\overline{\text{REFRESH}}$ signal indicates that the present bus memory-read cycle is a dynamic memory-refresh cycle. This signal can be used to refresh dynamic memory installed in the MCA expansion slots.

CHRESET

The CHRESET (channel reset) signal is driven from the system board and is activated when the system is powered on. It is used to reset the adapter to a known state before operation. This signal can be activated also under program control.

32-Bit Extension Bus Signal

The 16-bit MCA can be extended to 32 bits with the addition of the following signals to the slots.

A24-31

A24 through A31 (address bits 24–31) are used to extend the MCA memory addressing range from 16 megabytes to 4 gigabytes.

D16-31

Signals $\overline{\text{D16}}$ through $\overline{\text{D31}}$ (data bus bits 16–31) extend the data bus width from 8 or 16 bits to 32 bits.

$\overline{\text{BE0-3}}$

$\overline{\text{BE0}}$ through $\overline{\text{BE3}}$ (bus enable bits 0–3) are used to enable data transfers on the data bus for each individual byte of the 32-bit bus. BE0 enables the low-order byte, EB1 the next byte, EB2 the next byte, and EB3 the high-order byte. These signals are similar to SBHE and A0 signals, which enable 8-bit and 16-bit bus transfers.

$\overline{\text{CD DS 32}}$

The $\overline{\text{CD DS 32}}$ (card data size 32) signal is from the MCA slave slot device and indicates a 32-bit operation is possible on this adapter. This signal is similar in function to the $\overline{\text{CD DS 16}}$ bus signal, except it is used for 32-bit operations.

$\overline{\text{DS 32 RTN}}$

The $\overline{\text{DS 32 RTN}}$ (data size 32 return) signal indicates to the present bus master that the addressed adapter supports a 32-bit data transfer. This signal is similar to the $\overline{\text{DS 16 RTN}}$ bus signal used for 16-bit bus operations.

MCA Video Extension Signal

MCA supports access to the integrated PS/S system board's video adapter signals. The following signals are provided.

VSYNC	Vertical sync timing signal (output)
HSYNC	Horizontal sync timing signal (output)
BLANK	Video blanking timing signal (output)
P0-P7	PEL (picture element) digital DAC input data (output)
DCLK	PEL clock indicating new DAC data (output)
ESYNC	Enable horizontal and vertical sync signal outputs (input)
EVIDEO	Enable P0–P7 video outputs (input)
EDCLK	Enable video dot clock output (input)

Basic MCA Bus Cycle

Figure 12-3 illustrates the basic signal flow for an MCA bus cycle. The following is the sequence of signal events for a basic bus cycle.

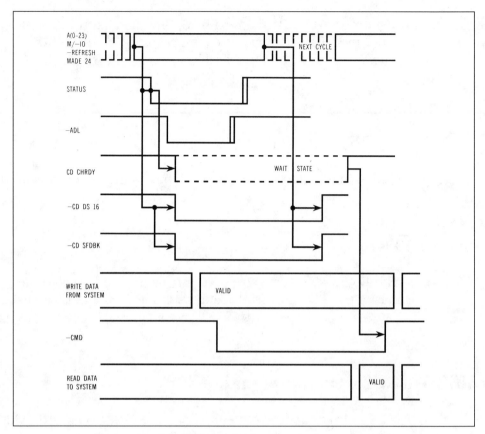

Figure 12-3. Basic MCA bus cycle. *(Courtesy International Business Machines Corporation)*

1. The address bus, including MADE24 and I/O/M signals, becomes valid immediately after the S0 and S1 bus status signals become valid.

2. The ADL signal becomes active. This is the first indication to the adapter of the start of a new bus cycle. On the trailing edge of the ADL signal, the bus adapter decodes the address and command, and determines if the bus cycle is for this slot adapter.

3. If the bus decode is valid for this slot adapter, it returns the CD SFDBK and CD DS 16 signals if appropriate. The adapter also determines if it will require a bus cycle extension by driving CH RDY inactive.

4. If the bus cycle is a write operation, the data bus becomes valid.

5. The CMD signal is activated, indicating valid bus data.

6. The address bus and status signal become invalid in preparation for the next bus cycle.

7. As the address bus and status become invalid, the adapter removes the $\overline{\text{CD SFDBK}}$ and $\overline{\text{CD DS 16}}$ signals.

8. If the bus operation is a read cycle, the adapter places read data on the data bus.

9. If $\overline{\text{CH RDY}}$ was inactive, it is now activated.

10. The $\overline{\text{CMD}}$ signal is deactivated, indicating the end of the present bus cycle.

MCA Enhancements

At present, MCA supports a 32-bit bus with a maximum 20M transfer rate using two 100-nanosecond clocks. IBM has indicated that several enhancements to improve MCA performance are forthcoming. These enhancements include the addition of a data-streaming mode that supports block data transfer in one clock cycle. This scheme would increase MCA performance to 40M per second. It is also rumored that IBM will introduce a version of MCA that uses the address bus in multiplexed mode to support a 64-bit data bus mode. This scheme uses the address bus in multiplexed mode to support a 64-bit data bus mode. This scheme would increase bus performance to 80M per second. Also reported are new bus drivers and receivers that will permit bus cycle times as low as 50 ns. Combined with the other enhancements, this would support a bus performance level of 160M per second.

Chapter 13

PS/2 Interrupts, DMA, Timer Counters, I/O, and Memory

THIS CHAPTER REVIEWS the support devices on the IBM PS/2 system boards: interrupt support, DMA support, timer counter support, and real-time clock support. PS/2 I/O and memory maps are presented also. These support devices and features are similar to those on the original PC and AT systems. The information presented here identifies the differences and enhancements in the PS/2 implementations.

Interrupts

PS/2 interrupts are nearly identical to interrupts on the PC AT. See Table 13-1. The primary difference is the use of the level-sensitive feature of the 8259A controllers. The 15 levels of 8259A-equivalent interrupts are software accessible at the same I/O port addresses as in the PC AT. Controller 1 is at I/O port address 20H, and controller 2 is at I/O port address A0H. For detailed information on the operations and programming of the interrupt controllers, see Chapters 6 and 11.

In the PS/2 design, the NMI interrupt has additional functions. It is used to accept interrupts from the following sources:

System memory parity check circuits

Watchdog timer timeout circuits

MCA arbitration timeout circuits

MCA channel check signal activated

The NMI interrupt can be masked using an OUT instruction to the real-time clock address port. Because only 6 bits of port address 70H data

Table 13-1.   PS/2 Interrupts

Level	Function		
NMI	Parity, watchdog timer, arbitration time-out, channel check		
IRQ0	Timer 0 output		
IRQ1	Keyboard interrupt input		
IRQ2	Interrupt input second controller	IRQ8	Real-time clock
		IRQ9	Redirect cascade
		IRQ10	Reserved
		IRQ11	Reserved
		IRQ12	Mouse
		IRQ13	Math coprocessor exception
		IRQ14	Fixed disk
		IRQ15	Reserved
IRQ3	Serial alternate		
IRQ4	Serial primary		
IRQ5	Reserved		
IRQ6	Diskette		
IRQ7	Parallel port		

IRQ8 through IRQ15 are cascaded through IRQ2.

is used to address the real-time clock functions and CMOS memory, the high-order bit is used to mask the NMI on and off. With bit 7 on, an OUT instruction to real-time I/O port address 70H enables the NMI. With bit 7 off (equal to zero), an OUT instruction to I/O port address 70H masks the NMI off. This function of NMI masking is identical in the PC AT and the PS/2 systems. Note that when using I/O port 70H to control the NMI mask, all accesses to I/O port address 70H must be followed quickly with an access to I/O port 71H to insure the proper continued operation of the real-time clock MC146818 chip.

DMA

From a software point of view, the PS/2 implementation of DMA has two modes of operation: 8237 compatible mode and extended mode. 8237 compatible mode is nearly identical to the PC AT implementation using the 8327 DMA devices. The primary software difference is that eight DMA channels are in the PS/2. (Channel 4, which is used for cascading in the PC AT, is available for use in the PS/2.)

DMA channels 0 through 7 are mapped to MCA arbitration levels 0 through 7. The program control and status registers of the 8237 are mapped to the same I/O port addresses as in the PC AT. The DMA page registers also are available at the same I/O port addresses. The extra DMA page register required for the new channel 4 is at I/O port 8FH. For detailed information on the operation and programming of the 8237 DMA controller, see Chapters 6 and 11. Table 13-2 defines the I/O addresses used to program and control PS/2 DMA.

Table 13-2. PS/2 DMA I/O Address Map

Address (Hex)	Description	Bit Description	Byte Pointer
0000	Channel 0, memory address register	00–15	Yes
0001	Channel 0, transfer count register	00–15	Yes
0002	Channel 1, memory address register	00–15	Yes
0003	Channel 1 transfer count register	00–15	Yes
0004	Channel 2, memory address register	00–15	Yes
0005	Channel 2, transfer count register	00–15	Yes
0006	Channel 3, memory address register	00–15	Yes
0007	Channel 3, transfer count register	00–15	Yes
0008	Channel 0–3, status register	00–07	
000A	Channel 0–3, mask register (set/reset)	00–02	
000B	Channel 0–3, mode register (write)	00–07	
000C	Clear byte pointer (write)	NA	
000D	Master clear (write)	NA	
000E	Channel 0–3, clear mask register (write)	NA	Yes
000F	Channel 0–3, write mask register	00–03	Yes
0018	Extended function register (write)	00–07	
001A	Extended function execute	00–07	Yes*
0081	Channel 2, page table address register**	00–07	
0082	Channel 3, page table address register**	00–07	
0083	Channel 1, page table address register**	00–07	
0087	Channel 0, page table address register**	00–07	
0089	Channel 6, page table address register**	00–07	
008A	Channel 7, page table address register**	00–07	
008B	Channel 5, page table address register**	00–07	

Table 13-2.   *(cont.)*

Address (Hex)	Description	Bit Description	Byte Pointer
008F	Channel 4, page table address register**	00–07	
00C0	Channel 4, memory address register	00–15	Yes
00C2	Channel 4, transfer count register	00–15	Yes
00C4	Channel 5, memory address register	00–15	Yes
00C6	Channel 5, transfer count register	00–15	Yes
00C8	Channel 6, memory address register	00–15	Yes
00CA	Channel 6, transfer count register	00–15	Yes
00CC	Channel 7, memory address register	00–15	Yes
00CE	Channel 7, transfer count register	00–15	Yes
00D0	Channel 4–7, status register	00–07	
00D4	Channel 4–7, mask register (set/reset)	00–02	
00D6	Channel 4–7, mode register (write)	00–07	
00D8	Clear byte pointer (write)	NA	
00DA	Master clear (write)	NA	
00DC	Channel 4–7, clear mask register (write)	NA	
00DE	Channel 4–7, write mask register	00–03	Yes

*Depends on the function used.
**Upper byte of memory address register.

The PS/2 also supports an extended mode of DMA operation that adds capability to the DMA functions. The extended mode is accessed through two new DMA I/O port register definitions. I/O port address 18II, the function register, is used to address a channel and specify a function to be performed. The data sent to I/O port address 18H is formatted as follows:

Bits 0–2   Specify the DMA channel for which the command is targeted

Bit 3   Not used

Bits 4–7   Specify a direct or indirect command to the specified channel

Table 13-3 defines the valid commands defined by bits 4 through 7 of I/O port address 18H.

If the command is indirect and has associated data, the data is written to I/O port address 1AH, the extended function execution register. You can fully set up and control DMA functions using the 1AH and 18H I/O

Table 13-3. Commands Specified by Register 18H, Bits 4–7

Register/Bits Accessed	Bits	Program Command (Hex)	Byte Pointer
I/O address register	00–15	0	Yes
Reserved		1	
Memory address register write	00–23	2	Yes
Memory address register read	00–23	3	Yes
Transfer count register write	00–15	4	Yes
Transfer count register read	00–15	5	Yes
Status register read	00–07	6	
Mode register	00–07	7	
Arbiter register	00–07	8	
Mask register set single bit*		9	
Mask register reset single bit*		A	
Reserved		B	
Reserved		C	
Master clear*		D	
Reserved		E	
Reserved		F	

*Direct commands to the function register.

port registers. Note that the extended function memory address registers, transfer count registers, and status register are 8237-equivalent registers. In extended mode, the mode register is redefined and the I/O port address transfer register is added. This register allows the specification of an I/O port address as a target for the I/O DMA operation. In 8237 mode, the I/O address is forced to 0000H for the I/O DMA bus cycle. The high byte of the memory address register in extended mode is equivalent to the DMA page register value set in 8327 mode.

In extended mode, the 8237 mode register specified by command 7 in I/O port address 18H and loaded by a write to I/O port 1AH supports new functions not present in 8237 mode. Table 13-4 defines the bits and functions for the new mode command in extended mode. The primary additions are support for 8- or 16-bit transfer specifications and the use of the I/O address during I/O DMA bus cycles to address the target I/O port. As with the PC AT, PS/2 DMA does not support 16-bit operations from 8-bit memory or I/O devices.

Table 13-4. Extended Mode Register Definition

Bit	Function
7	0 = Reserved (must be set to 0)
6	0 = 8-bit transfer
	1 = 16-bit transfer
5	0 = Reserved (must be set to 0)
4	Reserved (must be set to 0)
3	0 = Read memory transfer
	1 = Write memory transfer
2	0 = Verify
	1 = Transfer data
1	0 = Reserved (must be set to 0)
0	0 = I/O address equals 0000H
	1 = Use programmed I/O address

DMA channels 0 and 4 can have their arbitration levels programmed in extended mode. The other DMA channels have their arbitration levels fixed; the channel number corresponds to the arbitration level. The arbitration levels for channels 0 and 4 are specified by using the extended mode register command 8 and specifying either channel 0 or 4 in the I/O port write to address 18H. After the command is set, the arbitration level is written to the function execution register at I/O port address 1AH. All arbitration values except FH, which is the microprocessor level, are valid.

Although the software interface to the PS/2 DMA feature is close to the PC AT, the implementation on the MCA is quite different. DMA on the PC AT expansion slots uses a special single bus cycle to accomplish a transfer between memory and an I/O port. Thus, data is read and written in the same cycle, with no intermediate storage in the DMA device. This is possible because the PC AT provides separate signals for memory and I/O read and write operations and uses the DACK signals on the bus to identify the DMA source device.

The MCA has only one signal that specifies I/O or memory operations, and only one read or write operation at a time can be specified. Simultaneous read and write cycles are not possible on the MCA. Thus, a DMA transfer on the PS/2 MCA requires two cycles: a read followed by a write. On the MCA, memory-DMA cycles are two clocks in length and I/O-DMA cycles are three clocks in length. Thus, a PS/2 MCA DMA transfer is five clocks in length, or approximately 500 ns. A PC AT DMA transfer with a simultaneous read and write is also five clocks in length and is also 500 ns in length (at a 10-MHz bus clock speed).

Timer Counters

The timer counters in the PS/2 are similar to 8253 and 8254 devices used in the PC XT and AT, respectively. The PS/2, however, has two major changes. First, channel 1, which was used to request memory refresh bus cycles, is eliminated. All bits in control registers used to access and control this counter in the 8254 are now reserved and invalid. For example, I/O port address 41H, which is used to read and write to channel 1, is an invalid I/O port address in the PS/2. The PS/2 uses and programs channels 0 and 2 the same as the PC AT.

Second, a new channel was added; channel 3 is a watchdog timer. This channel is only 8 bits in length and operates only in timer counter mode 0 (interrupt on terminal count). The input to this timer is the clock out signal from channel 0. The gate input is IRQ0. The output is tied to the system microprocessors' NMI input. Timer 3, the watchdog timer, is used to detect when the IRQ0 input is active for more than one period of the timer 0 output. When timer 3 is incremented through a program set value of FFH, an NMI is generated. This scheme allows the detection of the loss of software service to the system timer interrupt and the detection of a possible system error condition.

The new channel 3 is read and written using I/O port address 44H. The control byte for the new timer 3 is at I/O port address 47H. Following are the valid control commands for timer 3:

Command 1 at 00H   Latch counter 3

Command 2 at 10H   Read or write bits 0–7

All other values are invalid for counter 3 commands. For further information on the operation and programming of the timer counter function in the PS/2, consult Chapters 6 and 11 and the 8254 Intel timer counter chip specifications.

Real-Time Clock and the Audio System

The PS/2 implementation of the real-time clock function is identical to that of the PC AT. See the PC AT real-time clock description in Chapter 11.

The audio systems on the PC, XT, AT, and PS/2 are nearly identical.

The only difference is on the PS/2, in which access to the audio system is provided by the MCA bus. Figure 13-1 illustrates the implementation of the audio system on the PS/2.

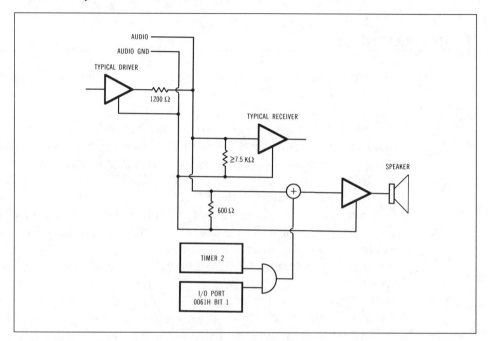

Figure 13-1. PS/2 audio system block diagram. *(Courtesy International Business Machines Corporation)*

Parallel Port

The PS/2 enhanced the parallel port functions over that provided in the PC XT and AT systems. Using the programmable option select capability of the PS/2's on-board I/O, you can define the parallel port's base I/O address and select PC XT and AT compatible mode or extended mode. In extended mode, the port can be defined as an input port, output port, or bidirectional port. POS register 102H is used to select the base I/O address for the parallel port and select compatible or extended mode. Table 13-5 defines POS 102H control fields for setting up the parallel port on the system board.

Table 13-6 defines the status input signals and control output port signals for the parallel port. Note that these are identical to the PC and AT parallel port definitions with the exception of the direction control signal, bit 5, in the control port. This bit is enabled in extended mode and allows the software to set the direction of the data transfer on the data port.

Table 13-5. POS Register Setup

Bit 6	Bit 5		Function
0	0		Parallel 1
0	1		Parallel 2
1	0		Parallel 3
POS Mode Bit	**Parallel Control Bit**	**System Reset Bit**	**Function**
0	0	1	Extended write
0	0	0	Extended write
0	1	0	Extended read
1	NA	0	Compatible write

Table 13-6. Parallel Port Status and Control Port Definitions

Status Port	
Port Bit	**Port Data**
7	$\overline{\text{BUSY}}$
6	$\overline{\text{ACK}}$
5	PE
4	SLCT
3	$\overline{\text{ERROR}}$
2	IRQ status
1	Reserved
0	Reserved
Parallel Control Port	
Port Bit	**Port Data**
7	Reserved
6	Reserved
5	Direction
4	IRQ EN
3	Pin 17 (SLCT IN)
2	Pin 16 ($\overline{\text{INIT}}$)
1	Pin 14 (AUTO FD XT)
0	Pin 1 (STROBE)

Memory and I/O Maps

The memory map of the PS/2 is illustrated in Figure 13-2. The upper limit of memory depends on the system and the microprocessor implementation.

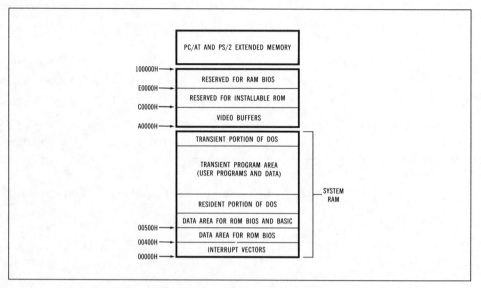

Figure 13-2. PS/2 memory map.

The I/O map of the PS/2 is similar to the PC XT and AT I/O map, with the addition of a new register to support the enhanced features of the PS/2 architecture. Table 13-7 lists the I/O port map for the IBM PS/2 system.

Table 13-7.   PS/2 I/O Map

Hex Addresses	Device
0000–001F	DMA controller
0020, 0021	Interrupt controller 1, 8259A
0040, 0042, 0043, 0044, 0047	System timers
0060	Keyboard, auxiliary device
0061	System control port B
0064	Keyboard, auxiliary device
0070, 0071	RT/CMOS and NMI mask
0074–0076	Reserved
0081–0083, 0087	DMA page registers (0–3)

Table 13-7. *(cont.)*

Hex Addresses	Device
0089, 008A, 008B, 008F	DMA page registers (4–7)
0090	Central arbitration control port
0091	Card selected feedback
0092	System control port A
0093	Reserved
0094	System board setup
0096, 0097	POS, channel connector select
00A0, 00A1	Interrupt controller 2, 8259A
00C0–00DF	DMA controller
00F0–00FF	Math coprocessor
0100–0107	Programmable option select
0278–027B	Parallel port 3
02FE, 02FF	Serial port 2 (RS-232C)
0378–037B	Parallel port 2
03BC–03BF	Parallel port 1
03B4, 03B5, 03BA, 03C0–03C5	Video subsystem
03CE, 03CF, 03D4, 03D5, 03DA	Video subsystem
03C6–03C9	Video DAC
03F0–03F7	Diskette drive controller
03F8–03FF	Serial port 1 (RS-232C)

Bibliography

Altera Corporation, *Altera Micro Channel Handbook*, May 1988.

Intel Corporation, *iAPX 88 Book*, July 1981.

Intel Corporation, *iAPX 86, 88 User's Manual*, August 1981.

Intel Corporation, *i486 Microprocessor*, April 1989.

Intel Corporation, *Microprocessors and Peripherals Handbook, Volume 1—Microprocessors*, 1989.

Intel Corporation, *1982 Component Data Catalog*, January 1982.

International Business Machines Corporation, *BASIC, First Edition*, August 1981.

International Business Machines Corporation, *Disk Operating System*, 1982.

International Business Machines Corporation, *IBM Personal System/2 Model 80 Technical Reference, First Edition*, 1987.

International Business Machines Corporation, *IBM Personal System/2 Models 50 and 60 Technical Reference, First Edition*, April 1987.

International Business Machines Corporation, *IBM Personal System/2 Models 50, 60, 80 MCA Architecture, Revision 5.3*, May 1987.

International Business Machines Corporation, *Macro Assembler, First Edition*, December 1981.

International Business Machines Corporation, *Technical References PC, First Edition*, August 1981.

International Business Machines Corporation, *Technical Reference PC XT, Revised Edition*, April 1983.

International Business Machines Corporation, *Technical Reference Personal Computer AT, First Edition*, 1984.

Mostek Corporation, *Mostek 1980 Bytewide Memory Data Book*, 1980.

Motorola Inc., *Motorola Microprocessor Data Volume II, Microprocessor, Microcontroller and Peripheral Data, Series A*, 1988.

National Semiconductor Corporation, *Interface Data Book*, 1980.

Que Corporation, *Networking Personal Computers, Third Edition*, 1989.

Signetics Corporation, *Bipolar and MOS Memory Data Manual*, 1980.

Texas Instruments Inc., *TTL Logic*, March 1988.

Winchrest Books, *MS-DOS Beyond 640K, First Edition*, 1989.

Index

0WS (0 wait states) signal, 280-81
32-bit extension bus signals
  A24–31 (address bits 24–31), 312
  BE0–3 (bus enable bits 0–3),
    312-13
  CD DS 32 (card data size 32), 313
  D16–31 (data but bits 16–31), 312
  DS 32 RTN (data size 32 return),
    313
386 performance accelerator board, 40
486 performance accelerator board, 40
6502 microprocessors, 45
8237-5 DMA controller chip, 91,
  96-97, 112-13, 155
  initialization process, 157-59
  PC AT use of, 287
  PS/2 use of, 321
  registers
    address, 166-67
    clear byte pointer flip-flop, 164
    clear mask, 165
    command, 159-61
    count, 166-67
    master clear, 164
    mode, 162-64
    page, 167-68, 287, 289
    read/write, 159
    status, 165

    table of addresses for control and
      status, 160
    temporary, 165-66
    write all mask-register bits, 165
    write request, 161-62
    write single-mask bit, 162
8253-5 timer-counter chip
  address decode and bus buffers for,
    184
  attaching, 183-85
  circuit diagrams, 186-89
  extended gating and control circuits
    for, 185-90
  gate input control summary table,
    183
  modes of operation, 181-83
  port control bit definitions, 190-91
  timer-counter functions
    implemented with, 175, 179-81
8254 timer-counter chip for PC AT,
  291
8259A interrupt controller, 131-33,
  135-36
  addition of eight 8259A controllers
    possible to create 64 interrupt
    levels using, 152-53, 155
  block diagram, 151-52
  initialization, 138-40

of the expansion, 151-52, 154
initialization command words
    (ICWs), 135, 139-40
    bit definitions for, 140-44
    impact of changing, 148
as interrupt-expansion device,
    150-51
MCA use of, 303
nested mode, 152, 154
operation control words (OCSs),
    135, 139-40
    bit definitions for, 144-48
    impact of changing, 148
second
    PC AT's use of, 289-90
    PS/2's use of, 317
8288 bus controller, 111
68000 microprocessor (Motorola), 46
80385 cache controller, 63, 80
82380 integrated system support
    device, 63

A

Access time of hard disks, 32-33
Adapters, communications
    COM1 RS-232C, 37
    COM2 asynchronous data
        communications, 37
    multiprotocol, 37
Adapters, diskette drive, 123, 169
Adapters, game control, 123
Adapters, graphics
    Color Graphics Adapter (CGA)
        memory decoded by, 205
        resolution of 640 x 200 pixels,
            28
        used in PC, 28
    Enhanced Graphics (EGA)
        introduced in PC AT, 7
        resolution of 640 x 350 pixels,
            28
    Hercules Monochrome Graphics
        Adapter (HMGA), 28

        Hercules resolution of 720 x 350
            pixels, 28
    Monochrome Display Adapter
        (MDA)
        memory decoded by, 205
        used in PC, 28
    Multi Color Graphics Adapter
        (MCGA), 29
        resolution of 640 x 480 2-color
            and 320 x 200 256-color
            pixels, 28
        used in PS/2 model 25, 11, 28
        used in PS/2 model 30, 13, 28
    Video Graphics Array (VGA)
        integrated in PS/2 model 30 286,
            15
        integrated in PS/2 model 50 and
            model 50Z, 17
        integrated in PS/2 model 55SX,
            18
        integrated in PS/2 model 60, 20
        integrated in PS/2 model 70, 21
        integrated in PS/2 model 70P, 23
        integrated in PS/2 model 80, 25
        introduced in PS/2, 10
Adapters, hard drive, 82-83
Adapters, interfacing, 42-43
Adapters, MCA, 305-6
Adapters, memory expansion, 39-40
Adapters, multifunction, 43
Adapters, performance accelerator, 40
Adapters, Video Frame Capture, 40
All Points Addressable (APA) color
    graphics, 28
Analog Devices, 245
Analog-to-digital converter (ADC)
    bits of resolution provided, 243-44
    characteristics of, 243-44
    device manufacturers, 244-45
    input range, 243
    length of time for conversion by,
        244

Arbitration priority level
  assignments for the MCA, table of, 304
  channel numbers corresponding to, 322
Assembly language, data transfer using, 172-73
AT extension slot signals
  +5VDC, 273
  DACK5–7 (DMA acknowledge 5–7), 271
  DRQ5–7 (DMA request 5–7), 271
  GND (ground), 273
  I/O CS16 (input/output chip select 16), 272
  IRQ10, 11, 12, 14, and 15 (interrupt requests 10, 11, 12, 14, 15), 272
  LA17-23 (unlatched addresses 17-23), 273
  MASTER, 272
  MEM CS16 (memory chip select 16), 272
  MEMR (memory read), 271
  MEMW (memory write), 271
  SBHE (system bus high enable), 270
  SD8–15 (system data bus bits 8–15), 273
Audio system
  block diagram of PS/2, 324
  of PS/2 similar to PC, PC XT, and PC AT, 323-24
Average access times of disks, 32-33

B

Backup devices, 42
Base address of a segment, 55
BASIC language, data transfer using, 170-72
Benchmark programs' evaluations of system performance, 85-86
Bibliography, 329-30
Binary Synchronous Communications (BSC) protocol, 37

BIOS, timer channels initialized by, 176-77
Boards for prototyping, sources of, 125
Bus arbitration with MCA, 302-3
Bus architecture. *See also* Extended Industry Standard Architecture (EISA) *and* Micro Channel Architecture of the PS/2
  386 AT, 9, 11, 60
  Industry Standard Architecture (ISA), 87, 267-68, 284
  as key attribute in evaluating merits of PC model, 3
  PC, 89-128
  PC 286 AT, 1, 10, 15, 26
  PC AT, 267-85, 300
  PC XT, 89-128
  performance levels of, 88
  PS/2 model 30 286 used of AT's, 10
  of PS/2 models, 11, 298-301
Bus bandwidth capabilities of Intel microprocessors, 74-75
Bus buffer circuit, 213-15
Bus cycle
  8088-driven, 89-91
  MCA, 300, 313-15
  times
    AT, 276-77, 279
    PC, 78
  types, 91, 274
    DMA, 89-91, 95-100, 103-7, 120-21, 168-69, 208, 213, 275, 278, 280
    I/O-port-read, 93-95, 101-4, 119, 275, 277
    I/O-port-write, 94-96, 101-4, 119, 275, 277
    memory-read, 92-93, 100-102, 118, 275-76
    memory-write, 92-94, 100-102, 118, 275-76
Bus extender design
  enhanced (longer length), 251-54
  simple, 247-51

Bus extension and monitoring for PC and XT, 247-65
Bus loading
    PC AT, 279-80
    table of, 122-23
Bus operation, asynchronous MCA, 298-301
Bus parameters, programmable 286, 386SX, and 386, 283-84
Bus power levels, 114-15
Bus signals
    for alternate bus master feature in bus arbitration of MCA
        ARB/GRT, 303
        ARB0–ARB3, 303
        BURST, 303
        PREEMPT, 303
    input specifications, 123
        IIH, 121
        IIL, 121
    output specifications
        IOH, 117-18, 122-23
        IOL, 117, 122-23
Bus system. *See* Bus architecture, Extended Industry Standard Architecture (EISA), *and* Micro Channel Architecture of the PS/2

C

Cache controllers, 9
Card(s)
    extenders, 254-64
    for interfacing, 227-33
    maximum dimensions for insertion in expansion slots of, 125, 127
Cassette
    connector signals, 227
    drive circuit modified for TTL output, 228
    input circuit modified to accept TTL levels, 229
    port, interfacing with, 227-29

Circuit for interfacing to I/O bus interrupt-request line, 149-50
Clock cycles. *See also* Wait state
    at 4.77 MHz, 5
    at 10 MHz, 5-6
    for 286 processor, 59
    inserted in bus cycles to use memory boards, 39
Clock speed (rate), 75
    386 AT bus system, 9, 63
    as key attribute in evaluating merits of PC model, 3
    PC AT, 7-8
    PC XT, 5, 115, 117
    of PS/2 models, 11
    third-party products to extend the PC XT's, 5
CMOS battery-backup
    nonvolatile memory, 283
    real-time clock chip, 291
CMOS RAM, 291-92
COM ports
    adapters for, 37
    overcoming maximum speed of 9600 baud for, 84
    uses of, 37, 83
Communications performance measurement, 83-84
Compare equal latch, 260, 262
Compatibility with IBM product line as key attribute in evaluating merits of PC model, 3
Coprocessors. *See* Numeric coprocessors
CPM operating system, 45-46
Customer Service Units (CSUs) network interface units, 38

D

Data compression and decompression of color images, 40
Data Terminal Equipment (DTE), 37

Data transfer, high-speed, 170-75
   DMA. *See* Direct memory access
      (DMA)
   ping-pong buffer approach for,
      174-75
   programmed I/O
      using assembly language, 172-73
      using BASIC language, 170-72
   two ports for, 174
DEBUG program, DOS, 264-65
Decode circuit, 213-15
Decoupling device, 128
Digital input (DI) registers, 211,
   212-15
   design, 218-19
   interrupts from, 223
   level-latching, 219-21
   to read output of DO register, 230
   testing bits in, 226
   transaction-detection, 221-22
Digital I/O
   devices useful in interface design,
      226-27
   registers, 212-26
      address decoding for, 213
      bidirectional, 223-24
Digital output (DO) registers, 211
   design, 215-18
   output
      drive, 224
      reading output from, 230
   pulsed-output, 223-25
   setting and resetting bits in, 225-26
   setting switches in, 256-59
   shifting and counting functions with,
      216-18
Digital-to-analog conversion (DAC),
   244
   device manufacturers, 244-45
Direct memory access (DMA). *See also*
   DMA controller
   channels
      0-3, 156, 166-68, 288-89

      0-7 in PS/2, 318-20
      reusing, 169
   for data transfers
      block diagram, 156-57
      between diskette and system
         memory, 31, 33
      at high speeds, 173-74, 211-12
   to drive bus cycles, 89-91, 95-100
   latency, 169
   modes
      block transfer, 163
      cascade, 132, 164
      demand transfer, 163
      single-byte transfer, 163
   operation
      in PC and PC XT, 156-59
      extended mode in PS/2, 320-22
   in PC AT, 287-89
   performance, 168-69
   in PS/2, 318-23
   to solve high data-rate transfer
      problems, 153-56
   usage in the PC, 156
Disk performance (average access
   time), 32-33
Diskette capacity
   PC, 30-31
   PC AT, 7, 30-31
   PC XT, 4, 30-31
   PS/2, 12, 30-31
Diskette controller integrated on
   system board for PS/2s, 9
Diskettes supported as key attribute in
   evaluating merits of PC model, 3
Display adapter, 27-30. *See also*
Adapters
   integrated on system board for
      PS/2s, 9
   as key attribute in evaluating merits
      of PC model, 3
   performance measurement, 81
Display modes supported by PC video
   adapters, 29

Display regen buffer, 205
Display type, 27-30
    gas plasma, model 70P's, 23
    IBM Color Graphics, 122
    IBM Monochrome, 122
    as key attribute in evaluating merits
        of PC model, 3
    multisync, 29
    VGA, 29
DMA controller, 95-97. *See also*
    8237-5 DMA controller chip *and*
    Direct memory access (DMA)
    initialized by ROM BIOS, 113, 161
    PC AT, 289
    purpose of, 155-56
DMA memory-read cycle, 98-99
DMA memory-refresh cycle, 99-100
DMA memory-write cycle, 97-98
DOS, DEBUG program of, 264-65
DTE. *See* Data Terminal Equipment
    (DTE)
Dynamic memory devices to add large
    blocks of memory, 208
Dynamic RAM memory chips
    (DRAMs), 77-80
    to use to "late write" or "CAS
        write" feature, 112

E

EOI (end of interrupt), 135-36
Expansion slots
    arrangement and location in system
        unit of, 126
    as key attribute in evaluating merits
        of PC model, 3
    MCA, 302
    mechanical restrictions on, 124-25
    PC AT, 267-68, 273-74, 292
    PC XT, 4, 267, 274
        signal additions and changes in,
            268-70
    pin and signal definitions for, 126
    PS/2 model 25, 11-12

PS/2 model 30, 12-13
PS/2 model 30 286, 10, 12, 15
PS/2 model 50/50Z, 12, 17
PS/2 model 55SX, 12, 18
PS/2 model 60, 12, 19
PS/2 model 70, 12, 21
PS/2 model 70P, 12, 22-23
PS/2 model 80, 12, 24
spacing, 125
system-bus load in, 121-23
EXT 1 through EXT 4 external signals,
    255-56
Extended Industry Standard
    Architecture (EISA), 2
    486 system use of, 26
    compatibility with ISA bus of, 87
    ISA specification included in, 284
    performance levels of, 88
    sources of, 284

F

Fax boards, 40
Fixed disk adapters for PC AT and PC
    XT, 33
Fixed disks. *See* Hard disks

G

Game control card, interfacing with,
    232-33
Ground, frame, 115
GROUP SELECT signal, 197-98, 201

H

Hard disk
    capacities, 12, 32
    data transfer rates, 82
    formats for PC and PS/2 systems,
        32
    interfaces to system controller
        ESDI (Enhanced Small Device
            Interface), 33-34, 82

SCSI (Small Computer Systems Interface), 33, 82
ST506 (Segate Technologies), 33-34
sector buffering and file caching on, 82-83
selection criteria, 32-33
subsystem performance measurement, 82-83
Hardware
for testing designs, 254-64
wait-state generation, 281-82
High-level Data Link Control (HDLC) protocol, 37-38
High-order address bit usage for expanding port addressing, 201
Hit ratio for measuring cache design effectiveness, 80-81
HOLDA signal, 158
HRQ signal, 158

I

Idle state of DMA controller, 97
Indicator driving
incandescent lamp for, 239-40
LEDs for, 239
Initialization command words (ICWs). *See* 8259A interrupt controller
Instruction set of Intel microprocessors, 67-72
Interface design
components, 211-12
functions used in, 211-12
Interface signal conditioning, 233-37
current-loop data transmission, 236-37
RS-232C, 234
RS-422, 235-36
RS-423, 234-35
Interface signal pins, 8088
A8–A15 (pins 2–8 and 39), 51
A16/S3–A19/S6 (pins 35–38), 51

AD0–AD7 (pins 9–16), 51
CLK (pin 19), 51
INTR (pin 18), 52
LOCK (pin 29), 52
NMI (pin 17), 52
pin definition diagram of, 50
QS0 and QS1 (pins 24 and 25), 53
READY (pin 22), 52
RESET (pin 21), 52
RQ/GT0 (pin 31), 51-52
RQ/GT1 (pin 30), 52
S0, S1, and S2 (pins 26–28), 53
TEST (pin 23), 53
Interfacing
cards and ports for, 227-33
cassette, 227-29
game control, 232-33
parallel printer, 229-31
techniques, PC, 211-45
Interleave factor of drive adapters, 82-83
Interleave memory designs, 79-80
Interleave mode, 34
Interrupt(s)
from DI register, 223
expanding, 150-53
housekeeping, 134-35
initialization, 136-44
input ports, maskable and non-maskable (NMI), 130-31
in an interface to a microprocessor, 211-12
MCA, 303-5
PC AT expanded, 289-90, 304
performance, 148-49
PS/2, 317-18
sequence of events in, 132-34
system initialization for, 135-36
Interrupt latency time, 148
Interrupt registers
in-service register (ISR), 131
interrupt mask register (IMR), 131
interrupt request register (IRR), 131

Interrupt-service routine, 136-37, 148-49, 151

Interrupt system. *See also* System interrupts
of 8088 microprocessor, 130-31
uses of, 130

Interrupt vector pointer, 137-38

Interrupt vector table initialization, 137-38

I/O port address. *See also* Port addressing
decoding techniques, 196
fixed address, 197-98
PROM select, 199-200
switch-selectable, 197-99
map, 195-96

L

L brackets to mount adapter boards, 125
source of, 127

LAN performance measurement, 84

Landmark CPU Speed Test (Landmark Software), 86

Laser disc technology, 42

Light emitting diodes (LEDs) to visually indicate interface event, 239

M

Mass storage devices, 42

MC146818 real-time clock chip (Motorola), 291

MCA signals
A0–23 (address bits 0–23), 307
ABR0–3 (arbitration priority bus bits 0–3), 310
ALD, (address decode latch), 307-8
ARB/GNT (arbitration/grant), 310
AUDIO, 311
AUDIO GND (audio ground), 312

BURST, 310

CD CHRDY (card channel ready), 310, 315

CD DS 16 (card data size 16), 309, 314-15

CD SETUP (card setup), 311

CD SFDBK (card select feedback), 309, 314-15

CHCK (channel check), 311

CHRESET (channel reset), 312

CHRDYRTN (channel ready return), 310

CMD (command), 308, 314-15

D0–15 (data bus bits D0–D15), 307

DS 16 RTN (data size 16 return), 309

IRQ3–7, 9–12, 14, and 15 (interrupt level requests 3–7, 9–12, 14, and 15, 311

M/I/O (memory/input/output), 308, 314

MADE24 (memory address enable 24), 309, 314

PREEMPT, 310

REFRESH, 310

S0 and S1 (status bits 0 and 1), 308

SBHE (system bus high enable), 309

TC (terminal count), 311

MCA video extension signals
BLANK, 313
DCLK, 313
EDCLK, 313
ESYNC, 313
EVIDEO, 313
HSYNC, 313
P0–P7, 313
VSYNC, 313

Memory
adding small and large blocks of, 207-8

CMOS battery-backup nonvolatile, 283
devoted to the interrupt function, 137
dynamic, refreshing, 99-100, 208-9
expanded, schemes for, 39, 60
extended
    access with 286, 60
    management with 386, 63
programmable read-only, 199-200
reserved for enhancements, 205-6
speed and location, 77-79
Memory address decoding, PC and XT, 206-8
Memory addressing
    8088, 53-59, 135
    80286, 59, 61, 287-88
    80386, 63, 65
Memory cycle of the 8088 microprocessor, 5-6
Memory management of the 286 microprocessor, 59-60
Memory protection in the PC AT, 7
Memory refresh function, timer-counter channel 1 to support, 177
Memory size
    base PS/2 models', 11
    expansion PS/2 models', 11
Memory subsystem architecture, 79-81
Memory usage map, 205-6
Micro Channel Architecture (MCA)
    of the PS/2, xv, 297-315
    286 models, 10-11, 15
    386 processor technology implemented through, 1, 9-11
    486 models based on, 26
    adapter board dimensions, 306
    bus arbitration feature, 302-3
    capabilities and characteristics, 298-307
    chip set manufacturers, 297-98
    competitors of
        EISA, 2, 87

ISA, 87
    enhancements, 315
    power and ground, 305, 307
    programmable option select (POS)
        feature, 301-3, 324
        registers, 301-2, 325
Microprocessors, Intel, 45-72
    8048 used for IBM keyboards, 47
    8080 used as communications controller for IBM 5100 portable computer, 47
    8085 used for the IBM 5250 terminals, 47
    8086, 8-MHz, 48
        features of, 58-59
        instruction queue of 6 bytes, 58
        used for IBM Display writer, 47
        used for PC XT and compatibles, 6, 49, 58
        used for PS/2 model 25, 10-11, 49, 58
        used for PS/2 model 30, 6, 10-12, 49, 58
    8088, 4.77-MHz, xv
        block diagram, 50
        clock speed, 5-6
        competitors of, 45
        data-bus width, 47-48
        as derivation of 8086, 47
        features of, 49
        instruction queue of 4 bytes, 58
        interface signal pins, 50-53
        memory addressing, 53-55
        memory usage map, 205-6
        registers, 55-58
        used for PC, 3, 45-47, 49
        used for PC XT, 5, 49
    80286
        block diagram, 61
        data types, 62
        features of, 59-60
        memory map, 292-94
        registers, 62
        used for PC AT, 7, 49

used for PS/2 model 30 286,
14-15, 49
used for PS/2 model 50 and
model 50Z, 15-16, 49
used for PS/2 model 60, 19-20,
49
80386
block diagram, 64
data-bus width, 65
data types, 63, 66
features of, 60, 63
memory addressing, 65
Micro Channel Architecture in
PCs using, 9
registers, 64
used for PC AT, 49
used for PS/2 model 70, 21, 49
used in PS/2, 9
used in PS/2 model 80, 23-24,
49
used in PS/2 model P70, 22, 49
80386SX
data-bus width, 65
as low-cost version of 386 that
uses 16-bit bus, 17, 65
memory supported, 292
used for PC AT, 49
used for PS/2 model 55SX, 17,
49, 65
80486, 25-MHz, 26
block diagram, 68
data cache system, on-chip, 67,
80
features of, 67
memory supported, 292
registers, 66-67
used as optional processor for
PS/2 model 70, 21, 49
used for PC AT, 49
80486, 33-MHz, xv, 26
as key attribute in evaluating
merits of PC model, 3
instruction set, 49-50, 67-72
migration strategy, 46-47

new PC models follow
introductions of new Intel, 3
Modems
data rates of, 37
to interface serial ports to analog
telephone lines, 37
Motorola Semiconductor Products,
Inc., 245
Mouse
buttons, 41-42
resolution of 100 to 200 dots per
inch, 41
Mouse port, PS/2 integrated, 10

N

National Semiconductor Corporation,
245
NEC V20 microprocessor, CLK signal
and, 108
NS8250B UART, NS16450, and
NS16550 (National Semiconductor),
83-84
Numeric coprocessor
8087, 85
80287, 85
data types supported by, 62
80387, 63, 85
data types supported by, 66
80387SX, 85
80486 chip's integrated, 67
performance, 85
used by PS/2 family, 11

O

Offset defined, 55
Open architecture of IBM PC and
PS/2, xv
Operation control words (OCWs).
See 8259A interrupt controller
Output bus signals
capacitive loading on, 124
INT, 150

P

Packaging, desktop, portable, floor-standing tower, and laptop, 2-3
Page mode memory management with 386 microprocessor, 63
Parallel port
  added as standard equipment to PC XT, 4
  printer attachment to, 36-37
  PS/2, 324-25
Parallel printer port card
  4-bit input/output port, 230-31
  5-bit input port, 231
  8-bit output port, 229-30
  address modification, 229
PC family
  attributes of models in, 3
  enhancement versions available in desktop, portable, floor-standing tower, and laptop packages, 2-3
  options and enhancements, 27-43
  product descriptions of, 1-26
PC AT, IBM. *See also* PC 286 AT bus system
  data throughput measurements with, 84
  enhancements to previous products of, 7, 267
  interrupt controller configuration, 290
  interrupts, DMA, timer counters, I/O, and memory, 287-95
  I/O map, 293-95
  new models of, 2
  processor of, 7, 49
  programmable bus and system parameters, 283-84
  system and bus architecture, 267-85
PC, IBM
  bus extension and monitoring, 247-65

displays and display adapters for, 28
  hardware description, 3-4
  interfacing techniques, 211-45
  introduction in September 1981 of, 1
  I/O, memory, and decoding, 193-209
  processor of, 45-47, 49
  system interrupts, DMA, and timer counters, 129-92
PC XT, IBM
  bus extension and monitoring, 247-65
  data throughput measurements with, 84
  diskette and disk drives of, 5
  enhancements to previous products of, 3-4
  I/O, memory, and decoding, 193-209
  new models of, 2
  processor of, 5, 49
  size of, 4
  system interrupts, DMA, and timer counters, 129-92
  timings, 115-21
Performance, 73-88
  factors that contribute to system, 73
  measurements of 8088 and 8086 microprocessors, 6
Personal computer (PC), open architecture of, xv
Port addressing, 193-94. *See also* I/O port address
  expanding, 201-5
  indirect, 201-3
  memory-mapped, 202-5
Power supply
  decoupling capacitors to supply transient power instead of, 128
  PC AT, 284-85
  PC XT, 4

PS/2 model 30, 13
    total power from, table of, 127
Printer
    dot-matrix, 34-35
    engrave, 36
    IBM Parallel, 122
    interfacing with. *See* Printer
        interfaces
    laser, 36
    for original IBM PC, 34
    resistive ribbon thermal transfer,
        36
Printer interfaces, 229-31
    Centronix parallel, 36
    RS-232C serial asynchronous, 36
Programmed I/O, 33
Protected mode, 7-9, 18
    386 microprocessor's 8086, 63
    features of the 286, 59-61
    systems' use of expanded memory,
        39
Prototyping boards, 125
PS/2 family
    comparison charts, 11-12
    diskette drives of, 10
    features common to all members
        of original, 9-10
    initial offering of, 10-11
    interrupts, DMA, timer counters,
        I/O, and memory, 317-27
    introduced in 1987, 9
    I/O map, 326-27
    memory map, 326
    Micro Channel Architecture used
        in, 9. *See also* Micro Channel
        Architecture of the PS/2
    mouse, 42
PS/2 model 25
    processor of, 10-11, 49
    standard features of, 11-12
PS/2 model 30
    as PC XT in a PS/2 cover, 6
    processor of, 6, 10-11, 49
    standard features of, 13

PS/2 model 30 286
    processor of, 10, 49
    standard features of, 15
PS/2 model 50, 18
    as Micro Channel Architecture
        version of PC AT, 15
    processor of, 17-18, 49
    standard features of, 16-17
PS/2 model 50Z, 18
    processor of, 18, 49
    standard features of, 16-17
PS/2 model 55SX
    announced in May 1989, 17
    processor of, 17-18, 49, 65
    standard features of, 17-18
PS/2 model 60
    processor of, 19-20, 49
    standard features of, 20-21
PS/2 model 70
    processor of, 21, 49
    standard features of, 21-22
PS/2 model 80
    processor of, 23-24, 49
    standard features of, 24-25
PS/2 model P70
    processor of, 22-23, 49
    standard features of, 23

Q–R

Quietwriter printer series, 36

RAM
    CMOS, 291-92
    decoding, 205
    dynamic, specifying, 283
    fixed disk data buffered in, 33
    low, initializing addresses in,
        135-38
RAM capacity
    as key attribute in evaluating
        merits of PC model, standard and
        maximum, 3
    PC XT, 4

READ REGISTER signal, 197
Real mode, 7, 9, 60
Real-time clock
    PC AT, 291
    PS/2, 323
Registers, 8088 16-bit
    data group, 55
    flag, 135-36
        AF auxiliary carry, 57
        CF carry, 57
        DF direction, 57
        IF interrupt-enable, 57
        OF overflow, 57
        PF parity, 57
        SF sign, 57
        TF trap, 57
        ZF zero, 57
    implicit use of
        AH byte multiply and byte
            divide, 56
        AL byte multiply, byte divide,
            byte I/O, translate, and
            decimal arithmetic, 56
        AX word multiply, word divide,
            and word I/O, 56
        BX translate, 56
        CL variable shift and rotate, 56
        CX string operations and loops,
            56
        DI string operations, 56
        DX word multiply, word divide,
            and indirect I/O, 56
        SI string operations, 56
        SP stack operations, 56
    IP instruction pointer, 56, 133,
        135-37
    pointer and index group, 55
    segment, 54-55
        CS code segment, 133, 135-37
Registers, 80286, 62
Registers, 80386, 64
Relay driving, 240-41
REQUEST signal, 173

ROM
    decoding, 205
    shadowing, 81, 283
RTN instruction, 135

S

S clocks, 97
Scanners, 40
Segment register defined, 54
Serial port
    added as standard equipment to
        PC XT, 4
    printer attachment to, 36-37
Set/reset latch, 219-21
SI clocks, 97
Signal conditioning, 212
Smart card extender design, 254-64
SN74LS688 octal compare device,
    260
SN74S240 and SN74LS240 octal
    buffers and line drivers (TI), 249,
    253
SN75475 dual peripheral-driver
    device, 240
Software for testing designs, 264-65
Speaker, timer-counter channel 2 to
    drive, 177-78
Stack pointer, initializing, 135
Stepper motors, 240-41
    bifilar, 242
    manufacturers of, 241
    permanent-magnet, 241-42
    pulse, 242
    variable-reluctance, 242
Streaming tape units for backups, 42
Switch debounce circuit, 238
Switch sensing, 237-38
Synchronous Data Link Control
    (SDLC) protocol, 37-38
Synchronous digital service networks,
    38
System board of PS/2s, 9-10

System-bus card slots. *See* Expansion slots

System-bus driving, 117-21

System-bus loading to cards, 121-24

System-bus mechanical and power characteristics, 124-28

System-bus signals, 107-8, 120, 122-23

  A0-19, 109, 198, 255

  AEN (address enable), 96, 105, 114, 198, 207, 213

  ALE (address latch enable), 92-93, 110

  CLK (clock), 108, 270, 275

  D0–7, 109-10

  DACK0–3 (direct memory access acknowledges 0 through 3), 96, 105-6, 113-14, 158, 170, 173, 208-9, 256

  DRQ1-3 (direct memory access requests 1 through 3), 96, 113, 158

  I/O CH CK (I/O channel check), 110-11

  I/O CH RDY (I/O channel ready), 111, 280

  IOR (I/O read), 97, 110-13, 158, 197, 249-50, 255, 257, 260, 279

  IOW (I/O write), 95, 98, 110-12, 158, 197, 219-20, 255, 257, 260

  IRQ2–7 (interrupt requests 2 through 7), 111, 270

  MEMR (memory read), 92, 98, 101, 110-11, 113, 158, 249-50, 255, 257, 260, 279

  MEMW (memory write), 93, 97, 101, 106, 110-12, 158, 255, 257, 260

  OSC (oscillator), 108

  RESET DRV (reset driver), 109

  TC (terminal count), 114

System-bus timings, 115-17

System Information (SI) (Peter Norton), 86

System interrupts
  advantage of, 129
  purpose of, 130

System timer, timer-counter channel 0 as, 176-77

T

T clocks, 95, 97

Tape backup units, 42

Testing, hardware and software for, 254-65

Timer counters
  channel 0
    as PC and PC XT general system timer, 176-77
    PC AT, 291
  channel 1
    eliminated in PS/2, 323
    in PC and PC XT to support memory refresh, 177
    PC AT, 291
  channel 2
    in PC and PC XT to output serial data to audio cassette port and to drive speaker of system unit, 177-78, 227-29
    in PC AT, 291
  channel 3, watchdog timer, added in PS/2, 323
  control function, circuit diagram of I/O port registers for, 185
  design of, 183-92
  implementation of, 175-76
  I/O address, 179
  mode control registers of, 179-80
  modes
    0: interrupt on terminal count, 181
    1: programmable one-shot, 181
    2: rate generator, 181-82
    3: square-wave rate generator, 182
    4: software-triggered strobe, 182

5: hardware-triggered strobe, 182
PC AT, 291
programming, 178-81
reading and writing, 180-81
Timing and counting functions, adding extended, 182-83
Trillium Network Systems COM 64 adapter, 38-39
TW clock, 94

U–V

Unique interface circuits, 211-12

Video interface types
analog RGB, 30
direct drive, 30
RGB direct drive, 30
RGB direct drive-composite, 30
Video interfaces supported by display adapters, 30

W

Wait state
of 8088 microprocessor, 5-6, 76
of 80286 PS/2 models (30 286 and 50), 16
adding and removing, 76
in DMA and I/O cycles, 76
effects dependent on microprocessor type, 76-77
generation
8088, 100-104
80286, 280-82
in DMA bus cycles, 103-7
in instruction fetch cycles, 75-76
Wattage, total PC, 127
Windows 386, 63
Write once, read many (WORM) technology for laser disks, 42
WRITE REGISTER signal, 197
WRT REG0 control signal, 215

Z

Z80 microprocessors, 45-46
Z8000 microprocessor, 46